Buddhism in the Krishna River Valley of Andhra

Edited by

Sree Padma

A. W. Barber

State University of New York Press

The three photos used in Chapter 3, "Amaravati as Lens: Envisioning Buddhism in the Ruins of the Great *Stūpa*," by Jacob Kinnard are used with the permission of the British Museum. © The Trustees of the British Museum.

Published by
State University of New York Press, Albany

Printed in the United States of America

For information, contact State University of New York Press, Albany, NY
www.sunypress.edu.

Production by Eileen Meehan
Marketing by Fran Keneston

Library of Congress Cataloging in Publication Data

Buddhism in the Krishna River Valley of Andhra / edited by Sree Padma, A. W. Barber.
p. cm.
Material culture and the emergence of urban Buddhism in Andhra / Sree Padma—Of tempted arhats and supermundane Buddhas : abhidharma in the Krishna Region / Bart Dessein—Amaravati as lense : envisioning Buddhism in the ruins of the great stūpa / Jacob N. Kinnard—Buddhism in Andhra and its influence on Buddhism in Sri Lanka / Sree Padma and John Clifford Holt—Candrakīrti on the medieval military culture of South India / Karen Lang—Two Mahāyāna developments along the Krishna River / A. W. Barber— Dhanyakataka revisited : Buddhist politics in post Buddhist Andhra / Jonathan S. Walters.
Includes bibliographical references and index.
ISBN 978-0-7914-7485-3 (hardcover : alk. paper)
1. Buddhism—India—Andhra Pradesh—History. 2. Buddhism—India—Krishna River Valley—History. I. Sree Padma, 1956– II. Barber, A. W. 1952–

BQ349.A56B83 2008
294.30954'84—dc22 2007036637

10 9 8 7 6 5 4 3 2 1

This volume is dedicated to John Holt and Theresa Barber.

Contents

Illustrations

Maps

Figures

Location of Andhra

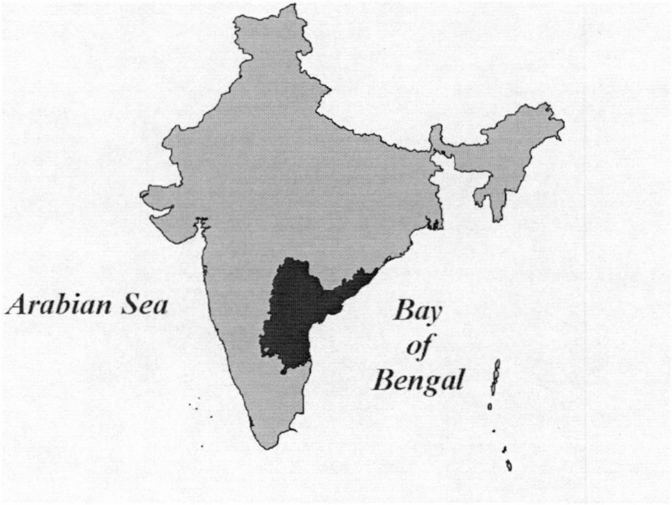

Buddhist Settlements

1	Saripally	26	Jaggaiahpeta
2	Kalinga Patnam	27	Guntupally
3	Dantapuram	28	Arugolanu
4	Sali hundam	29	Adurru
5	Ramatirtham	30	Alluru
6	Mangamaripeta	31	Gummadidurru
7	Bavikonda	32	Yeleswaram
8	Sankaram	33	Manchikallu
9	Dharapalem	34	Goli
10	Kottur	35	Nagarjunakonda
11	Gopalapatnam	36	Grandisiri
12	Kapavaram	37	Amaravati
13	Kodavali	38	Rentala
14	Lingarajupalem	39	Buddam
15	Pithapuram	40	Gudivada
16	Pashigam	41	Ghantasala
17	Kotilingala	42	Bhattiprolu
18	Dhulikatta	43	Chinnaganjam
19	Kondapur	44	Chandavaram
20	Tirumalagiri	45	Dupadu
21	Gajulabanda	46	Peddaganjam
22	Panigiri	47	Kanuparti
23	Nelakondapally	48	Uppugundur
24	Aswaraopet	49	Ramatirtham
25	Wadhamankota	50	Nandalur

51 Pavurallakonda

Location of Andhra

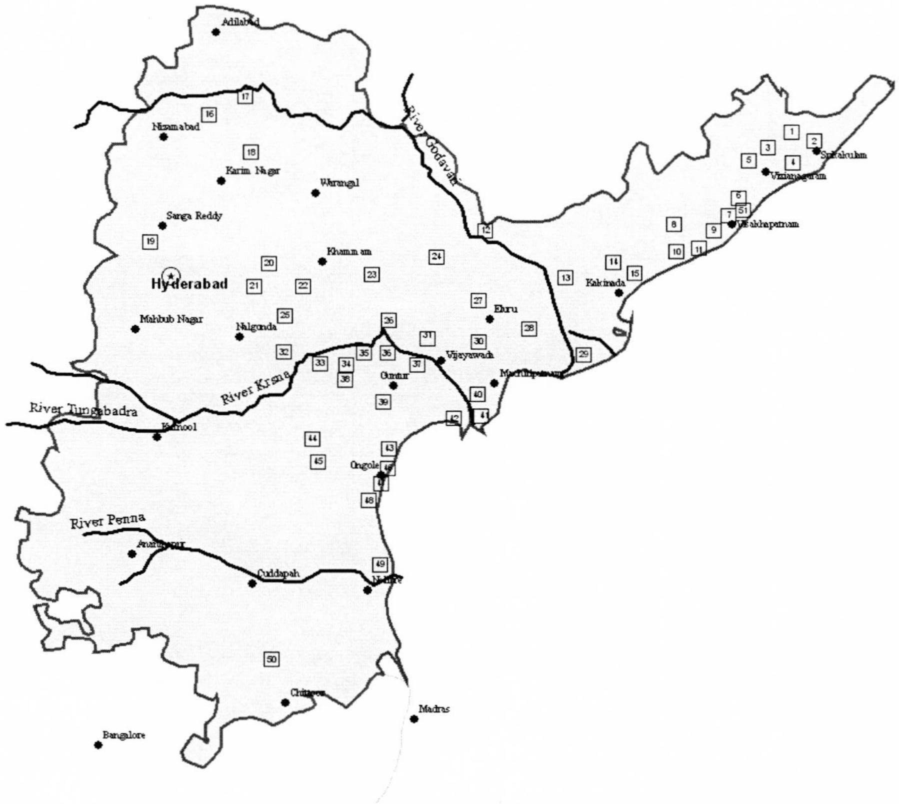

Ancient Buddhist sites in modern Andhra

Acknowledgments

We would like to acknowledge many people who helped to make this volume possible. First, we thank each of our contributors for their patience and cooperation throughout the process of manuscript preparation. Second, Sree Padma worked closely with archeologists at the Department of Archaeology, Andhra Pradesh, in Hyderabad, particularly its retired Director, Dr. V.V. Krishna Sastry, but also Drs. E. Siva Nagireddy, and B. Subrahmanyam. She acknowledges her indebtedness to them. Third, in preparing the manuscript, we received helpful assistance from the technical personnel at Bowdoin College, especially William York who assisted with software issues, and Nancy Grant who enthusiastically prepared our maps. We are grateful for their help. Our thanks are also due to the officials at the British Museum for permission to use their photos of Amaravati sculpture. Finally, we acknowledge our deep appreciation to our editor Nancy Ellegate who helped us bring this volume into the light.

Introduction

Despite popular and scholarly perceptions of Magadha in northeastern India (modern Bihar) as the center of Indian Buddhism, the essays in this volume collectively make a strong case that the Buddhism of the Krishna River Valley in southeastern India (modern Andhra Pradesh) likewise played a pivotal role in the rise and development of the religion, and profoundly impacted subsequent Buddhist traditions, not only in India and the Indian subcontinent but throughout Southeast and East Asia as well. We are particularly interested in this theme, not only because one of us is originally from Andhra, grew up in the shadow of many of its famous archaeological sites and had an opportunity to study them as a part of pursuing academic degrees, but also because Buddhism in this region has been largely neglected within the scholarship to date. The impetus for this volume also stems from conversations between the editors about the present revival in interest about Buddhism now taking place in Andhra Pradesh among archaeologists, historians, politicians, and the general public. During our conversations, we also realized how a number of our own friends from various disciplines in the scholarly community, archaeologists, art historians, epigraphists, historians of religion, and philosophers, shared interests with us in the significance of Buddhism in the Krishna River Valley. We invited some of these colleagues to participate in panels at the meetings of Association for Asian Studies and the University of Wisconsin South Asia Conference. Most of the chapters in this volume grew out of these panel presentations.

Various factors account for the relative neglect of Andhra's significance in buddhological circles, both in India and abroad. For example, in Europe and the United States, historians of Buddhist thought have been aware for quite some time that such pivotally important Mahāyāna Buddhist thinkers as Nāgārjuna, Dignāga, Candrakīrti, Āryadeva, and Bhāvaviveka, among many others, formulated their theories while living in Buddhist communities in Andhra, but such a premium has been placed on the study of religious doctrine or philosophy that the historicity of Buddhism, in both its material and social expression, has not been emphasized to any great degree. Similarly, we have been aware of some of the significant contributions Buddhist communities of this region made to world Buddhist praxis, but we still know very little about these communities per se.

In India, many scholars are not very aware of the history of Buddhism beyond the South Asian context, whereas it is in considering Buddhism as a whole that Andhra's special significance becomes apparent. While Indian scholars have devoted considerable attention to the study of Buddhist art and other material culture that has been excavated and exposed in Andhra Pradesh during the past two centuries, and some of them have studied the influence of the Amaravati school of art in South and Southeast Asian Buddhist traditions, these studies tend not to go beyond the identification of technical and stylistic details characteristic of this art. Simultaneously, especially in the context of Asian scholarship, the nationalist mythology of a pure Buddhist tradition being preserved in various Buddhist nations led to a refusal to admit the contributions of outside influences such as those coming from Andhra; if recognized at all, they were considered problematic and or even repellant.

Among the regional historians of India, especially those who have studied the regions south of the Vindhya Mountains, there has been a trend to trace connections between Buddhist communities of the south with the history of Buddhist communities in the north of India in the earliest eras of Buddhist history. This has been the case especially with many historians of Andhra. These historians have relied heavily on literary sources and travelogues to assert these connections. Considerable energy has been expended to match modern place names in Andhra with names of places mentioned in Buddhist literary sources and in foreign sources such as Pliny's *Natural History*, Ptolemy's *Geography*, and in the Chinese sources provided by Fa-Xian, Xuanzang, and Yiqing. In the absence of precise material evidence, the claims of these historians have often been debated and doubted in scholarly circles outside of Andhra. Some of these historians have asserted that Buddhism entered Andhra as early as the lifetime of the Buddha. References from the *Suttanipāta* and the *Mahāvagga* are cited to warrant these assertions. While claims of this nature by these historians have not been sufficiently substantiated, it is clear that many of the ancient Buddhist sites that have been explored and excavated by archaeologists in the twentieth century, including Amaravati, Nagarjunakonda, and Jaggayyapeta in the lower Krishna River Valley, can be traced to at least to the third century BCE, if not earlier. Moreover, the great array of Buddhist sects that are mentioned in inscriptions at Nagarjunakonda and other places has made it clear that Andhra was a lively historical venue at which numerous institutional schisms and novel doctrinal developments occurred. The study of these inscriptions, as well as the consideration of art, architecture, and other forms of material culture in the excavated sites, have been of enormous help in supporting or rejecting the claims made by earlier historians. In spite of all of the material evidence that has been weighed, there are still a large number of unanswered questions to ponder.

The holistic approach of the present volume—which embraces both Indian and extra-Indian Buddhist traditions, and treats Buddhism as a religion not only of philosophy but also of art, politics, and praxis—enables a new appraisal of Buddhism in Andhra. Together, the various chapters—each focused on specific dimensions of Andhra's long and rich history involving Buddhism, and treating it from a variety of disciplinary and methodological angles—contribute a uniquely comprehensive picture of Buddhist culture from even before its emergence in the historical record (third century BCE) up to and beyond its final decline in about the twelfth century CE, and make the general case that the Buddhism that developed in Andhra's Krishna River Valley played a catalytic role for the history of Buddhist tradition in other cultural milieus; its creativity in art, philosophy, praxis, and political theory became at times paradigmatic for, or at least a factor of significant influence on communities in other regions of the world that embraced Buddhism in its various forms.

Sree Padma's lead-off chapter traces the background leading to the history of Buddhism in Andhra, especially in its lower Krishna River Valley, to show how the Buddhist culture that developed in Andhra from the third century BCE to the third century CE was unique to the region. Citing recent archaeological reports, she traces out the movements of protohistoric communities in Andhra and their interactions with communities in other regions to show how this shared knowledge led to gradual progress in metallurgy and building technology as they advanced from pastoral to agricultural stages, to developing trade, and then into the process of urbanization. A common theme throughout each of these stages was the veneration of the dead. To express their respect for the dead, these communities built substantial commemorative structures. The building methods of these structures increased in complexity as the communities progressed in their technology. By the time of the arrival of Buddhism, protohistoric communities had developed a religious culture that had anticipated important aspects of Buddhist cult. Specifically, the communities who were successful in building complicated monuments to venerate their dead in what we might call "proto-*stūpa*s" were not only poised to build Buddhist *stūpa*s and *caitya*s, but to add their own religious symbols and indigenous cultic practices into the Buddhist mix. This creativity, as it was expressed in art, architecture, and religious ideas, Sree Padma states, functioned as a kind of fulcrum that eventually proved attractive to Buddhist communities beyond Andhra.

Details of Mahāsāṃghika literature, philosophy and the practice of *caitya* worship in the Krishna region have been dealt with at length in the next chapter by Bart Dessein. Dessein draws information from both Indian and Chinese sources using previously unstudied materials in his development of this theme. The chapter's main focus is the study of śrāvakayāna schools which, as he says, constituted different subgroups of the Mahāsāṃghikas. Dessein uses epigraphical records to determine the identity of various schools that existed in the Krishna River Valley. He analyses the history of these schools and their doctrinal viewpoints as revealed through their textual sources in order to show how the Mahāsāṃghikas in Andhra were more innovative and held a slightly different view from their northern counterparts regarding the supermundane nature of the Buddha and *bodhisatvas.* In order to understand the historical and doctrinal significance, he provides specific information about the Mahīśāka, Bahuśrutīya, Caityaka, Pūrvaśaila, and Aparaśaila schools. He discusses, at length, the Mahāsaṃghika *abhidharma* after conceptualizing it within the greater body of Mahāsāṃghika literature. His article also contributes to our understanding of the controversial discussion about distinguishing characteristics between *arhats* and the Buddha.

Jacob Kinnard's chapter focuses on the interpretation of Buddhist sculptural scenes. His attention centers on the issue of aniconic and iconic representations of the Buddha and the possible historical meanings of these representations. He focuses his study on the Amaravati *stūpa* and its most conspicuous symbols, such as the footprint, the tree or the *dharmacakra.* He discusses how the representation of these symbols has been interpreted by earlier scholars as symbolic of the Buddha's presence in aniconic form. The popular view among these scholars has been that the aniconic tradition of symbolic representation was succeeded by the iconic anthropomorphic tradition coinciding with the emergence of Mahāyāna ideas. Kinnard questions this standard interpretive conception and proceeds to demonstrate, with the help of visual examples from Amaravati, that this was not quite true. Noting that Susan Huntington has proposed that aniconic representation of the Buddha commemorates post-*nirvāṇa* events, ongoing ritual practices, and the places associated with these events, Kinnard understands the sculptures at Amaravati as documenting early Buddhist ritual action and thereby constituting a kind of lexicon of cultic activity that eventually became paradigmatic for Buddhist communities in other parts of India. Kinnard finds that this paradigm is especially reflected in the Pāla art of the later northeast. He argues convincingly that these sculptures were intended to be narratives, objects of veneration, and ritually mimetic images. For Kinnard, then, the art at Amaravati represents not just an "Amaravati School of art," but a whole set of rituals in which various objects were venerated that later inspired the practice of Buddhism in other parts of India, Sri Lanka, and Southeast Asia.

John Holt and Sree Padma's joint chapter on "Buddhism in Andhra and Its Influence on Buddhism in Sri Lanka" discusses the development of Buddhist ideas, practices, and the artistic portrayal of the Buddha in Andhra and their possible impacts on Sri Lanka's burgeoning Buddhist culture. The chapter begins with noting how national myths of origin have often occluded aspects of social and political history when rendered authoritative by historians of a nationalist bent. It then reviews various scholarly findings about the early schism between the Sthāviravādins and Mahāsāṃghikas and notes the likely possibility that dissident Mahāsāṃghika sects made Andhra their home. Citing inscriptions issued at two famous Buddhist centers and canonical writings produced in the early centuries CE in the lower Krishna River Valley, the chapter then describes how the emerging Buddhist culture of Andhra gave rise to ideas and practices congenial to the eventual Mahāyāna that were later spread to Sri Lanka, a development further reflected in the growing distinction between the rival Theravāda Mahāvihāra and more eclectic Abhayagiri monasteries in Anuradhapura, Sri Lanka. The chapter refutes claims made by Sri Lankan nationalist scholars that the Buddha image originated in Sri Lanka. It notes, by means of Ulrich von Schroeder's detailed analysis of Buddhist sculpture, that many limestone images, made from a particular type of stone only found within the Krishna River Valley, were directly imported from Amaravati and used for ritual purposes in monasteries throughout the island and it further notes the extent of the influence of Amaravati on sculptural representations of the Buddha and on *caitya* building activity, citing examples at famous Buddhist centers in Sri Lanka and the impact of Mahāyāna philosophy on conceptions of the Buddha and *bodhisattva.* What we see throughout Sri Lankan history, as it has been understood within Theravāda monastic circles and recapitulated through nationalist historians, is that there was a constant struggle to retain the so-called purity and originality of Buddhist teaching that translated into controversies between the Abhayagiri and Mahāvihāra monasteries. In spite of this view that there was a stiff resistance by Theravāda monks to outside influence and their victory over the other group that advocated change, there was always, to be sure, a certain amount of ideas and practices that seeped into emergent Sinhala

Theravāda Buddhism, nationalist claims for purity notwithstanding. This chapter concludes by raising questions regarding the impact of all of this on contemporary Sri Lankan public and political consciousness.

The next chapter takes up the study of Candrakīrti, an important Mahāyāna commentator on Nāgārjuna and Āryadeva's works. Karen Lang studies some of Candrakīrti's assertions made in his commentary on Āryadeva's *Catuḥśataka* in which he vehemently refutes Brahmanical and Jain beliefs and practices while vigorously defending Buddhist ideas of kingship. Candrakīrti questions the Brahmanical concept of the king's divinity, noting the fact that the king's power was dependent on his subjects' revenues. Candrakīrti warns that the king who abuses his power for wealth and ill treatment of women would be reborn in a far less exalted stage. (Candrakīrti's criticism of military culture is quite classic in its substance and could even be compared to the conceptual underpinning of contemporary pacifist movements!) Why did Candrakīrti so severely critique Brahmanical and Jain beliefs and practices? Why did there seem to be such a compelling need for him to defend Buddhism? To understand Candrakīrti's rather harsh criticisms, Lang looks at the contemporary political and religious map of South India through the inscriptions issued by both Buddhist and Saivite Brahmanical kings. In her hypothesis, she situates Candrakīrti in the seventh-century delta region between the two great rivers of the Deccan, the Krishna and Godavari. This was the time when many Buddhist monasteries fell out of use while political rulers were embracing Saivism. Lang documents, through an examination of inscriptions, the historical survival of some Buddhist monasteries under the patronage of the Viṣṇukuṇḍins, monasteries that were later were taken over by the Saivite Cālukyas. She compares the content of these inscriptions with a long donative inscription of the Saivite Cālukyas to show the changing religious culture of the Deccan and South India and its impact on the notion of an ideal ruler. The Viṣṇukuṇḍin records, consistent with Buddhist expectations of kinghood, show how the donor king wanted the resultant merit of his donations to be transferred to not only himself, but also to his parents and to all sentient beings, a development, we would note, that seems to find its quintessential expression ultimately in the construction of temples by the Khmers at Angkor from the ninth through the twelfth centuries CE. Furthermore, these records mention the benevolence and generosity of the king and his rightfully acquired wealth. Saivite Cālukyan inscriptions, on the other hand, celebrate the rulers' achievements as warriors, but do not emphasize their accomplishments as donors. The poet author of a Cālukyan inscription, for example, praises the king for pillaging the opponents' territories and wresting their wealth. While Lang mentions that glorification of the battlefield was not unique to Saivite kings alone, she also quotes Davidson on how the Saivite kings and their poets were particularly susceptible to this kind of rhetoric. Lang also examines eulogies found in both Viṣṇukuṇḍin and Cālukyan inscriptional records to ascertain a conception of "the world ruler" and then compares this with Candrakīrti's ideology. According to Candrakīrti, the world ruler must be the moral exemplar, not the powerful king who devastates the world through waging wars. Lang has successfully demonstrated how Buddhist Viṣṇukuṇḍin records meet Candrakīrti's standards of kingship while Candrakīrti's scathing criticisms are aimed directly at what Cālukyan inscriptions claim. She also notes that other Buddhist works by scholarly monks like Candrakīrti advocated the idea of an ideal ruler who could be simultaneously a *bodhisattva*, by means of compassion. She further demonstrates through inscriptions how the notion of ideal Buddhist king traveled to Sri Lanka, thus complementing assertions made by Sree Padma and Holt in their essay.

Building on the trajectory established by Dessein and using Indic, Tibetan, and Chinese sources, A. W. Barber explores the development of the *tathāgatagarbha* concept and *tantra* traditions to show how Andhra's Buddhist culture played a seminal role in their inceptions. He does this by developing doctrinal, historical, and geographical arguments in support of his thesis. *The Lion's Roar of Queen Srimala*, a seemingly Mahāsāṃghika influenced text discussed by Dessein in his chapter, is taken up once again by Barber within the context of how it appears to sustain the tenets of the Mahāsāṃghika while also articulating the new notion of *tathāgatagarbha*. Viewing Vajrayāna as another way of practicing Mahāyāna, Barber discusses the possible connection of various Vajrayāna Buddhist scholars and practitioners to the Andhra region, specifically to the Krishna River Valley. While cautioning his readers about textual inconsistencies and the hagiographic nature of the vast material that he has had to work through, Barber lists only a selected few Vajrayāna teachers for whom the evidence seems compelling. He divides these teachers into two groups on the basis of the *tantras* that they practiced and cites specific references from Tibetan sources to show how the teachers of the two groups practicing various *tantras* either originated from Andhra or spent considerable amounts of time practicing and composing various *tantric* treatises in Andhra. The treatises that were composed in Andhra would play a crucial role in the development of Mahāyāna ideas in Tibet, China, and Japan.

The final chapter, by Jonathan Walters, discusses Buddhist politics in Andhra in an era when Buddhism had definitely lost its popular support. Walters refers to this as the "post-Buddhist period" in Andhra history. He begins his chapter by challenging the validity of claims made regarding the dating of an important inscription purportedly issued by a king called Siṃhavarman Pallava. Walters raises the question of how Siṃhavarman could have been a Pallava ruler belonging to an earlier period when the language and the script employed in this inscription betray a much later origin. He discusses the inscription's shared similarities with some twelfth century CE inscriptions issued at Amaravati by the Koṭa king Keta and his wives within the context of their donations to the "god" Buddha, in the process coming to the conclusion that the Siṃhavarman inscription was actually manufactured by the Koṭa king Keta. Walters argues that the plausibility of this hypothesis, or Keta's rationale for inventing an "older" inscription while issuing donations to the temple of the Buddha, was rooted in Keta's desire to impress his Buddhist ally, the powerful King Parākramabāhu I of Polonnaruva in Sri Lanka, so that Parākramabāhu would know that the Buddha had received continuous patronage in the past and that he would continue to receive patronage under Keta's rule. Walters situates this argument in the background scenario of political geography in southern India and in Sri Lanka wherein the Saiva king Keta and the Buddhist king Parākramabāhu were brought together in an alliance to face their common enemies in southern India. To further his argument, Walters has mentioned and reviewed a number of issues within the broader history of Andhra, noting what happened to Buddhism in "post-Buddhist Andhra" under various dynasties and the historical implications of these developments for Sri Lanka.

Thus, though the articles cover a wide range of issues from various perspectives, all of them enhance our general understanding of Andhra's significance for Buddhist history worldwide. As suggestive as these essays may be, one of the interesting questions of a general nature to pursue in the future would be. What forces in Andhra's own cultural milieu gave rise to its creative activities in art, philosophy, religious practice, and politics, a creativity that was obviously widely admired? In some cases, we have provided some specific answers relevant to specific developments, but that more general question regarding the specific types of impetus responsible for the fruition of Andhra's own Buddhist culture per se remains. Our modest goal is that our reflections will stimulate further sustained inquiry.

The editors would like to extend our deepest appreciation to the authors of the articles contained in this volume. We understand the nature of the work that went into to each of these articles and the difficulty of finding the time to research and develop each contribution. We further hope that the readers will find our modest effort something of use in their own pursuit of understanding Buddhism not only as a doctrine of major significance in the world but as a cultural force that found expression in every aspect of human endeavors in the past and still inspires those of us so far removed in time and space.

Because of the problems brought about by modern versus ancient place names and the use of various languages, except in quotations, all geographic place names appear without diacritics. At the end of the volume, there is a list of place names wherein diacritics are provided.

CHAPTER 1

Material Culture and the Emergence of Urban Buddhism in Andhra

SREE PADMA

The presence of Buddhism in Andhra coincides with Andhra's first urbanization processes. Whether Buddhism was somehow responsible for urbanization in the Andhra region or whether urbanized society was congenial to the spread of Buddhism are not easy questions to answer with precision. Most of the explored and excavated Buddhist ruins in Andhra suggest that Buddhist institutions functioned for almost six hundred years, roughly from the third century BCE to the end of the third century CE. From a study of the majority of these sites, it seems as if Buddhism entered Andhra in a surge that inundated almost the whole populace but then disappeared almost as suddenly as it had made its presence, though there were isolated sites in Andhra, such as Amaravati, Nagarjunakonda, Jaggayyapeta, Salihundam, and Sankaram, where Buddhism lingered perhaps as late as the fourteenth century CE.[1] However, finding the reasons for the demise of the vast majority of Buddhist sites by the end of the third century CE in Andhra has also remained an intriguing problem for scholars of religion and archaeology alike. Some theories have been put forward to account for the relative disappearance of Buddhism in Andhra, but none have proved to be very satisfactory so far. What has been accepted, however, is that the spread of Buddhism and the first urbanization processes in Deccan and south India coincided with each other. Trade, especially oceanic trade, was one of the major features of this urbanizing culture, activity which no doubt abetted the spread of Buddhism. Moreover, some scholars have pointed out that indirect trade with Rome or with Roman subjects came to an end in the entire subcontinent sometime in the third century CE, coinciding with the disappearance of Buddhism.[2]

The aim of this chapter is not so much to see how and when oceanic trade ended and how it affected Buddhist establishments. Neither is this chapter focused on the continuing controversy of whether or not Andhra had direct trade relations with Rome and Roman subjects. Instead, my aim here is to trace out the first urbanization process in Andhra in order to see how Buddhism came to be associated with it. In this study, the lower Krishna River Valley is given a special attention, as this particular region offers a continuum of evidence from the late stone age through its transition to historic ages. This continuity creates a scope to assess the nature of historical vicissitudes that occurred in this fertile valley in which urbanization and Buddhism played concomitant roles. Here, in this context, the term "Andhra" corresponds to the present political unit of Andhra Pradesh, the Telugu linguistic state of modern India. The lower Krishna River Valley includes the fluvial area of the River Krishna and its estuaries comprising the present administrative divisions of Krishna, Guntur, Prakasham, and parts of Nellore and Kurnool districts.

I will begin my survey with the pastoral communities in neolithic societies of the lower Krishna River Valley, people who gradually settled into agricultural communities, the communities that eventually developed extensive networks with the rest of the subcontinent and beyond. Here my first inquiry is to see how these relations helped to spread ideas and goods from other regions of the Indian subcontinent to the south, in the process facilitating the spread of Buddhism to Andhra and its lower Krishna River Valley, a development that served as a springboard for its further dissemination to other regions in the subcontinent and beyond. In each phase leading to the historical period, I will note technological progress, contacts with neighbors, and the evidence of emerging religiosity. My second inquiry is to see under what circumstances Buddhism came to be accepted by these local communities. By doing so, I propose to address two different specific questions: (1) What factors contributed to Buddhism being so popular among the urbanizing populations in Andhra? (2) Were modifications of the same factors somehow responsible for its eventual demise from the land? Considering the scope of this chapter, the first issue will form the main focus of this study while the second is left largely to the hypothesis that I derive from the study of the first.

Archaeological sources indicate that Andhra, particularly the lower Krishna River Valley, witnessed all of the traditionally recognized pre- and protohistoric phases of cultural development that precede the early historical period.[3] This simply indicates that the region was continuously inhabited for centuries and perhaps for even thousands of years before the period of time with which I am concerned. While the archaeological evidence from the early historic sites often has been subordinated to what we might ascertain from textual accounts, I aim to emphasize the former.

Neolithic and Neolithic-Chalcolithic

Archaeological evidence suggests that from 2000 BCE onward, all of the protohistoric communities of Andhra, with few exceptions, had entered the region from neighboring Karnataka by gradually moving east along the banks of the rivers Krishna and Tungabhadra.[4] Depending on their cultural backgrounds and the availability of resources in their surrounding areas, various communities of neolithic, chalocolithic, and megalithic cultures practiced different ways of disposing of their dead. In general, their burial structures were better built than their homesteads and hence better preserved over time. They provide an excellent source for the study of these cultures, especially due to the fact that they often contained goods that the dead used while living. These worldly possessions that accompanied the dead are referred to as "grave goods" or "burial goods" in archeological terminology. The study of these burial structures and their accompanied goods lead us to think that these protohistoric communities believed in some form of life after death. Megalithic burials with their complicated building methods signal the communities' respect to their ancestors. These protohistoric burial monuments were succeeded in the historical stage by monuments containing the relics of the Buddha or famous Buddhist monks. Unfortunately, little effort has been made by scholars to connect the afterlife beliefs associated with the burials of protohistoric communities with that of later *stūpa* cults associated with historic Buddhism. Instead, scholarly focus based on literary analysis has often tended to project a picture of how Buddhism and Brahmanism suddenly spread from the north of India to the south thereby exposing the southern tribes for the first time to "civilization." There were some discussions by archaeologists about the architectural and conceptual similarities between the megalithic burial and a *stūpa* (as I will quote in the following pages), but there was no attempt to show the continuity in the development of ideas and local genius from prehistoric to historic ages. The disjunction between accounts based on literary and archaeological bases has been reflected in various attempts to account for the appearance of urbanization and the historical manifestation of religious behavior.

Indeed, some Andhra sites, such as Amaravati and Nagarjunakonda, reveal successive layers of prehistoric, protohistoric, and historic stages of lifestyle reflecting a very gradual transition from rural, pastoral habitation to urban life. Maurizio Tosi, tracing out early urban evolution in the Indo-Iranian borderland, mentions several background factors for the emergence of a city in that context:[5]

> The city, taken as the nucleus of demographic and economic concentration, is necessarily the direct expression of a productive economy. As such, it can hardly be defined as a cultural model or type in itself, since it has no alternatives worthy of consideration . . . The different stages of evolution of human communities—agricultural-pastoral, mercantile and industrial—have created different formulas; nevertheless, the city remains a point of confluence in its initial phase, and its growth is closely linked to possibilities of concentration and cohabitation, as well as to its capacity for attracting external groups.

Amaravati, and Nagarjunakonda in the lower Krishna River Valley witnessed several evolutionary stages (agricultural-pastoral, mercantile, and industrial) through their pre- and protohistoric ages before they emerged as cities during the pre- and early Christian era. Specifically, some of the ancestors of those people who later worshiped Buddhist *stūpas* in Amaravati and Nagarjunakonda can be traced back to neolithic communities who entered Andhra leading pastoral lives. Around 1500 BCE, these neolithic communities began to make use of copper and emerged as characteristically chalcolithic. That is, they used agricultural tools like hoes as well as food-processing equipment, suggesting that they had left behind their pastoral lifestyle and had begun to settle down practicing agriculture. Pieces of jewelry made of copper, as well as copper tools recovered at places like Guttikonda, and Cinnamanur,[6] indicate their interaction with their northern neighbors, such as the cultures that flourished in Vidarbha in Madhya Pradesh.[7] For copper was not an easily available metal in these parts. The evidence shows that metallurgy at this period was developed only in the Vidarbha region by chalcolithic and megalithic communities from where the implements must have been imported. Although we don't have any evidence to prove how they imported copper implements, it is plausible that these neolithic communities in Andhra exchanged their surplus agricultural produce. Agricultural production and its surplus must have given these communities some leisure time as evidence points to the development of certain skills in organizing their society and developing arts and crafts. They showed interest in decorations and paintings, as is revealed from their pottery, terracotta objects, and rock brusings.[8] Dhavalikar who worked on neolithic sites in the Western Deccan, was of the opinion that these communities were organized into "chiefdom societies" where the surplus was controlled by a few.[9] His assumption was made on the basis of studying unearthed public buildings, fortifications, granaries, and irrigation structures at Diamabad and Inamgoan in Maharashtra. However, in Andhra, there is no evidence of monumental buildings belonging to neolithic-chalcolithic communities, although we know that these communities were branches of the same stock of people who lived in Karnataka. The kind of structured societies that Dhavalikar encountered in Karnataka were seen in Andhra only during the next stage, the megalithic period.

Be that as it may, I am primarily concerned here with the earliest structures built for the living and the dead. At Nagarjunakonda, the communities who had arrived by 2000 BCE lived in underground dwellings aligned with postholes.[10] They buried their dead in pits and filled them with cairn heaps. Although we don't have enough proof to show that these cairn heaps were venerated in the same way as Buddhist *stūpa*s were in the later periods, one can argue that the origins for the concept of the *stūpa* would seem to be traceable to these early burial forms. At the same time, it is hard to miss the similarity between the shapes of Buddhist *stūpa*s and the early dwellings of the neolithic communities in the southern part of Kurnool District, people who lived in huts of an apsidal, oval, and circular type.[11] The apsidal and circular shapes were so sustained in popularity in later periods that the same huts have continued to be built even to this day in many parts of Andhra.

The newly migrated groups of neolithic-chalcolithic people in Andhra followed a postexcarnation system of burial. A majority of them attempted to arrange the bones of their dead in their original anatomical order thus reflecting their ritualized care towards the dead.[12] The fact that some of these communities buried their dead children either in pots or in pits within their houses may also reflect their belief in afterlife, since these arrangements would seem to indicate that they believed that the children needed to be provided with safety and protection even after their deaths.[13] From the study of the skulls of the dead, Murthy has argued that the majority of these early communities can be identified as Mediterraneans of the Protoaustraloid complex whose continued presence can be traced up to the early historical period when Buddhism was the dominant form of religious expression.[14]

Megalithic Phase (800 BCE–300 BCE)

The Megalithic period in Andhra falls between 800 and 300 BCE. The transition from chaclolithic-neolithic culture to the megalithic was very smooth as far as Andhra and the lower Krishna River Valley is concerned. The evidence shows that there is a continuum in many cultural practices while the new period was characterized by the use of iron and further developments in agriculture, crafts, and building technology. Just like its preceding culture, megalithic culture witnessed many different communities arriving in different parts of Andhra who overlapped each other at times. Although all of them built megalithic monuments for their dead, these communities were differentiated according to the types of these sepulchral monuments.

While chalcolithic-neolithic culture in its final stage witnessed agriculture and settled village life, it was the megalithic culture that would set the stage for urbanization in the first historical period (third century CE forward). The examination of skulls in the lower Krishna River Valley and elsewhere in Andhra shows that the population of megalithic culture was mixed. Some of these mixed groups shared racial affinities with the earlier chacolithic-neolithic communities while others with those of megalithic cultures from Karnataka.[15] This racial mixing of communities resulted in the development of a new subculture in the lower Krishna valley and elsewhere in Andhra.

The most significant new development in the megalithic period marking this new subculture was the construction of reservoirs at many places in Andhra.[16] While spacious storage granaries dug into the earth suggest that these tanks were used for irrigation, their proximity to living areas may indicate their use as drinking water reservoirs.[17] Spacious platforms built inside and outside of houses may also have been used for temporary storage of grains and other produce just in the same way as platforms in the contemporary Andhra village houses are used today.[18] The houses during this time had enclosure walls with stone slabs probably erected to provide protection for produce from wild animals and thieves.[19] The late phase of megalithic culture also witnessed the use of sun-dried mud bricks thus marking the innovation of brick making technology in Andhra.[20]

Findings of burial goods suggest that there were further developments in crafts and the trade network during this period. In addition to the usual pottery and personal ornaments, Andhra megalithic burials invariably contained iron implements and terracotta figurines. Although implements of copper continued to be sparse in Andhra, especially in the lower Krishna River valley, the use of iron for a variety of purposes, from agricultural, domestic tools to defensive weapons, is evident from the findings of these burial goods.[21] Indigenous technology among these megalithic folk is known from the remains of a number of ancient iron working spots and iron ores found in Karimnagar, Mahaboobnagar, Nizamabad, and Adilabad Districts.[22] The bead-making industry known from findings at Kondapur and other places also belonged to this period.[23] Jewelry made of copper and bronze continued to appear in this period. In addition, ornaments made of silver, gold, and ivory have been noticed in burial goods in both lower Krishna River Valley and elsewhere in Andhra indicating their importation from other areas. These imports and exports helped to share ideas resulting in the advancement of technological skills.[24]

Megalithic burials grew dramatically in size and shape owing to an increasing complexity in building methods when compared to the burials of the earlier period. This development serves as a marker for assessing the amount of skills and resources that this culture had developed. In the study of other pre- and protohistoric cultures in other parts of the world, there has been quite a bit of debate among scholars about the possible spread of megalithic cultures from one region to another, even from one continent to another. Colin Renfrew, for instance, has found himself in a dilemma about whether or not to label similar types of contemporary burial structures found in different parts of Europe during megalithic period as "megalithic tombs":[25]

> It is important, then, to recognize that it is a taxonomic decision of our own which leads us to apply the term 'megalthic tomb' to monuments as different as the *dysser* of Denmark and the passage graves of Almeria. And yet, at the same time, it is difficult to escape from the feeling that there *is* a certain homogeneity, both in time and in space, of the distribution of these monuments once so defined.

In Andhra, we also have a variety of "megalithic tombs" reflecting different cultural traits. But because of proximity, these Andhra cultures had undoubtedly interacted with each other and in the process had created a greater amount of homogeneity when compared to the cultures of disparate regions of Europe. All of the megalithic communities in Andhra continued the tradition of extended burial practices of the dead handed down from their predecessors but employed new techniques that they learned through interaction with other neighbors to provide more secure and elaborate abodes for their ancestors. In Europe, the relative heterogeneity of megalithic cultures sharing a common feature of building stone monuments has generated debates among scholars about whether or not a single culture was originally responsible for the diffusion and eventual variegation of burial practices. Debating the hypotheses that European megalithic culture originally had "a single focal area" from which it spread to different parts of the world, Renfrew says this:[26]

> A widespread, Atlantic distribution in the absence of a single colonising movement of megalithic spread need not be a paradox. It requires simply that a particular set of conditions existed in the Atlantic region at this time, conditions which were not seen elsewhere in Europe, and that these favored the construction of stone monuments by the small-scale societies of the time. Such a general formulation, if it can be achieved, would explain for us the essentially independent genesis of stone monuments, no doubt of widely different forms, in several areas. It might also explain for us the essentially independent genesis of stone monuments, no doubt of widely different forms, in several areas. It might also explain the adoption of similar customs in adjacent areas, and do so in such a way as to give detailed, locally-operating reasons for such an adoption, rather than appealing to migration or diffusion as adequate explanation that is, in the traditional sense, non-diffusionist, in no way denies the mutual influence of neighbouring communities.

What Renfrew argues in relation to the European context appears to be true as far as the different streams of megalithic cultures in Andhra are concerned. While difference might be attributed to geographical and ecological factors abetting independent developments, the common features that tie these different and independent streams in Andhra had been a result of constant interaction of contemporary communities rather than an imposition of one dominant culture over others. If so, this view works against the more conventional understanding that the diffusion of religious culture from the north, be it Brahamnical or Buddhist, simply established itself in the south.

As far as independent innovations are concerned, megalithic communities in Andhra adapted different building methods for their burials depending on the material available in the localities in which they lived. In the lower Krishna River Valley, these communities buried their dead in cairns, cists, pits, urns, and terracotta sarcophagi.[27] The origins of the sarcophagus can be traced to the neolithic communities of the Deccan,[28] and its further development in Andhra took place in the alluvial plains of Krishna basin at places like Agiripalli and Tenneru[29] where stone is sparse for building. Stone troughs, however, were developed in hilly areas like Dongatogu in the Khammam District.[30] Whatever their construction methods, it is evident from these structures that not only did these communities believed in afterlife but also that they venerated their dead and spent a lot of time and energy to build structures that were far superior to their homes. Local people still refer to these structures as *rakshasa gullu,* the literal translation being the "temples of demons."[31] But here "demons" refer to souls who become active during the night and wander about unless they are provided with secured abodes. At the risk of being anachronistic, if this popular belief is somewhat akin to the understanding of the megalithic community, then it would seem as if they were providing more than what would be practically expected for the dead to continue on in their "afterlives." For, it was unnecessary to expend so much effort and to employ so many skilled people to build these relatively large and well-constructed monuments unless it was really their intention to venerate or placate their dead, and not just to provide for their welfare in the afterlife. Buddhist literature gives us some clues regarding what might have been the preexisting beliefs about the dead before Buddhism took over the land. The Mūlasarvāstivāda *Vinaya*[32] mentions ghosts in the context of one of its discussions on how to dispose of the dead. It mentions how the dead, if not ritually disposed of properly, can return as ghosts to their previous abodes and cause harm. If there was a similar belief among the megalithic communities of Andhra, its presence would help to explain why they built elaborate abodes for their dead. Yet, the architectural complexity and the skill involved in constructing these monuments suggest that there may have been additional motivations at work. It is well known that many tribal societies in India built special structures in specific places that they revered as sacred. This was certainly the case in early historic Andhra culture. Some of the megalithic structures in Andhra have served as precursors to Buddhist *stūpa*s not only in their shape, plan, and constructional methods, but also in the manner in which we can see a deliberated selection of given natural spaces for their constructions. Buddhist literature itself refers to a long-standing tradition of enshrining the relics that predates the religion. Gregory Schopen,[33] in his essay on the cult of the monastic dead, cites archeological evidence indicating the construction of *stūpa*s predating the cult of the Buddha:

> Archeologically and epigraphically, the two types of *stūpa* appear now as roughly contemporary with, in some cases, some indication that *stūpas* of the local monastic dead may actually have predated those of the Buddha.

He goes on to say:[34]

> It is interesting to note, moreover, that if we look at the internal chronology or narrative time taken for granted in our Buddhist literary sources, it would appear that their redactors also considered *stūpas* for the local monastic dead to predate those of the Buddha. Both of the *stūpa*s mentioned in *Udāna* and *Apadāna*, and that referred to in the Pali *Vinaya*, for example, long preceded—according to the narrative time assumed by our texts—those erected for the Buddha.

In the case of megalithic monuments, we do not know for sure that these contained the relics of any dead monks, but it is very possible that the dead in whose commemoration these monuments were built were highly respected by the community.[35] What we do know is that the monastic cult that Schopen is discussing was prevalent in Andhra's Krishna River Valley in places like Amaravati, Nagarjunakonda and Guntupalle where a number of small *stūpa*s containing the relics of monks were set up close to other major *stūpa* constructions.[36] These structures may be the direct result of transformations originally derived from megalithic religious activities.

The megalithic culture in Andhra falls between the eighth and third centuries BCE, and there are, of course, overlaps with the urbanizing historical period that starts as early as the fourth century BCE. This overlap of megalithic culture with the historical period is signaled, for instance, by the continuous but very rare presence of megalithic burials into the early centuries of common era, such as those found at Muktyala[37] and at Galabhagutta[38] where Brāhmī characters are noticed. There are several examples to show the influence of these megalithic burials on Buddhist *stūpa*s that started appearing in Andhra as early as the fourth to third centuries BCE, signaling the beginning of the early historic period.

Early Historic Phase (400–100 BCE)

In some ways, the transition between the megalithic culture and the early historical period might not seem so significant. The gradual technological development achieved by megalithic communities in construction, metallurgy, and agriculture is what really advanced them into the early historic phase. The catalytic urbanizing revolution that did occur was, in addition to trade, the result of a vast increase in food production made possible first by the introduction of iron tools, such as the plough, sickle, hoe, spade, and so on, and then with the construction of reservoirs and irrigation channels.[39] This surplus of food, turned into a surplus of wealth through trade, is what helped to fund the patronage of skilled craftsmen and specialized labor. Not only were these developments conducive to the growth of brisk trade relations, but also to the formation of a complex form of government, a government that needed to protect the interests of various professions while providing safety and security from outside invasions by maintaining a standing army. Fear of outside invasion is what probably necessitated the building of fortified cities and more sophisticated ways of organizing defense systems. All of this occurred simultaneously with the introduction of Buddhist religious culture.

While these forces of the urbanization process gathered more momentum starting from the fourth century BCE, small cities headed by chiefs grew out of villages situated along rivers and rivulets. The *Milindapañha*, an early Buddhist text that was composed around this time in northern India, mentions an elaborate plan for building towns and cities.[40] At the same time, sculptural constellations at sites like Amaravati and Nagarjunakonda begin to reflect urban scenes. Corroborating this evidence, a number of very early cities and towns have been unearthed at Dhulikatta, Kotilingala, Budigapalle, and Dharanikota which belong to the early fourth century BCE and contain remains of fortifications, palatial buildings, subterranean sewage systems, well-laid-out roads, managed water supply systems, and metallurgy works. Several port cities that also later became famous Buddhist centers in the Krishna River Valley, such as Amaravati, Nagarjunakonda, Ghantasala, and Bhattiprolu also date precisely to this time.[41] All were well planned with specified places for common dwellings, workshops, public structures, palaces, good roads and covered drainage systems. Some of the dwellings dating to this time were multistoried with tiled roofs.

These fortified cities and towns were ruled over by chieftains (with titles such as *Mahārathi, Mahātalavara,* and *rājaya*) either independently or possibly through power delegated from a political center. In either case, we know that these rulers controlled local resources and then attempted to regulate the value of trade by minting coins on their own.[42] Many of these rulers might have been Buddhist laity or possibly even monks as two Brāhmī inscriptions found at the Satavahana level of digging at Pedda Vegi, mention the name of one Mahārāja Kākichi who is said to have been an inmate (*antevāsaka*) of a Buddhist monastery.[43]

Almost all of the towns and cities mentioned above became well known Buddhist centers and all of them were located along ancient trade routes and hence connected to the network of land routes and navigational channels leading to different parts of the subcontinent. The port towns and cities not only were well connected to the land routes but also carried on coastal and inland trade using the sea and river systems. There is abundant evidence to show that contacts with the north and the rest of the subcontinent increased during this time. That these trade routes linked the north and Andhra is also inferred from the presence and spread of northern black polished ware (NBPW).[44] The evidence of a limited use of a special variety of NBPW treated with copper riveting and luting produced in the Ganga-Yamuna Doab makes its specific presence in many Buddhist sites in Andhra, indicating the ongoing relations that these Buddhist institutions maintained with their northern counterparts.[45]

Apart from pottery, the uniformity of punch-marked coins from the fourth century BCE found in many regions of the north as well as many places in Andhra further suggest the region's connection through trade.[46] In addition, industries like bead making from semiprecious stones at Peddabankur and terracotta figurines and a mould found at Yelesvaram also add to my argument about how these cities and towns were well positioned to supply merchandise through a distribution network.[47]

Though less reliable owing to uncertainties of dating the redaction of texts, there is a variety of literary references suggesting the presence of Buddhism in Andhra at this time.[48] Further, early epigraphic evidence dating to the reign of Aśoka in the third century BCE reveals that some Andhras were already followers of the Buddha by this time.[49] This is by far the earliest epigraphic reference to the population of Andhra termed as "Andhakas."[50] Thomas identifies these Andhakas as the Mahāsāṃghikas who were said to have played a significant role in the discussions that took place at the third Great Buddhist Council convoked by Aśoka at Pataliputra.[51]

Given the presence of Buddhism that emerged along with increased trade and urbanization in Andhra possibly as early as the fourth century CE or even earlier, some have taken the position that the local megalithic culture of Andhra was simply replaced by a triumphant Buddhism. Others have argued that Buddhism integrated forms of practice from the indigenous traditions into its evolving religious culture. Schopen, for instance, argues how Buddhist monks when moving into foreign lands incuding Andhra had "to forge some links with the local land, to find a place in the local landscape."[52] As a part of this strategy, he says that monks "sought out . . . already occupied" places by the protohistoric dead.[53] It is true, as is seen in the following examples that most cases, *stūpa*s were built in the same spaces that were used by megalithic folk. In fact, not just the use of space, but also the form and architectural patterns of megalithic burials were assimilated into Buddhist *stūpas*. Other popular religious symbols as I show below were also incorporated as well. Looking at the evolution of Andhra culture through its material remains, the presence of its local genius and its adaptability is unmistakable even after its Buddhist transformation. This is evident not just in how the Buddhist cult was expressed through assimilated local beliefs and traditions but also in how they shared their genius with other regions of the subcontinent and beyond.

I have already indicated how Buddhist *stūpas* in the Krishna River Valley were built in the same spaces that were used earlier for megalithic burials of the proto-*caitya* type. Examples can be cited from Yeleswaram and Amaravati where megalithic burials of different types such as cairns, cists, and urns were found immediately beneath the tier of Buddhist *stūpas*.[54] This leads us to the possibility that the community accorded a similar kind of ritualized sanctity to the *stūpa* as they had earlier accorded to the places of their own dead. In the past, archeologists have mentioned the structural similarities between megalithic burials and *stūpas* noting, as I would argue, that the *stūpa* evolved from a more primitive custom of burying the dead.[55] In fact, the etymological meaning of *stūpa* is "a pile" or "a heap."[56] What follows are some instances that further illustrate the significant links. A burial at Chagatur has a stone pavement with four upright stones at each of its four cardinal points, the architectural feature that was seen adopted in the construction of many Buddhist *stūpas*.[57] The *stūpas* at places like Amaravati and Yelesvaram were adorned with an *āyaka* platform and pillars at the four cardinal points just like the burial at Chagatur.[58] Another popular form of apsidal plan used in building early Buddhist *stūpas* can be seen in a dolmenoid cist at Padra, where the base is built in an apsidal plan, the plan that was used to build huts since neolithic times.[59] This apsidal plan has been borrowed in building *caitya gṛhas* to house the *stūpa* or other Buddhist symbols. Early forms of *caityas* that were built in the apsidal plan are also evident at Bhattiprolu, a Buddhist site of the third century BCE[60] and Guntupalli from the second century BCE.[61] One of the other forms of *stūpa* construction in Andhra is in the shape of a *svastika*. The megalithic communities often used the *svastika* pattern in the construction of multichambered cists.[62] Examples of these are the *stūpas* at Nagarjunakonda[63] and Peddaganjam containing *svastika*-shaped bases.[64]

While the architectural borrowings from the earlier megalithic period gave some uniqueness to Andhra Buddhist structures, the popular sculptural motifs such as tree and *nāga* (hooded serpent) as part of Buddhist symbols are well known beyond the boundaries of Andhra. Fergusson has discussed very elaborately the prevalence of the *nāga* and tree cults among pre-Buddhist societies including Andhra and its consequent and frequent depiction in the *stūpa* decoration at Sanchi and Amaravati.[65] Especially at Amaravati, Fergusson felt that the representation of *nāga* dominated the temple, making it difficult at times to determine whether the shrine was meant for the Buddha or the *nāga* himself. While both *nāga* and tree cults received veneration independently by the common folk throughout many parts of India, their association with the cult of the goddess is universal. Particularly in the context of Andhra, it is common for the rural populations to worship goddess in the form of tree or *nāga* into the present day.[66]

What is interesting however, is how this seemingly ubiquitous worship of goddess was integrated into Buddhist institutions.[67] The auspicious symbol *pūrṇakumbha*, the full pot of grains or water or vegetation, symbolizes abundance and is often taken to represent work of the mother goddess. Some of the nude mother goddess figurines were depicted with *pūrṇakumbha* as a kind of womb. This *pūrṇakumbha* is seen portrayed in bricks on the doorjambs of monk cells in Thotlakonda and Bavikonda and other Buddhist sites elsewhere.[68] The goddess Hārītī, a protective mother figure in the Buddhist pantheon who symbolizes monastic prosperity can be seen perhaps as a Buddhist adaptation of the mother goddess.[69] The extent images of Hārītī located outside of refectories among the ruins of Buddhist monasteries in Nagarjunakonda and Sankaram would seem to attest to the popularity of this goddess cult at this time. Even to this very day in Andhra, the goddess continues to be worshiped in various forms and the worship of the goddess in the form of a vessel containing water remains very popular among Andhra population.

The architectural forms, symbolism, imagery, and sentiments that were held sacred by the local population were carefully integrated into Buddhism and its establishments. The structure and function of megalithic burial reappeared with few variations in the form of Buddhist *stūpa*. The *nāga* becomes *Mucilinda nāga*, the protector of the symbols of the Buddha which in the later period was portrayed as the protector of the Buddha himself. The symbols of the goddess such as *pūrṇakumbha* have been appropriated as auspicious symbols adorning the doorjambs of monks' cells, while some of the monasteries constructed separate shrines for the goddess where monks and laity made food offerings. Thus the Buddhism that spread among Andhra folk expressed itself using the local genius and popular belief system as though the religion itself was the local creation.

Śatavāhana and Ikṣvāku Periods (100 BCE—300 CE)

I have noted how literary references seem to suggest the spread of Buddhism to Andhra possibly as early as to the life time of the master. I have also tried to show how aspects of emergent Andhra Buddhism was, in some cases, literally built on indigenous religious cults. But, the forms of cultic behavior constitutive of Andhra Buddhism did not just stay in Andhra but also seem to have created a space for themselves among the Buddhist communities of the north as well. The continuous interaction of Andhra Buddhists with the north is known from Buddhist texts such as *Mahavāgga*, a text that refers to either monasteries or rest houses with the names Andhakavana near Shravasti and Andhakavinda at Rajagriha.[70] An Aśokan pillar inscription that was issued later speaks about the followers of *Dharma* from Andhra living in Rajavisaya. We know from these types of references that Andhras were collectively referred to as Andhakas. More details about these Andhakas come from later literature belonging to Śatavāhana period.

Two important tribes, the Nāgas and Yakṣas, are mentioned in this literature as forming the majority of the Andhra population. These tribes did not seem to live in isolation. On the contrary we see significant intermixing between these tribes, even with Brahmins from the north.[71] For instance, the *Kathāsaritsāgara* written during Śatavāhana times (second century BCE to third century CE), records the story of Dipakarni in which the origin of Śatavāhanas is mentioned.[72] According to this, the first Śatavāhana was born out of the union of a Yakṣa by name Śata and a Brahmin girl thus signaling how the dynasty perceived of its beginnings. Another text of the same period talks about Gunadhya, a minister to one of the Śatavāhana rulers who was born out of a wed lock between a Nāga prince and a Brahmin woman.[73] It is true that this evidence comes from later mythic sources, but it has some salience nonetheless. Given material evidence such as pottery, coins, and other sculptural representations, the frequent mention of Nāgas and Yakṣas in literature, one can deduce that the local tribes did share a lot in common with the north as early as the third century BCE.

While there are some records indicating royal support to Buddhist institutions, the majority of the evidence coming from inscriptions proves that it was common people, such as traders and craftsmen who were the main supporters of Buddhist tradition. Inscriptions found at the sites of ancient Buddhist *stūpa*s reveal that Buddhism seems to have been first patronized in Andhra by traders and then gradually attracted the attention of all sections of society, including royalty. The relationship between Buddhism and trade has been legendary since the beginnings of the religious tradition. Indeed, the literary tradition avers that the first converts of the Buddha after his enlightenment experience were not monks, but merchants who became the first lay supporters to take refuge. According to early textual accounts,[74] the Buddha first encountered two traveling merchants named Tapussa and Bhallika who, in later lore, were thought responsible for establishing the cult of the Buddha's hair relic in various Buddhist countries, including Afghanistan, Burma, and Sri Lanka.[75] While the story is more metaphoric in meaning than historical in fact, it underscores the perceived primary role played by merchants and traders in the early spread of the religion. Why Buddhism attracted the merchant class remains an interesting question to this day.

One view, probably more Buddhist apology than fact, is that it is possible that the Buddha's "casteless" ethic provided a certain appeal to those formerly dependent on brahmanical ritual and teaching for their spiritual practices and hopes. But more likely, it would appear that the cult of the *stūpa* honoring the remains of the Buddha struck a resonant cord among those with a cultural and religious penchant for honoring the dead, venerating *nāga*s, and venerating the powers of the goddess, all characteristics of proto-Andhra society that I discussed above. Moreover, the appeal of Buddhism for the artisans and traders who formed an important class of urbanizing people, can be clearly seen in the ideology of merit that serves as a conceptual underpinning for the practice of *stūpa* veneration. The cult of the *stūpa* provided a means for those who had recently acquired wealth to express their religious sentiments through material means. Donating to the *saṇgha* through the building of monasteries and by the construction of *stūpa*s was a highly meritorious act that signaled positive karmic consequences in at least two ways. The doctrine of *karma* legitimates one's social and economic status. By one's actions, one benefits or suffers consequences. Being able to contribute liberally to the interests of the religion can be taken as a sign of one's success. Second, the well-known practice of merit-transference provided a means to continue assisting and honoring one's departed ancestors. It is within this context that acquiring wealth, the chief preoccupation of the trading class, made possible the making and sharing of merit, the chief form of Buddhist religious activity for the laity. These religious actions do not require the intermediary services of brahmin priests and suggest much more of an ethic of independence, self-effort and work, an ethic thoroughly congenial to the attitudes of the trading class.

The success of traders and their religious association with Buddhism was not lost on the political rulers of Andhra at this time. Inscriptions issued by political chieftains during this time at Amaravati,[76] and Bhattiprolu,[77]announce their donations and support to the Buddhist *saṅgha*. At the same time, coins issued by these same rulers reflect their enthusiasm for growing trade relations.[78] It is clear that by embracing and supporting trade, they also saw it expedient to embrace and support the religion of the traders. Often the conversion of whole peoples is said to follow the conversion of their leaders. In the Andhra of this era, perhaps the reverse process occurred.

Following the conversion of political chieftains, we can also note, however, how other segments of Andhra society soon followed. We can see through further evidence of inscriptions that people of various castes belonging to agriculture and industry organized themselves into larger associations. The names of these associations and their flourishing states are known from the engraved records of donations they made to various Buddhist establishments. These include such groups who came to be known as *gāmas*[79] (village agriculturalists), *nigamas*[80] (traders), and *ghoṣṭis*[81] (professionals) at Bhattiprolu, Dhanyakataka, and Amaravati. The steadily increasing numbers of donations made collectively by people belonging to such *gāma*s, *nigama*s, and *ghoṣṭi*s indicates the sudden rise of their economic prosperity. This prosperity is also corroborated by the finding of many hoards of punch-marked coins dating to this time.[82] In addition, some of these punch-marked coins at places like Nasthullapur were found along with extensive hoards of Roman coins.[83] Foreign traders, who were residents at Amaravati, also apparently understood the connection between Buddhism and trade. Records of their donations made in support of Buddhist cave establishments are also now known.[84] By the preceding and early centuries of the Common Era, Buddhism through flourishing economic activity had proliferated into virtually all sections of Andhra society. Simultaneously, it spread to other countries as well.

Literary tradition abounds with stories of merchants from various parts of the subcontinent heading for Southeast Asian countries to amass wealth. Archaeological studies in Southeast Asia repeatedly mention the impact of Amaravati school of Buddhist art in these countries. According to Somasekhara Sarma, the script of some of the inscriptions found at Ghantasala's *stūpa* site, correspond exactly to inscriptions found in Java (Indonesia)[85] raising the possibility of established trade relations between Andhra and Java in the early centuries CE.

There is abundant archaeological evidence in Andhra as far as the trade beyond the Arabian Sea is concerned.[86] This evidence and the unearthed hoard of Roman coins in and around Buddhist establishments suggest the possibility that trade with countries beyond the Arabian Sea was conducted under the ageis of Buddhist institutions. The association of this pottery with Buddhist monastic sites may reveal the cosmopolitan nature of *saṇgha* during this time. At Nagarjunakonda, the names of various monasteries suggest that there were accommodations for monks coming from different regions of the subcontinent as far as Kashmir and Gandhara regions in the north and Sri Lanka in the Indian Ocean in the south. These monasteries must have had enormous resources to attract people from these far away lands. It was Kosambi[87] who first suggested that the monasteries might have facilitated the trade through trade caravans to make profits. Not many accepted Kosambi's view since some of the monasteries in question were away from towns and cities. Ray[88] talks about the Buddhist *saṇgha* holding a considerable amount of land and property in the early centuries of Common Era. Her argument was on the basis of the evidence for storage rooms at Nagarjunakonda, material remains of the presence of various industries and a large number of donations made by people from different walks of life. Buddhist *vihāra*s at places like Bavikonda and Thotlakonda also have remains of storage houses while local and foreign coins invariably have been included in the cultural remnants of almost all of the Buddhist sites. Furthermore, coin molds and coins in *vihāra*s at Nagarjunakonda show that these monasteries possessed separate mints of their own.[89] Schopen in his chapter on monks, nuns, and "vulgar" practices argues with the help of inscriptional evidence how monks and nuns constituted the majority in making donations to the image cult.[90] Obviously monks and nuns during the pre- and early centuries of Christian era were able to own property. If this was true, it would not have been difficult for them, if not on the behalf of the Buddhist monastery, to act on their own as private bankers to loan the money to traders.

Conclusion

The Buddhism that developed along with trade and urbanization in Andhra replaced the megalithic burial monuments with *stūpa*s. On the one hand it can be argued that the local megalithic culture of Andhra transformed Buddhism by integrating its forms of practice into the indigenous milieu. On the other hand, it may be surmised that Buddhism became the new status quo of religious culture and grafted some of the indigenous practices into its edifice. On the basis of the analysis of the material culture, we can assert with confidence that the tradition of ancestor veneration that started in the prehistoric ages within these Andhra communities eventually culminated in the worship of the Buddhist *stūpa* reflecting the undeniable fact that there was continuity between the earlier and the newer forms of religion.

The emergent Buddhist religious culture of Andhra reveals an inclusive sensitivity to indigenous religious cults and their symbolic expression. This inclusive ethos in which Buddhist institutions incorporated popular forms of religion abetted its appeal to a broad cross-section of urbanizing society. The forms of veneration of the dead that were predominant among pre- and protohistoric societies were successfully merged into Buddhist symbols and cultic forms of veneration. Other lesser forms of religious expression in the form of goddess and snake images also found their place within the Buddhist complex thus providing a wider venue to meet a full-scale religious needs of the population as a whole.

When the population experienced a transition from a self-sufficient, agrarian society to an urban one that was ambitious in acquiring skills, wealth, and self-respect, Buddhism came to its aid. It provided a matrix of values to meet these needs. This is seen very clearly in relation to the merchant community. Buddhist establishments were often set up in strategic places that would give shelters to merchant caravans and the sea voyagers. In conclusion, I want to briefly allude to some of the reasons behind the close ties between the trading class and Buddhist establishments.

The spread and vitality of trade was directly linked to the spread and vitality of Buddhism. As a religion appealing to commoners because of its "casteless" concerns and its religious ethic of giving, it proved attractive to a wide variety of people. Traders found that in Buddhism, there were fewer barriers between them and the other classes (cultivators and artisans) with whom they came into contact with in the business of trade. Business friendship included religious friendship. Buddhist traders erected *stūpa*s not only to honor the Buddha, but also to demonstrate that their material excesses were equated with spiritual success. These *stūpa*s also became important landmarks, beacons and lighthouses to mariners, and the larger *vihāra*s also provided shelter to itinerant traders. In this connection, it is interesting to note the role reversal that took place here: supportive laity had become those on the move in pursuit of economic success while the Buddhist monks had begun to live more of a sedentary existences. This last point does not ignore the fact that monks often accompanied traders in their far-flung voyages to regions of Southeast Asia and beyond where trade and Buddhism were also to flourish hand-in-hand.

Finally, with reference to the question of what was responsible for the relative demise of Buddhism in Andhra that I raised at the outset perhaps we can only ponder basic questions and speculate. Did the Buddhists outdo themselves in remaking the religion to make it congenial for so many of the masses? While Buddhist "inclusion" abetted its success as it spread across the depth and breadth of Andhra by meeting the needs of the changing society that was going through the evolution from pastoral through rural and urban forms, is it possible that it became too identified with the socioeconomic regimes of those times? While it was successful for more than 600 years in Andhra, did the factor of economic decline of the society within which it had become so intertwined and identified lead to its own decline? Buddhist institutions rather suddenly found themselves without much patronage in the fourth century CE. While there is some indication that it entered into another phase of change in association with the rise of the Mahāyāna, it also seems to have lost its great popularity in Andhra at a time when the society in general had retreated economically. By the time the economy recovered, had Buddhism changed itself so much that it lost its resonance with the deeper structures of religion in Andhra? Was this why, as a transformed institution, it became a very poor competitor to other forms of religion such as Śaivism that seems to have better catered to the needs of the another wave of urbanization? And why was it not able to reconnect with the rural communities of those times as well?

However these questions are answered, it cannot be denied that Buddhism came to Andhra at a time when conditions were such that it was able to create cohesiveness and order in the society that was going through a change. Newly emerged professional groups found social respect and spiritual satisfaction by associating themselves with Buddhist institutions. The concept of "*dāna*" helped not only to boost the morality of the public but also gave a further boost to the economy. While Buddhism flourished with the traders' patronage, it was also spread by these trading communities from the Krishna River Valley to other regions of India and across the seas to Sri Lanka, regions of Southeast Asia and beyond.

Notes

1. B. S. L. Hanumantha Rao, et al., *Buddhist Inscriptions of Andhradesa* (Secundrabad: Ananda Buddha Vihara Trust, 1998), pp. 10–12; B. S. Rajendra Babu, *Material Culture of the Deccan* (Delhi: Agam Kala Prakashan, 1999), p. 25. Babu states that an inscription of Dharmakirti dated 1344 CE mentions the repairs done to the main *stūpa* (*mahā caitya*) at Amaravati. But the existence of the Mahāstūpa until this late is controversial although there are references to the lingering Buddhist remnants in Amaravati and elsewhere. For the controversy about the Mahāstūpa see Jonathan Walters' chapter in this volume.

2. On the basis of the unearthed hoards of Roman coins along coastal Andhra and inland, scholars and archeologists in the past assumed that Andhra

conducted direct trade with Rome and that this trade was in its height from first century BCE to the third century CE. In fact, in one of my papers on maritime trade, I have discussed the presence of Roman coins, bullae, sculptural representations, and architectural features in Andhra due to intrinsic trade links with Rome, see Sree Padma, "Maritime Archaeology of Andhra Pradesh: Prolegomenon to a study of a Roman influenced Buddhist Culture in South India." *Bulletin Australian Institute for Maritime Archaeology* 17.1 (1993), pp. 39–44. Some scholars have disputed this view saying that "Roman ships did not venture often beyond the Malabar Coast (see, David Whitehouse, "Epilogue: Roman Trade in Perspective," in Vimala Begley and Richard Daniel De Puma, eds., *Rome and India: The Ancient Sea Trade* [Madison, Wisconsin: The University of Wisconsin Press, 1991], pp. 216–220) and that the trade on the east coast was carried out by mediators who brought the merchandise by land routes to the west coast. At the same time, analysis of pottery types that had been termed as Mediterranean were analyzed as local imitations of foreign prototypes that antedate Roman trade itself. Further, it has been argued that Roman coins were brought to India only after their long circulation in the Roman Empire and then they were only traded for their metal value. See, N. C. Ghosh. *Excavations at Satanikota, 1977–80* (Delhi: Director, Archaeological Survey of India, 1986), p. 2. It was contended that most of the material evidence that appeared to be of Roman origins such as pottery, sculptures, terracotta findings, seals, and sealings came either from the Persian Gulf, the Red Sea or were the local imitations of foreign types. See H. P. Ray, *The Winds of Change* (Delhi: Oxford University Press, 1998), pp. 62–79. According to this view the "*yavanas*" who were mentioned in inscriptions and literature were not Romans but consisted of several trading partners including the Greeks and Arabs from the Gulf region (ibid., 83–85). The reports of recent excavations conducted at places like Arikamedu in Tamil Nadu, south India (Vimala Begley, "Changing Perceptions of Arikamaedu," in Vimala Begley et al., eds., *The Ancient Port of Arikamedu* [Pondichery, India: Ecole francaise D'Extreme-Orient, 1996], vol. I, pp. 1–40) and Mantai in Sri Lanka (John Carswell, "The Port of Mantai, Sri Lanka," in Vimala Begley and Richard Daniel De Puma, eds., pp. 197–203; see also O. Bopearachchi, "Seafaring in the Indian Ocean: Archaeological Evidence from Sri Lanka," Himanshu Prabha Ray & Jean-Francois Salles, eds., *Tradition and Archaeology* [New Delhi: Manohar, 1996], pp. 59–78), and studies in Egypt, East Africa, and the east coast of Red Sea (Steven Sidebotham. "Ports of the Red Sea and the Arabia-India Trade," in Vimala Begley and Richard Daniel De Puma, eds., pp. 12–35) reinforce the view of extensive trade between the ports of peninsular parts of India including its east coast with that of the Roman world as far as Alexandria during the first three centuries of CE.

3. B. Subbarao, *The Personality of India* (Baroda: M. S. University Monograph Series 3, 1958), p. 77 reports that the chalcolithic culture was mainly confined to northern India while in central (including the Andhra region) and western India, the neolithic culture, in the absence of copper tools, developed a sophisticated stone blade industry. This is true to a large extant in Andhra as copper was not a locally available metal. Nonetheless, the neolithic culture in Andhra did assume

a chalcolithic character finally with the appearance of copper tools, although in a limited number, which were likely acquired through trade.

4. P. Ramachandra Murthy, *Megalithic Culture of the Godavari Basin* (Delhi: Sharada Publishing House, 2000), pp. 32–35, 58, and 113.

5. Maurizio Tosi, "Early Urban Evolution and Settlement Patterns in the Indo-Iranian Borderland," in Colin Renfrew, ed., *The Explanation of Culture Change: Models in Prehistory* (Pittsburgh, PA: University of Pittsburg Press, 1973), p. 429.

6. E. Siva Nagi Reddy, *Evolution of Building Technology* (Delhi: Bharatiya Kala Prakashan, 1998), vol. I, p. 73.

7. P. Ramachandra Murthy, p. 67; V. Rami Reddy, *A Study of the Neolithic Culture of Southwestern Andhra Pradesh* (Hyderabad: Government of Andhra Pradesh, 1978), p. 93: "In view of the relative priority of the southern Neolithic culture, it would appear that the traits like grey ware, urn burial and polished stone tools might be derived in the northern Deccan from the south. On the other hand, painted pottery and use of copper are much more marked features of the Deccan chalcolithic. Their scarcity in the Neolithic culture in the south might suggest that these items were imported from the northern Deccan into the southern Deccan and other parts of south India."

8. V. V. Krishnasastry, *The Pre and Early Historical Cultures of Andhra Pradesh* (Hyderabad: Government of Andhra Pradesh, 1983), p. 46; V. Rami Reddy, p. 90.

9. M. K. Dhavalikar, "Cultural Ecology of the Chalcolithic Maharashtra," in S. B. Deo and K. Paddayya, eds., *Recent Advances in Indian Archaeology* (Poona: Deccan College Post Graduate and Research Institute, 1985), pp. 65–73, has an explanation about how the protohistoric communities evolved themselves into urban population in south Indian scenarios: "The early agricultural societies are characterized by a social organization which are different from that of the earlier hunter-gatherers. Agriculture brought large communities together for subsistence activities which further led to division of labour for efficient farming and craft specialization. This could be possible because of greater concentration of people at one place and also because of increased food supply with irrigation and consequent increased food production, new forms of redistributive mechanisms come into being. This, in turn, created the need for a centralized authority for controlling the distribution of water for storing surplus grain for lean years. Craft specialization led to trade and exchange. Increased wealth created a class of men of means who, together with the ruling elite, specialized craftsmen and tillers of the land, formed a class structured society" (p. 69).

10. P. Ramachandra Murthy, pp. 33–34.

11. Ibid., 34

12. Ibid., 64.

13. V. V. Krishnasastry, 1983, pp. 40–42.

14. P. Ramachandra Murthy, p. 169.

15. Ibid.

16. V. V. Krishnasastry, 1983, p. 106.

17. *Indian Archaeology—A Review, 1983–84*, Annual Report of Archaeological Survey of India, Delhi (here on wards *IAR*), pp. 3–4.

18. Ibid.

19. E. Siva Nagi Reddy, vol. I, pp. 116–117.

20. Ibid.

21. M. L. Nigam, *Excavation Report of Two Megalithic Burials at Hashmathpet*, (Hyderabad: Government of Andhra Pradesh, 1978), p. 6.

22. V. V. Krishnasastry, 1983, pp. 213, 219, and 237.

23. M. G. Dikshit, *Beads from Kondapur* (Hyderabad: Government of Andhra Pradesh, 1952), p. 27.

24. R. Subrahmanyam, *Nagarjunakonda (1954–60)*, Memoirs of Archaeological Survey of India, No. 75 (1975), vol. I, pp. 179, 194.

25. Colin Renfrew, *Approaches to Social Archeology* (Cambridge, MA: Harvard University Press, 1984), pp. 166–167.

26. Ibid., p. 168.

27. For the description of each of these megalithic monuments, see V. V. Krishnasastry, 1983, pp. 49–50; Bridget and Raymond Allchin, *The Rise of Civilization in India and Pakistan* (Cambridge: Cambridge University Press, 1982), p. 342.

28. *IAR, 1974–75*, pp. 33 and 34. During excavations at Inamgaon in Pune district in early Jorwe levels belonging to 1400–1000 BC, a burial pit was discovered with two four-legged urns of unbaked clay. While in the later Jorwe period of 1000 BC another four-legged urn of unbaked clay with a shape of human torso on its southern side containing an adult male skeleton. The burial offering suggests that it represents the current Hindu belief that the departed soul has to cross waters in a ferry in the heaven.

29. Ibid., pp. 70 and 113–114.

30. P. Ramachandra Murthy, p. 125.

31. A number of archaeologists mentioned this name as being prevalent among locals. See P. Ramachandra Murthy, p. 2.

32. Gregory Schopen, "On Avoiding Ghosts and Social Censure," in his *Bones, Stones, and Buddhist Monks* (Honolulu: University of Hawai'i Press: 1997), pp. 209–213.

33. Gregory Schopen, "An Old Inscription and the Cult of the Monastic Dead," in *Bones, Stones, and Buddhist Monks*, 181.

34. Ibid., pp. 181–182.

35. Archaeological reports reveal that a number of megalithic burials and Buddhist *stūpas* in Andhra and elsewhere were devoid of human mortuary remains, but some of them contained animal bones. No satisfactory explanation has been advanced so far to explain why. See Gregory Schopen, "Immigrant Monks and Protohistorical Dead: The Buddhist Occupation of Early Buddhist Sites in India," in his *Buddhist Monks and Business Matters* (Honolulu: University of Hawai'i Press: 2004), pp. 370–373.

36. Ibid., pp. 183–184.

37. V. V. Krishnasastry, 1983, pp. 13–24.

38. *Annual Report of the Archaeology and Museums, Andhra Pradesh, 1982–83* (here on wards *ARAM*), p. 7. About 200 dolmens are located on the hillock known as Peddapurapugutta. The arthostats of some of the dolmens in this group have marks quite similar to the graffiti marks noticed on megalithic burial pottery.

39. B. S. Rajendra Babu, p. 49.

40. *Milinda's Questions*, Tr. From Pali by I. B. Horner (London: Luzac & Company, 1969 reprint), vol. I, p. 46.

41. E. Siva Nagi Reddy, vol. I, p. 120. He further reports that wells and drainage systems were constructed to take the waste water away from the wells. Public structures included ampitheaters, rest houses, public baths, *ghāts*, and palaces with moats and fortified walls. In this context, we can recall Megasthenese account about Andhras possessing thirty walled cities.

42. A terracotta seal from Peddabankur and a potin coin from Polakonda refer to "Mahātalavara" and some coins from Kondapur bear the name or title of "Mahārathi." (Krishnasastry, 1983, pp. 130.) Coins unearthed at places like Kotilingala (N. S. Ramachandra Murthy, "Kotilingala, an early Historic Site," *Proceedings of Andhra Pradesh History Congress* [Karimnagar: A. P. History Congress, 1992], pp. 33–34) Nagarjunakonda (*IAR*, 1954–55 to 1960–61), and so forth mention other names for these rulers or chieftains.

43. Krishnasastry, 1983, p. 19.

44. H. Sarkar & B. P. Sinha, "Ancient Magadha: The Cradle of the Northern Black Polished Ware," in P. C. Pant and Vidula Jayaswal, eds., *Ancient Ceramics* (Delhi: Agam Kala Prakashan, 1997), pp. 85–115. Sarkar and Sinha state that the NBPW that was prevalent in the north and western parts of the subcontinent from 700–350 BCE, gradually spreading to various parts of Andhra around 350–250 BCE. The NBPW recovered at places like Kesarapalle (H. Sarkar, "Kesarapalle, 1962," *Ancient India* 22 [1966]: 43–44), Amaravati (*IAR* [1962–63], pp. 1–2) and Dhanyakataka (*IAR* [1964–65], p. 2) in the early layers belonging to the third and fourth centuries BCE shows the continuous interaction of these sites with their northern neighbors, along the coast and inland along the water channels.

45. Pisipaty Rama Krishna, "Megalithic Pottery: Cultural Contacts," in *Ancient Ceramics*, editors, P. C. Pant, Vidula Jayaswal (Delhi: Agam Kala Prakashan, 1997), p. 127.

46. P. L. Gupta, *Punch Marked Coins in the Andhra Pradesh Museums* (Hyderabad: Government of Andhra Pradesh, 1960), pp. 1–3. More recent excavations at Vaddamanu in the Guntur District also reveal both black and red ware as well as punch-marked coins. See *IAR* (1981–82), p. 2. Some of the earliest punch-marked coins recovered in Raichur and Karimnagar districts belonging to pre-Mauryan periods and the recovery of two different kinds of molds at Kondapur further support this view. See, A. W. A. Khan, *Monograph on Yelesvaram Excavation* (Hyderabad: Govt. of Andhra Pradesh, 1963), p. 45. The occurrence of copper punch-marked coins containing ship symbols at the earliest levels of occupation at Chandraketugarh in the lower Ganga Valley (*IAR* [1960–61], p. 70; *IAR* [1961–62], p. 107: and *IAR* [1962–63], p. 46) and forty-eight more varieties of these coins found at Amaravati would seem to indicate clearly the existence

of trade along the coast of the Bay of Bengal. Amaravati not only carried on trade during this time with the north and east coast communities, but also with Sri Lanka, as attested by the presence of sixty-two pearls found at Bhattiprolu, the type of which are found only off the northwest coast of Sri Lanka. See Alexander Rea, *South Indian Buddhist Antiquities* (Madras: Archaeological Survey of India, 1894), XV, pp. 7–11.

47. Alexander Rea, pp. 7–11 and 49–50.

48. For instance, the Pāli *Suttanipāta* (H. Saddhatissa, trans., *The Suttanipāta* [London: Curzon Press Ltd., 1985], pp. 114–133) contains what may be an early mythic account about how people from Andhra became followers of the Buddha even during the lifetime of the master. According to this myth, a certain brahmin from Sravasti by name of Baveri came to the south (the land of the Assakas beyond Pratishtana) and settled on the banks of the Godavari River in search of a life of detachment. Suffering from an illness, he was advised by a *yakṣa* to find the nature of his illness (*duḥkha*) from the Buddha. Hearing the *Dharma* preached by the Buddha, Baveri's followers were enlightened and became *arhant*s. Subsequently, they returned to Baveri and together, they began converting others to the Buddha's teaching. The reference to a *yakṣa* in this account can be taken to mean a person belonging to the *yakṣa*s, one of the important tribes in Andhra who were referred to as such. Another early literary reference to Buddhism in Andhra is found in the commentary of the *Vimānavatthu* where it is asserted that the King of the Assakas in Andhraratta (the Andhra country) was ordained as a member of the *saṇgha* (B. S. L. Hanumantharao, *Religion in Āndhra* [Hyderabad: Dept. of Archaeology and Museums, Govt. of Andhra Pradesh, 1993 rev. ed.], p. 55). This particular reference is similar in substance to the inscriptional evidence regarding how some rulers like *Mahārāja* Kākichi were ordained into the Buddhist *sangha*.

49. Rock Edict XIII; *Epigraphia Indica* (here onward *E.I.*), xxxv, p. 40: A fragmentary pillar inscription from Amaravati reveals that it is a part of an inscribed pillar of Aśoka; it contains a reference that would seem to attest to the antiquity of Buddhism in Amaravati as early as the third century BCE.

50. *Corpus Inscription Indicarum* 1: 66ff. (66–70); *E.I.* 35, p. 40 Rock Edict XIII mentions Andhras as followers of Aśoka's *dharma*.

51. See the discussion in E. J. Thomas, *History of Buddhist Thought* (London: Kegan Paul, Trench, Trubner & Co., 1963), pp. 33–37. Here, it is interesting to entertain a theory that the Caityaka sect of the Mahāsāṃghikas originated in Andhra [B. S. L. Hanumantha Rao, op. cit., pp. 79–85]. The Caityakas are so called because the decoration and worship of *caitya*s formed an important part of their cult. In light of our discussion, there would appear to be some plausibility to this theory as the worshipers of the indigenous cult of the dead, the Caityakas would have abetted the rise of *stūpa* cultic activity. Moreover, the term adapted "*Andhaka*" used to denote the people living in Andhaka or the Andhra region is sometimes used in Buddhist literature synonymously with the term "Caityaka," suggesting that the followers of Buddhism from Andhaka belonged to the Caityaka sect, a name given for one of the Mahāsāṃghika denominations. The sculptural carvings at Amaravati depicting *yakṣas* carrying flower garlands to

decorate the *stūpas* is also quite explicit regarding their form of worship. It may signal how *yakṣas*, either as supernatural figures or as members of indigenous tribal communities, were fused into the worship of the Buddhist *stūpas*.

52. Gregory Schopen, "Immigrant Monks and Protohistorical Dead: The Buddhist Occupation of Early Buddhist Sites in India," in his *Buddhist Monks and Business Matters*, pp. 360–361.

53. Ibid.

54. V. V. Krishnasastry, 1983, p. 88.

55. V. V. Krishnasastry, *Roman Gold Coins, Recent Discoveries in Andhra Pradesh* (Hyderabad: Govt. of Andhra Pradesh, Archaeology and Museums, 1992) pp. 18–20; E. Siva Nagi Reddy, vol. II, pp. 230–231; Lawrence S. Leshik, *South Indian Megalithic Burials: The Pandukal Complex* (Weisbaden: Franz Steiner Verlag GMBH, 1974), pp. 31–32, who says: "No students with a knowledge of both types of monuments can overlook the close resemblances of the two. These are emphasized by the fact that originally, if not exclusively in later times, the *stūpa* too was a funerary structure. The circular railing surrounding the brick vault at Amaravati or Sanchi, for example, can reasonably be derived from the simple boulder ring around the cairns and the dome is analogous to the raised cairn. *Stūpas* are usually associated with Buddhism, but there are passages in the Pali annals of the north which indicated that they were erected over cremated remains of sages or monarchs in pre-Buddhist times. Ordinary people, whose dead were exposed rather than cremated, revered these shrines, and this practise was encouraged and continued by the Buddha. Sometimes these tumuli were placed in cemeteries, although more usually they stood alone on private grounds, and in cases where a particular honor was intended, the *stūpa* was built at the crossing of four principal roads. The earliest extant *stūpa* is a brick structure located near the Nepalese border, dated to about 450 BCE. A more plain but related burial mound, also pre-Mauryan, was found at Lauriya in the same region and it is undeniable that all the oldest *stūpas* occur in the north . . . While the *Yajur Veda* mentions the Āryans using them [burial mounds], the tribal peoples of middle India still today preserve the practise and numerous cremation burials covered by mounds in Baluchistan and along the northwest frontier fall under this category. The use of cairns and circles was fairly common in the ancient world and so the resemblance of the *stūpa* to the Pandukal [in the South] cairns may be understood as not merely coincidental, but due to a remote common ancestry which here is not insignificant."

56. S. Nagaraju, "Buddhist Stupas," in V. V. Krishnasastry ed., *Archaeology of Andhra Pradesh* (Hyderabad: Dept. of Archaeology and Museums, Govt. of Andhra Pradesh, 1987), p. 23.

57. E. Siva Nagi Reddy, vol. II, p. 230.

58. B. S. Rajendra Babu, pp. 25 and 29.

59. E. Siva Nagi Reddy, op. cit.

60. B. S. Rajendra Babu, p. 27.

61. Ibid., 39.

62. E. Siva Nagi Reddy, vol. II, p. 228.

63. H. Sarkar and B. N. Misra, *Nagarjunakonda* (New Delhi: Archaeological Survey of India, 1987), p. 36.

64. Alexander Rea, p. 3.

65. James Fergusson, *Tree and Serpent Worship: From the Sculptures of the Buddhist Topes at Sanchi and Amaravati* (Delhi: Indological Book House, 1971 [rev. ed.]), pp. 92–226 and 235–238.

66. Sree Padma Holt, "Serpent Symbolism in the Mythology of Andhra Folk Goddesses," Fiftieth Annual Meeting of Association for Asian Studies, Washington D.C., 1998; Sree Padma, "From Village to City: Transforming Goddesses in Urban Andhra Pradesh," in Tracy Pintchman ed., *Seeking Mahadevi* (Albany: SUNY, 2001), pp. 115–144.

67. For instance, figurines of nude mother goddesses made of terracotta are prolific as early as the fourth century BCE, a fact that leads us to think that the worship of goddesses was prevalent. In fact, there is an argument that the worship of goddess goes back to stone ages. Paintings of the Chalcolithic period depict the figure of mother goddess as is reported by Veena Datta (Veena Datta, *Chalcolithic Pottery Paintings* [Delhi: Sharada Publishing House, 2000] p. 236). Figurines of the goddess come from almost all of the places (B. S. Rajendra Babu, pp. 156–157) from where terracotta art has been documented. A stone sculpture of the mother goddess with jewelry from Nagarjunakonda during the Ikṣvāku period may indicate not only the continuity of goddess worship into the common era but also its popularity among the royalty. An inscription on the bottom of the sculpture says that one of the queens of Ikṣvāku dynasty and her family members were devotees of the mother goddess.

68. *IAR*, 1974–75, p. 6: Excavation at Chandavaram, Dist. Prakasham recovered carved stone slabs with symbols like *Purnakumbha.*

69. Sree Padma Holt, "The Cult of Hariti," Twenty-seventh Annual Conference of South Asia, University of Wisconsin, Oct. 16–18, 1998.

70. B. S. L., Hanumantharao, p. 55.

71. Ibid., p. 48.

72. *Kathasaritsagara,* C. H. Tawny, trans. (Delhi: Munshiram, 1968), vol. I, pp. 36–37.

73. B. S. L., Hanumantharao, op. cit.

74. E. J. Thomas, *History of Buddhist Thought* (London: Kegan Paul, Trench, Trubner & Co., 1933), p. 139.

75. See John C. Holt, *Buddha in the Crown* (New York: Oxford University Press, 1991), p. 69.

76. H. Luders, "A List of Brahmi Inscriptions from the Earliest Times to about A.D. 400," in *E.I.* X (1909–10), no. 1266, p. 150. See also P. L. Gupta who notes a recently discovered inscription by Siri Siva Maka Sada. "Coins from Archaeological Excavations in the Deccan," *Colloquim on South Indian Archaeology* (Hyderabad: Birla Archaelogical and Cultural Research Institute, 1990), pp. 292–93.

77. A. Buhler, "Bhattiprolu Inscriptions," *E.I.* 2 (1894), no. 6, p. 328 and no. 9, p. 329. These two inscriptions record donations given by a ruler called Kubiraka to the Buddhist *stūpa.*

78. Krishnasastry, 1983, pp. 11, 130, and 202.

79. R. Chanda, "Some Unpublished Amaravati Inscriptions," *E.I.* 15 (1925), no. 2, p. 262 and no. 15, p. 265: The text of the first inscriptions reads ". . . gamasa

pato" which was translated as (this) slab (is the gift of) the village. The text for inscription no. 15 is: ". . . (ni) gamasa" translated as "of the city" read as "of the village" not of the city. It is possible that a group of agriculturists who form the backbone of village economy represented "*gama*" or a village.

80. Ibid., no's. 4 and 5, pp. 262–263: The text in these two inscriptions read as "Dhamnakataka nigamasa" or "Dhamnakadakasa nigamasa." The word *nigama* was translated as "city." Usually the word *nigama* is translated in other inscriptions as a body of traders. If we go by the latter meaning, then the translation would be: (the gift) of the traders (*nigama*) of Dhanyakataka.

81. A. Buhler, "Bhattiprolu Inscriptions," *E.I.* 2, no's. iii & v, pp. 327–328: These two inscriptions contain "*ghoṣṭi*" as a common word that was translated as "committee," that donates collectively to the Buddhist *stūpa*.

82. P. L. Gupta, *Punch Marked Coins in the Andhra Pradesh Museums* (Hyderabad: Government of Andhra Pradesh, 1960), pp. 2–3.

83. Ibid., pp. 27–28.

84. *IAR* (1977–78), pp. 60–61: mentions Prakrit inscription of second century CE from Gummadidurru which records the gift of a rail by Sidhthaya, the female pupil of Purima. A Prakrit inscription of third century CE on a mound near the North canal records a gift by a Sramanaka along with his wife; pp. 61 and 62: Two Prakrit inscriptions of first to second century CE from Guntupalle: the first one records the gift of a pillar by a lay worshiper, the wife of the householder Hamgha of Sa[ku]he. The second one records a pillar and a cave gifted by a Nataga, son of the householder, the son of a servant cook, and the lady Duhusa.

85. The letters of estampages in the inscriptions at Ghantasala and in Java share the same shape of floral designs. See the discussion and edited versions of these inscriptions in *E.I.* 22: p. 4ff and *Epigraphia Andhrica* 2: p. 2. Further, the contents of the one of the inscriptions mention that this place served as a port. Another inscription records the donation made by a master mariner.

86. As mentioned in the beginning of this chapter, there is a scholarly controversy about the presence of foreign pottery and other objects associated with the Greco-Roman Empire, such as Roman gold and silver coinage found in Andhra and elsewhere in the subcontinent. Earlier scholarship attributed these findings to a direct trade relationship with the Roman Empire. Later, special studies on pottery revealed that a significant amount of foreign varieties such as rouletted ware, mold-made ware, red polished ware, arretine ware, and amphorae ware, were imitated and produced locally. This was to meet the demand made either by the local populace or those western traders who resided in Andhra whoever wanted imported varieties from the west [*IAR* 1977–78:71]. These locally produced wares usually have auspicious symbols like the *svastika*, *triśūla*, or *Brāhmī* letters inscribed on them as at Amaravati [*IAR* 1958–59 and 1961–62 to 1964–65; Annual reports of Archaeological Survey of India 1905–1906 and 1908 to 1910].

87. D. D. Kosambi, "Dhenukataka," *Journal of the Asiatic Society of Bombay* 30 (1955), pp. 60–61.

88. H. P. Ray, 1998, p. 150.

89. B. Subrahmanyam, *Buddhist Relic Caskets in South India* (Delhi: Bharatiya Kala Prakashan, 1998), p. 105.

90. Gregory Schopen, "On Monks, Nuns, and 'Vulgar' Practices," *Bones, Stones and Buddhist Monks*, pp. 238–257.

CHAPTER 2

Of Tempted *Arhats* and Supermundane Buddhas

Abhidharma in the Krishna Region

BART DESSEIN

In the present article, textual records on the history of the Buddhist schools are discussed in the light of the evidence revealed by epigraphical sources of the Krishna valley region. This discussion concentrates on the position of the person of Mahādeva in the history of Buddhism. After a brief introduction to the various sources to study the Mahāsāṃghika philosophical viewpoints, an analysis of their philosophy is given. This treatment envisages the "five points" of Mahādeva. The analysis of the Mahāsāṃghika doctrine brings us to the practice of *caitya* worship among the Buddhists in the Krishna valley region, and to some reflections on *caitya* worship in Śrāvakayāna and Mahāyāna circles.

Epigraphical and Textual Records

Precise determination of which school was present in which region and at what time, primarily has to rely on epigraphical evidence.[1] For the Krishna valley region of what is now Andhra Pradesh, the majority of the inscriptions concerned are those found at Nagarjunikonda and Amaravati, both located on the right bank of the Krishna River.[2] In these places, we find inscriptions that date back to the reigns of the Śatavāhanas (second century AD) and the Ikṣvākus (third century AD). For these periods, the presence of the Mahīśāsakas,[3] Bahuśrutīyas,[4] Caitikas,[5] Pūrvaśailas,[6] and

Aparaśailas[7] is attested. Although none of these inscriptions refers to the Mahāsāṃghikas directly, there is textual evidence that of the above mentioned schools and sects, the Bahuśrutīyas, Caitikas, Pūrvaśailas, and Aparaśailas, issued from the Mahāsāṃghikas.[8] In Xuanzang's translation of AD 662 of the *Samayabhedoparacanacakra* (henceforth *Sbc*) (*Yibuzong lun lun*), a work attributed to the Sarvāstivāda master Vasumitra,[9] for example, we read:

> In the course of the two hundred years [following the Buddha's *parinirvāṇa*], three schools issued from the Mahāsāṃghikas: the Ekavyāvahārikas, the Lokottaravādins,[10] and the Kukkuṭikas.[11] Thereafter, equally in the course of these two hundred years, still another school issued from the Mahāsāṃghikas: the Bahuśrutīyas.[12] After this, still in the course of these two hundred years, a further school issued from within the Mahāsāṃghikas: the Prajñaptivādins.[13] When these two hundred years had passed, there was a heretic who had given up heterodoxies and had returned to the right [doctrine]. Also he was called Mahādeva. He had gone forth in the Mahāsāṃghika school and had received full ordination. He was well-versed and diligent, and resided on Caityagiri. With the monks of this school, he again studied the five points. This caused discussion and a split into three schools: the Caityaśailas, the Aparaśailas, and the Uttaraśailas.[14]

That Vasumitra lays the cause of the schism "also" with Mahādeva who "again" studied the five points with the Caityagiri monks, is because he also connected the original schism of Mahāsāṃghikas and Sthaviras with Mahādeva.[15] It is, in this respect, noteworthy that the *Śāriputraparipṛcchāsūtra*, a text that, as the above quoted is claimed by André Bareau to belong to the earliest group of texts dealing with the affiliation of the early Buddhist schools,[16] only mentions Mahādeva in connection with the further split of the Mahāsāṃghika school, that is, at a moment when the Mahāsāṃghika school already existed for about one century:

> In the two hundred years after *nirvāṇa*, because of dogmatic reasons, from within the Mahāsāṃghikas, the following schools arose: Ekavyāvahārika, Lokottaravāda, Kukkuṭika, Bahuśrutaka, and Prajñaptivāda. In the three hundred years after *nirvāṇa*, due to other doctrines, within these five schools, other schools arose: the school of Mahādeva, the Caitras, and the Matarīyas.[17]

The second list of *Bhavya, included in the *Nikāyabhedovibhangavyākhyāna* (henceforth *Nbv*), belongs to a second period of texts recording the affiliation of Buddhist schools.[18] Taranātha attributes this list to the Mahāsāṃghika tradition.[19] It, more precisely, should then be situated in the Andhra region around Amaravati.[20] According to this text,

> Within the Mahāsāṃghikas, eight divisions occurred: the Mahāsāṃghikas,[21] the Pūrvaśailas, the Aparaśailas, the Rājagiriyas, the Haimavatas, the Caitiyas, the Saṃkrāntivādins,[22] and the Gokulikas.[23]

It is noteworthy that the four schools that Buddhaghosa in his fifth-century commentary to the *Kathāvatthu* I, 9 grouped under the name "Andhaka,"[24] are mentioned here: the Rājagirikas,[25] the Siddhatthikas (Saṃkrāntivādins),[26] the Pubbadeliyas, and the Aparaseliyas.[27]

Epigraphical evidence found in Mathura shows that the Mahāsāṃghikas were predominant in this region in the second half of the first century BC,[28] that is, a period that predates the inscriptions found in the Krishna valley region. This implies that the inscriptions of the Krishna valley region belong to a second period of Mahāsāṃghika inscriptions, that is, inscriptions that are posterior to the inscriptions in Northern India.[29] The textual evidence quoted thus affirms the epigraphical sources. According to the *Śāriputraparipṛcchāśāstra,* the Bahuśrutīyas issued from the Mahāsāṃghikas in the second century AB.[30] André Bareau hereby suggests that it is a controversy on the superficial and profound meaning of the scriptures, and on the relative and absolute truth that caused this schism.[31] In the third century AB, a group of Southern Mahāsāṃghika schools—Caitika, Uttaraśaila and Aparaśaila—arose.[32]

The Importance of Mahādeva

The accounts of the development of the Buddhist community after the death of the historical Buddha either mention the doctrinal position of Mahādeva—the "five theses,"[33] or the so-called ten points (*daśa vastūni*) of laxity in monastic behavior[34] as the cause of the first schism in the Buddhist community, that is, the schism between the Mahāsāṃghikas and the Sthaviravādins.[35] Janice Nattier and Charles Prebish (1977) convincingly claim that this schism, for which the date 116 AB is proposed,[36] was most likely caused by the expansion of the root Vinaya text by the future Sthaviravādins, an expansion that was not accepted by the later Mahāsāṃghikas.[37] If, indeed, the schism between Sthaviravādins and

Mahāsāṃghikas had a disciplinary basis, the connection of Mahādeva with the origin of the Mahāsāṃghikas becomes doubtful.[38] The five points of Mahādeva are the claim that:

> (1) (1) *Arhats* can be tempted by others (*paropahṛta*), (2) [some *arhat*s] are subject to ignorance (*ajñāna*), (3) [some *arhat*s] have doubts (*kāṅkṣā*), (4) [some *arhat*s] attain enlightenment through the help of others (*paravitīrṇa*), and (5) they obtain their path by emission of voice.[39]

As stated by Janice Nattier and Charles Prebish (1977), the five points as here formulated clearly demote the *arhat* from his status of near-perfection which the Buddhist tradition had ascribed him. There are two logical reasons that can explain such a position. If arhatship is still the goal to be pursued, this goal is made easier to attain. The other possibility is that the Mahāsāṃghikas wanted to highlight another ideal. The latter might be the more likely case. It seems awkward that a Buddhist school would demote the final goal of religious praxis, and, further, Mahādeva is referred to as a "*bodhisattva*" (*dashi*) in the *Fenbie gongde lun*, a half Mahāsāṃghika, half Mahāyāna commentary on the Chinese *Ekottaragāma*.[40] This epithet seems to indicate an attempt to replace the goal of arhatship with that of the *bodhisattva* (resulting in the eventual attainment of full Buddhahood).[41]

Not all Mahāsāṃghika groups, further, had the same opinion on the qualities of a *bodhisattva*. The so-called northern schools had a much more divinized concept of a *bodhisattva*, while the southern schools—with which we are concerned here—give a much more human description of a *bodhisattva*.[42] This helps to explain that a demotion of the *arhat*-ideal gradually also led to a more human concept of the *bodhisattva*, thus highlighting Buddhahood as the final goal to be achieved by the adept (*śrāvaka*).[43]

In the same line of argumentation, we have to mention the *Sanlun xuanyi*. In this—for Mahāsāṃghika history—relatively late text, it is stated that "in addition to advocating the heretical five points," Mahādeva also "tried to incorporate Mahāyāna *sūtra*s into the Tripiṭaka."[44] The latter opinion is also found in Paramārtha's treatise on the schools.[45]

It thus seems that within Mahāsāṃghika Buddhism, a gradual reinterpretation of the position of an *arhat* and a *bodhisattva* developed, and that this development was especially strong among the Andhaka subgroups. As textual evidence points to it that Mahādeva was only later connected to the original schism between the Mahāsāṃghikas and the Sthaviras, the position of Mahādeva and his five points thus shows to be an important element in the difference between the northern and southern groups of Mahāsāṃghikas.

Mahāsāṃghika Abhidharma

Sources

We do not possess one single work that systematically outlines the complete philosophy of the different Mahāsāṃghika groups. However, we do have a series of historical and philosophical works that provide us with a fairly clear picture of their viewpoints. Apart from the above mentioned accounts on the history of the different Buddhist sects and schools (Vasumitra, *Bhavya, Vinītadeva), these are the Bahuśrutīya **Satyasiddhiśāstra*,[46] and the *Mahāvastu*, a work that is connected to the Lokottaravāda subschool of the Mahāsāṃghikas.[47] The **Satyasiddhiśāstra* is a work by Harivarman who is supposed to have been a native of Central India and lived around the third century AD.[48] The Indian original of the work is lost, but it is preserved in its Chinese translation by Kumārajīva (T.1646).[49] The *Mahāvastu* is a compilation, probably finalized around the third or fourth century AD,[50] of which the material shows to have been derived from the Lokottaravāda *Vinayapiṭaka* and also shows connections with a *Sūtrapiṭaka* that must have consisted of texts that are identical or at least very similar to Pāli texts and were reworked for the *Mahāvastu*.[51] To these works have to be added the Pāli *Kathāvatthu*, the **Śāriputrābhidharmaśāstra*, and the Sarvāstivāda works **Abhidharmavibhāṣāśāstra* and **Abhidharmamahāvibhāṣāśāstra*.

As the title indicates, the *Kathāvatthu* is aimed at refuting the—according to Sthaviravāda viewpoint—heretical doctrines. Unfortunately, the different "points of controversy" are not attributed to some Buddhist sect/school in the *Kathāvatthu* itself. We do possess a commentary on the work by Buddhaghoṣa (fifth century AD), titled *Kathāvatthuppakaraṇa-Aṭṭhakathā*,[52] in which these doctrinal positions are attributed. Although this commentary is of a much later date, a comparison of the already mentioned works with the commentary by Buddhaghoṣa shows that he was very well informed on the diverging doctrinal opinions of the different schools.[53] It should, however, be kept in mind that it is not at all unlikely that some of the polemics were attributed to those schools that were vigilant at the time of compilation of the commentary, and were not based on material that had been transmitted over a few hundred years.[54] For the purpose of the present article, the importance of the *Kathāvatthu*, therefore, primarily lies in these later attributions.

The Chinese version of the **Śāriputrābhidharmaśāstra*, the *Shelifo apitan lun* (T.1548) was produced by Dharmayaśas and Dharmagupta, between AD 407 and 414 in Chang'an during the reign of the Qin Dynasty.[55] André Bareau claimed that the work to all probability is of Dharmaguptaka origin.[56] According to Vasumitra, the doctrine of the Dharmaguptakas was very close to the one of the Mahāsāṃghikas.[57] Analysis of the **Śāriputrābhidharmaśāstra* indeed shows that the work contains a great number of theses that were accepted by one or more of the Mahāsāṃghika groups. As some theses of the so-called Andhaka schools are denied,[58] the **Śāriputrābhidharmaśāstra* thus most likely postdates the rise of the schools that later settled in the Krishna valley region.

The **Abhidharmamahāvibhāṣaśāstra* should be dated roughly somewhere around the end of the first to the end of the second century AD.[59] The Chinese version by Xuanzang's translation team (T.1545) was produced between 656 and 659. Before that, a translation of the **Abhidharmavibhāṣaśāstra* had been completed by Buddhavarman together with Daotai between AD 437 and 439 (T.1546).[60]

In what follows, I will apply the scheme of the "path to liberation" to systematize the various opinions ascribed to the Mahāsāṃghikas or to one of the schools that issued from them at a later date. These opinions will be interpreted in the light of what appears to be a major development in Mahāsāṃghika philosophy: the status of arhatship and, related to this, the status of the *bodhisattva*, and the interpretation of the nature of and the peculiar characteristics ascribed to the Buddha. For obvious reasons, I will primarily base myself on those of the aforementioned works that refer to the Mahāsāṃghika schools directly, and use the other works—such as the *Kathāvatthuppakaraṇa-Aṭṭhakathā*—only as secondary information. Using these criteria, of all the above mentioned works, Vasumitra's *SBc* is our oldest source of information.

The Abhidharma of the Southern Mahāsāṃghika Schools

Origin of defilements

Humans (*manuṣya*) are endowed with faculties (*indriya*). As contact (*sparśa*) of these faculties with their respective objects (*viṣaya*) makes feelings (*vedanā*) arise, conditioning factors (*saṃskāra*) are formed. This defilement adds to the karmic result (*vipāka*), and, eventually, to a new birth and further suffering.

According to Vasumitra's *Sbc*, the Mahāsāṃghikas, Ekavyavahārikas, Lokottaravādins, and Kukkutikas shared the opinion that:

> (2) The group of such five types of consciousness (*vijñāna*) as the one of the eye[61] are both with attachment (*sarāga*) and without attachment (*vairāgya*).[62]

From *Kathāvatthu* X, 3, it is clear that we have to interpret this statement as "That one may develop the path while enjoying the fivefold cognitions of sense."[63] The argument with this is that one who develops the path, although possessing the five faculties, is not attracted by their respective objects. For this interpretation, according to Buddhaghoṣa's commentary on the *Kathāvatthu*, the Mahāsāṃghikas referred to *Aṅguttaranikāya* III, 16, where can be read that when a *bhikṣu*'s sensual faculties (*indriya*) come into contact with their respective objects (*viṣaya*), this *bhikṣu* does not grasp at the general or specific characteristics of it.[64] Also the following two related statement are, in the *Sbc*, attributed to the above four Mahāsāṃghika groups:

> (3) The realm of form (*rūpadhātu*) and the realm of formlessness (*ārūpyadhātu*) are both provided with the group of the six types of consciousness (*ṣaḍvijñānakāya*);[65]

and:

> (4) The nature of [the one of the] mind (*cittasvabhāva*) is clean (*śuddha*) in its origin: it becomes defiled (*kliṣṭa*) when it is stained by secondary afflictions (*upakleśa*), the "adventitious dusts."[66]

These statements imply that in the higher two realms, consciousness of the mind is still present, be that it is no longer stained. As the Mahāsāṃghikas further claimed that the existence of faculties presupposes the existence of their respective types of consciousness and vice versa,[67] this implies that, for the Mahāsāṃghikas, the eighteen elements exist throughout the three realms. This contradicts the general belief of the nonexistence of form in the realm of formlessness. The Mahāsāṃghikas therefore recurred to acknowledging the existence of "subtle form" (*sūkṣma rūpa*)[68] in the realm of formlessness. The subtlety of this kind of form is defined in relation to form of the other two realms.[69]

The picture that emerges from the above is that the Mahāsāṃghika path to liberation accentuates the intrinsic value of the elements, and especially of the mental factors, not the number of these elements: the Mahāsāṃghika path to liberation is a mental process of gradual interiorization, a process in which the external world is cut off from staining the adept's mind.[70]

Directly related to this process of "interiorization," is the question whether sensual perception is effectuated in the sensual faculties themselves, in the types of consciousness associated with their respective faculties, or in mental consciousness. This question further encroaches on the question in what way mental consciousness differs from the other five types of consciousness, and in what way the sensual faculties and the objects perceived act as conditions for the arising of perceptual consciousness.[71] The Mahāsāṃghikas, Ekavyāvahārikas, Lokottaravādins, and Kukkuṭikas are, according to the *Sbc,* claimed to have held to the following position:

> (5) The five material faculties (*rūpendriya*) are nothing but lumps of flesh. The eyes (*cakṣur*) do not see matter (*rūpa*), the ears (*śrotra*) do not hear sounds (*svara*), the nose (*ghrāṇa*) does not smell odors (*gandha*), the tongue (*jihvā*) does not taste flavors (*rasa*), the body (*kāya*) does not feel the tangible (*spraṣṭavya*).[72]

This statement clearly excludes the possibility that it is the sensual faculties themselves that perceive the objects. This is in full accordance with the acceptance of the eighteen elements throughout the three realms. That the sensual organs are "nothing but lumps of flesh" can hereby be understood as the sensual faculties that are like windows through which the sense-consciousness can acquire its sense-cognition.[73] The possibility that these are the sensual faculties themselves that perceive their objects excluded, leaves the possibility of sensual perception in the five types of consciousness, or in mental consciousness. On this issue, the **Abhidharmamahāvibhāṣaśāstra* informs us that, according to the Mahāsāṃghikas, in the process of apprehending their respective objects, two thoughts (*citta*) can arise simultaneously.[74] In view of the peculiar Mahāsāṃghika assignment of liberation to the mental domain, it is not unlikely that the idea here is that mental consciousness is active whenever one of the other five types of consciousness is active. This interpretation is sustained by the following two statements that in the *Sbc* are listed among those on which the Mahāsāṃghikas later came to hold to an opinion that diverged from the one of the Ekavyāvahārikas, Lokottaravādins, and Kukkuṭikas:

> (6) At one and the same time two thoughts can arise side by side.[75]

and:

> (7) Thoughts permeate the whole body, and [these] thoughts can contract and expand in accordance with the basis (*āśraya*) and the object (*viṣaya*).[76]

Although we do not have any precise information on the place of residence of the Ekavyāvahārikas and Kukkuṭikas,[77] we do know that the Lokottaravādins (who may actually be the same group as the Ekavyāvahārikas) resided in the region of Bamiyan.[78] This does not make it unlikely that it is especially among the southern Mahāsāṃghika groups that the aforementioned statements came to be accentuated. In the light of the above thesis (7), and in view of the Mahāsāṃghika interpretation of the process of the attainment of liberating insight as conceived as a process of interiorization, it is very likely that we have to give prominence to mental consciousness over the other—second—type of consciousness that is active whenever an object (*viṣaya*) is perceived.[79] This explains the following statement in the **Abhidharmamahāvibhāṣāśāstra*:

> (8) Some, among whom the Mahāsāṃghikas, adhere to [the opinion] that only thoughts and thought concomitants have a cause of retribution (*vipākahetu*) and a fruit of retribution (*vipakaphala*). In order to stop them [. . . this explanation is done].[80]

The *Sbc* further claims that the Mahāsāṃghikas later came to hold the following opinion, not shared by the Ekavyāvahārikas, Lokottaravādins and Kukkuṭikas:

> (9) The material [four] great elements (*mahābhūta*) that constitute the faculties (*indriya*) are subject to change: the thoughts (*citta*) and thought concomitants (*caitasikadharma*) are not subject to change.[81]

This means that material things are subject to change because they last for a longer period of time than thoughts and thought concomitants do. The latter are instantaneous, and hence do not transform from a previous to a later state.[82] In the light of the denial of the existence of the three time periods (see below), this again points to it that enlightenment was interpreted as a process of "interiorization" of the individual adept.

Analysis of defilements

The Buddhist path to liberation aims at the ultimate destruction of all impure influence (*āśravakṣaya*).[83] This is the quality that traditionally defines arhatship.[84] This explains why the concept of "defilement" has been a major topic in abhidharmic discussions in the different Buddhist schools. The problem of the nature of defilement is related to the concept of "time" (*kāla*). The question arose whether conditioned factors (*saṃskṛta dharma*) proceed through an eternal time, or whether "time" as such does not exist, but is an aspect of the conditioned factors themselves. In the latter supposition, it is the intrinsic value of the conditioned factors that determines their being present (*pratyutpanna*), past (*atīta*), or future (*anāgata*). This intrinsic value is labeled "activity" (*kāritra*).[85] For the Mahāsāṃghikas, Ekavyāvahārikas, Lokottaravādins, and Kukkuṭikas (*Sbc*), "past" and "future" as such do not exist.[86] It is in the conditioned things themselves that "time" is situated, the difference in the three stages of time (*adhvan*) being based on the "activity" (*kāritra*) of these elements. Given the fact that the past is without substance (does not "exist"), and that an action and its maturation by definition cannot exist simultaneously, the Mahāsāṃghikas came to the following interpretation of the relation of an action with its matured effect (*vipāka*): as long as an action is not exhausted, it exists in a kind of a perpetual present. Also its matured effect, being present, exists at the same time as the action itself. Once a part of an action matures, it is exhausted and no longer exists. It has disappeared into the past (it is no longer "active") and so no longer exists simultaneously with its matured effect.[87]

Judging from the *Sbc*, this idea was not shared by the Ekavyāvahārikas, Lokottaravādins, and Kukkuṭikas; and in the **Satyasiddhiśāstra*, the view that "the past action that has not yet received its matured effect exists, and that the rest [of the past] does not exist,"[88] is contradicted. According to the **Satyasiddhiśāstra*, the division of the past action into a part that has not yet received its matured effect and a part that already has, is meaningless.[89]

The idea that there is no strict demarcation between past and present does, further, not require the kind of factors characterized as "neutral," that is, factors that do not have a karmic effect. The existence of neutral factors (*avyākṛtadharma*) is denied by the Mahāsāṃghikas.[90]

We can summarize the above as follows: in the Mahāsāṃghika interpretation of the path to liberation, time is seen as inherent in the conditioned factors. Liberating insight, that is, termination of the karmic succession of causes (*hetu*) and fruitions (*phala*), and hence of the cycle of rebirths (*saṃsāra*), is, by consequence, situated in these conditioned factors themselves. The acceptance of all eighteen elements throughout the three realms, makes liberation the result of a mental process of interiorization. Attaining liberating insight hence implies that the contaminants are gradually made ineffective with regard to mind. This detachment from the contaminants is—as shown below—related to the acceptance of a latent and an active state of these contaminants, whereby these contaminants are situated in a kind of perpetual present. As indicated above, this interpretation appears to have become accentuated especially among the southern Mahāsāṃghika groups.

As stated, the notion of "activity" became fundamental in the Mahāsāṃghika interpretation of final liberation. The Mahāsāṃghikas, Ekavyāvahārikas, Lokottaravādins, and Kukkuṭikas differentiate a latent activity (= *anuśaya*) and a manifest activity (= *paryavasthāna*) in the defilements:

> (10) The contaminants (*anuśaya*) are different from the manifestly active defilements (*paryavasthāna*), and the manifestly active defilements are different from the contaminants. It must be said that the contaminants are dissociated from thoughts (*cittaviprayukta*), whereas the manifestly active defilements are associated with thoughts (*cittasaṃprayukta*),[91]

and:

> (11) The contaminants (*anuśaya*) are neither thoughts (*citta*) nor thought concomitants (*caitasikadharma*), and they do not take a supporting object (*ālambana*).[92]

That the "manifestly active defilements are associated with thoughts" is logically explained by the fact that, in the contrary case, their activity of defiling thought—the obstruction to attaining *nirvāṇa*—would be meaningless, and so also the whole process of "annihilation" of defilements would become meaningless. As the Mahāsāṃghikas claim the existence of the eighteen elements in all three realms, it has to be so that, for attaining liberating insight, the contaminants gradually have to be made ineffective with regard to mind, in which the process of enlightenment is realized. If past and future were "substantial,"[93] this also would make the "destruction of impure influence" impossible. It is precisely the concept of "activity,"that is, the acceptance of a latent and an active intrinsic nature of the defilements, that overcomes both problems. When the contaminants no longer become manifestly active, the result of what we called "a process of interiorization of the individual adept," they no longer add to karmic fruition (in their *anusaya* state, they do not take a supporting object).

Judging from the *Sbc*, the Ekavyāvahārikas, Lokottaravādins, and Kukkuṭikas later no longer agreed with the Mahāsāṃghikas who claimed the following:

> (12) The seeds (*bīja*) precisely are the sprouts (*aṅkura*);[94]

and:

> (13) Both the path and passions can exist side by side.[95]

These two position are both related to the theory of "activity" as sustained by the Mahāsāṃghikas. Statement (12) is likely to mean that the essence (*bhāva*) of contaminants (*anuśaya*) and manifestly active defilements (*paryavasthāna*) is the same. When their activity is latent, they are "seeds;" when this activity becomes manifest, they are "sprouts." As the contaminants are dissociated from thoughts (statement [11]), there is no objection to the existence of good (*kuśala*) and bad (*akuśala*) seeds side by side (statement [13]): only one of them becomes active at the same time. When bad seeds become active, they form a manifestly active defilement and stain the mind; when what is good becomes active, the path is developed. Also the denial of the existence of neutral factors is related to this.

Connected to the denial of the existence of the three time periods as such, the Mahāsāṃghikas (as well as the Ekavyāvahārikas, Lokottaravādins, and Kukkuṭikas) logically do not accept the existence of an intermediate state of existence (*antarābhava*), a type of existence in between this life and the future life, accounting for the transfer of karmic effects from one lifetime to the next.[96]

The above analysis of the nature of defilement shows that the Mahāsāṃghika interpretation of this nature is in line with their view on the presence of the eighteen elements throughout the three realms, and with their view of liberation as the result of a process of mental interiorization. This interpretation appears to have been adhered to especially by the Mahāsāṃghika groups who resided in the Krishna valley region.

Knowledge and meditative experience on the path to liberation

On the path to liberation, it is through the instrumentality of wisdom (*prajñā*)[97] that the devotee makes sure that the contaminants no longer become manifestly active. The last step before entering the path to liberation is called "the highest worldly factor" (*laukikāgradharma*). It is the moment of transition from being a worldling (*pṛthagjana*) to being a noble person (*āryapudgala*). This point of transition, according to the Mahāsāṃghikas, belongs both to the realm of sensual passion (*kāmadhātu*) and to the realm of form (*rūpadhātu*).[98] This refers to the fact that the Mahāsāṃghikas conceived the process of attaining liberation as a gradual process. This is affirmed in the following opinion that, according to the *Sbc*, was shared by the Mahāsāṃghikas, Ekavyāvahārikas, Lokottaravādins, and Kukkuṭikas:

> (14) From conversion onwards to the stage of transformation of personality (*gotrabhūmidharma*), there is in all stages the possibility of retrogression (*parihāni*).[99]

This means that a worldling (*pṛthagjana*) is subject to falling back from the moment of his conversion onward, up to the moment of transition from being a worldling to being a noble person, namely, the moment of the "highest worldly factor." As the "highest worldly factor" also belongs to the realm of sensual passion, the worldling and the noble person share some qualities. This opinion encroaches on the qualities of an arhat.

The actual noble path is twofold: it consists of the path of vision (*darśanamārga*), and the path of spiritual practice (*bhāvanāmārga*). The difference between both paths is based on the way in which defilement is annihilated: vision of the four noble truths and spiritual practice respectively. The path of vision, hereby, is divided into sixteen moments of which each time four moments correspond to the four aspects of one of the noble truths (*ṣoḍaśākāra*[100]). In the *Sbc*, we read that the same four Mahāsāṃghika groups claim that the adept, on entering the first moment of these sixteen moments (patience regarding the doctrine in relation to suffering (*duḥkhe dharmakṣānti*),[101] at once destroys every defilement to be abandoned through vision.[102] It is in this respect noteworthy that the oldest Chinese translation of the *Sbc* claims that "one does not destroy all bonds when entering the righteousness of the ability to arise free from beings."[103] This implies that the sixteen aspects are understood to be comprehended gradually. In *Kathāvatthu* II, 9, this idea of gradual higher realization is, among others, attributed to the Andhakas.[104] This is confirmed in the *Sbc*.[105] Related to this, is the idea that:

> (15) Also in the eighth stage (*aṣṭamaka-bhūmi*) one can abide for a long time.[106]

Kathāvatthu III, 5 attributes this position to the Andhakas,[107] and explains that the idea here is that, for one who goes to the fruit of the streamwinner (*srotaāpattipratipannaka*),[108] the contaminant perplexity (*vicikitsānuśaya*) and the contaminant views (*dṛṣṭyanuśaya*) no longer become manifestly active. It is precisely because perplexity and views are still latent, that it can take some time before the one who goes to the fruit of the streamwinner attains this fruit (*phalastha*). This opinion corresponds to the Andhaka acceptance of a gradual higher realization of the truths.

Also the opinion of the Mahāsāṃghikas, Ekavyāvahārikas, Lokottaravādins, and Kukkuṭikas, that:

> (16) Even in the state of meditative attainment (*samāhita*) one can utter words: there is also a subdued mind and also a quarrelsome mind.[109]

seems to be related to the Mahāsāṃghika opinion that the eighteen elements exist throughout the three realms.

The above section can be summarized as follows: The Mahāsāṃghikas interpreted liberation of the adept as a gradual process of interiorization, in the course of which the defilements are gradually made ineffective with regard to the mind. This process of attaining enlightenment is explained by their acceptance of a latent and an active state of these defilements, and, hence, of the fact that past and future as such do not exist. The idea that there are no past and future appears to have been contradicted by the Mahāsāṃghika groups that resided in the North. As the interpretation of time necessarily encroaches on the interpretation of the nature of defilements, and, hence, also on the attainment of liberation, this may explain why among the northern Mahāsāṃghika groups the concept of a "sudden enlightenment" developed. This may further be connected to the fact that the northern Mahāsāṃghika groups had a much more divinized concept of the *bodhisattva* than the groups that resided in the South had. The southern Mahāsāṃghikas, on the contrary, saw the transformation from being a worldling to being a noble person as a gradual process. This idea further influenced their interpretation of the *bodhisattva*. In the South, a more human interpretation of the *bodhisattva* prevailed.

The fruits of nobility

Three stages precede arhatship (*arhattvaphala*): the stage of the streamwinner (*srotaāpanna*), the stage of the once-returner (*sakṛdāgāmin*), and the stage of the nonreturner (*anāgāmin*). In the *Sbc*, only statements concerning the *srotaāpanna* and the *arhat* are found. We read:

> (17) A streamwinner is liable to commit all kinds of evil (*pāpa*) except the forms of proximate blameworthiness (*ānantaryavadya*);[110]

and:

> (18) A streamwinner is subject to falling back while an *arhat* is not.[111]

That a streamwinner is subject to falling back (statement 18) is exactly because he is liable to commit evil (statement 17). This is because he still possesses latent contaminants (*anuśaya*), and some evil may be done through the power of habit. Here, it is important to remark that the three versions of the *Sbc* we possess, all give a different opinion. According to the oldest version, "A streamwinner is subject to falling back and also an *arhat* is subject to falling back."[112] The second version states that "A streamwinner is subject to falling back, while an *arhat* is sometimes subject to falling back."[113] Only in Xuanzang's version do we read that an *arhat* is not subject to falling back.

An investigation of the Sarvāstivāda and Pāli philosophical literature shows that they share the ideal of arhatship as the final goal of the religious praxis. Hereby, the early Buddhist texts do not make much distinction between the liberation of the Buddha and the one of an *arhat*.[114] That very soon however, divergent opinions arose on the precise characteristics of an *arhat*, is seen already in the oldest texts, where some peculiar characteristics not shared with the *arhat* came to be ascribed to the Buddha.[115] The different Buddhist schools also came to accept different types of *arhat*. One of these is "the one who falls back" (*parihāṇadharman*). The "five points of Mahādeva" already repeatedly referred to above can thus be seen as an element in this discussion on the interpretation of the status of an *arhat*.

If, indeed, the status of an *arhat* is as fundamental to Mahāsāṃghika philosophy as the historical records persuade us to believe, it seems justified to ask the question why then the "five points of Mahādeva" are only listed as the twenty-seventh of the forty-eight theses that the *Sbc* ascribes to the Mahāsāṃghikas, Ekavyāvahārikas, Lokottaravādins, and Kukkuṭikas,[116] and why they are also not listed as first viewpoint of the schools that issued from them at a later date: the Bahuśrutīyas, Caityaśailas, Aparaśailas, and Uttaraśailas.[117] In the light of the two Chinese versions of Vasumitra's treatise, prior to Xuanzang's, which claim that *arhat* are (sometimes) subject to falling back, and in view of the fact that *Kathāvatthu* II, 1–5 ascribes this opinion to the Pūrvaśailas and Aparaśailas, the "five points" are likely to either be a rewriting of a previous issue, or to be a later opinion.

As mentioned, one of the types of *arhat* that is enumerated in the list of different types of *arhat*, is "the one who falls back" (*parihāṇadharman*). This shows that already in the early Buddhist schools, doubt arose on the infallibility of an *arhat* in contradistinction to the Buddha. The conditions depending on which such an *arhat* who falls back has attained his arhatship are mundane. This fact is similar to what P. S. Jaini remarked concerning Yaśomitra's commentary on the *Abhidharmakośa*. In this text, two kinds of ignorance are differentiated. The first type is the kind of ignorance that pertains to the worldly nature of things (as opposed to the true nature of *dharma*s). This kind of ignorance persists even after one has become an *arhat*. Most probably, it is this kind of knowledge that is referred to when claiming that "[some] *arhats* are subject to ignorance." Contrary to ordinary worldlings who have not attained liberating insight (*prajñā*) yet and for whom not meeting with the desired object causes frustration (and meeting with it causes delight), for an *arhat* it is so that, as his defilement has been destroyed, "ignorance of 'things' is unable to obstruct the purity of his mind. When a need arises to know something hitherto unknown (i.e., when he becomes aware of his ignorance), the *arhat* will be mindful and will dispel any delight that may accompany the act of knowing the new object. In the case of the Buddha, there is no such deficiency because he lacks all forms of curiosity and consequent delight, since the objects he wants to know become instantaneously known to him without any effort (*prayoga*) whatsoever."[118] From *Kathāvatthu* II, 2 and II, 3, we learn that according to the Pūrvaśailas, the *arhat* may still possess ignorance and doubt because he may be ignorant and doubtful about worldly things, such as names of men, trees, and so forth. In these matters, he may be even excelled by worldlings.[119] As with ignorance, also doubt has to be understood as doubt concerning worldly matters, not as doubt concerning the Buddha, his doctrine and his community.[120]

It may thus be evident that, actually, the "five points" do not much more than emphasize the differences between the interpretation of the enlightenment of the Buddha and the one of an *arhat* as it already existed. The "five points" thus appear to be a rewriting of a previous issue. This accounts for the fact that the "five points" are not the first item listed in Vasumitra's work, and also accounts for the differences in opinion with regard to the position of Mahādeva in the history of Buddhism.

Buddha and *Bodhisattva*

As already indicated, far more important is that—the fallibility of an *arhat* being accepted—arhatship as ultimate goal of the path of liberation became replaced with the *bodhisattva* ideal. Gradually, the reinterpretation of the state of arhatship also invoked a reinterpretation of the concept of the *bodhisattva*, and, consequently, of the notion of the Buddha to whom supermundane characteristics became ascribed. That, with the further fragmentation of the original Mahāsāṃghikas, the reinterpretation of the concepts of the *bodhisattva* and of the Buddha became more important than the "five points" may be evident from the fact that the *Sbc*, discussing the doctrinal positions of the Mahāsāṃghikas, starts from this tenet. Not only is this problem the first that is addressed, it also is the one most elaborately worked out: twenty of the total of forty-eight theses the *Sbc* attributes to the Mahāsāṃghikas, Ekavyāvahārikas, Lokottaravādins, and Kukkuṭikas, concern the concepts of Buddha and *bodhisattva*.

Concerning the *bodhisattva*, we find the following points in the *Sbc*, attributed to the Mahāsāṃghikas, Ekavyāvahārikas, Lokottaravādins, and Kukkuṭikas:

> (19) None of the *bodhisattva*s, when they enter their mothers' wombs (*garbha*), take on the specific nature (*svabhāva*) of a *kalala*, fetus in the second week (*arbuda*), fetus in the third week (*peśī*) and fetus in the fourth week (*ghana*) as one of the four embryonic stages, [stages] which ordinary people pass through.[121]

> (20) All the *bodhisattva*s assume the forms of white elephants when they enter their mothers' wombs.[122]

> (21) All the *bodhisattva*s are born from the right side when they come out of their mothers' wombs.[123]

The first thing that deserves our attention in the above three statements is that the phrasing in all three Chinese versions of the *Sbc* unmistakably refers to *bodhisattva*s in the plural.[124] This may refer to the *bodhisattva*(s) of the past, present, and future, but may equally already be presupposing the existence of many *bodhisattva*s, an idea that is universal for the Mahāyāna schools. A second element noteworthy in the above three statements is that the *bodhisattva*s are seen as superior to ordinary worldlings, and are, as such, characterized by an extraordinary birth. The superiority of a *bodhisattva* vis-à-vis ordinary worldlings, is also referred to in the following statement:

> (22) In none of the *bodhisattva*s, thoughts of desire (*kāma*), of malice (*vyāpāda*), or of violence (*vihiṃsā*) come up.[125]

This proposition does not only make a *bodhisattva* superior to a worldling, but, as statement (18) and (19) are also ascribed to the Pūrvaśailas and the Aparaśailas in the *Kathāvatthu*, also superior to an *arhat*.[126] Related to statement (18), is the following statement that in *Kathāvatthu* VIII, 11 is ascribed to the Pūrvaśailas and Aparaśailas:

> (23) The *arhat*, because of his actions, is subject to falling back.[127]

Just as statements (19–21) are similar to later Mahāyāna positions, also the following point (24) is similar to the Mahāyāna interpretation of a *bodhisattva*, and is further also related to the concept of the twofold truth (*dve satye*):

(24) For the benefit of sentient beings, *bodhisattvas* are born into bad states (*durgati*) at will, and can be born into any of them as they like.[128]

The first statement concerning the characteristics peculiar to a Buddha is that:

(25) All World-honored Buddhas are supermundane (*lokottara*).[129]

Parallel to what we remarked concerning the statements on the *bodhisattvas*, the three Chinese versions of the *Sbc* also refer to the Buddha in the plural.[130] In view of what was remarked in the previous passage, we may have to interpret the "supermundaneaity" of the Buddha as that Buddhahood is situated on the level of what the Mahāyāna came to term "absolute truth" (*paramārthasatya*), in contradistinction to the "conventional truth" (*saṃvṛtisatya*).[131] Above, it has been evidenced that the Mahāsāṃghikas interpreted liberation as to be attained through the instrumentality of liberating insight (*prajñā*), wisdom being the real body of the Buddha, his *dharmakāya*.[132] It thus is clear that some elements pointing to the philosophical concept of the twofold truth are also traceable in the Mahāsāṃghika interpretation of Buddhahood.

The idea that Buddha is "not of this world" is, in fact, already foreshadowed in the earliest Buddhist literature. In the *Anguttaranikāya* we can read that Gautama, when asked what kind of being he was, denied that he was human.[133] Since arhatship as the final goal to be attained through the process of liberation was gradually replaced with Buddhahood, Buddha not being subject to falling back, it is very likely that a need arose to highlight those peculiar characteristics of a Buddha that definitely make him excel over the *arhat*, that is, his "Buddha-like" characteristics (*āveni-kadharma*).[134] That is, the outerworldliness of a Buddha was accentuated. All other characteristics that, in the *Sbc*, are enumerated for a Buddha illustrate this first statement on the Buddha. That this difference with the *arhat* is linked to the "five points," is evidenced in, for example:

(26) The Buddha has neither sleep nor dream.[135]

The "five points" claim that it is in the state of dreams that an *arhat* has emission of semen. The Mahāsāṃghika claim that the Buddha does not sleep is related to the fact that, being in the Tuṣita heaven, he is always in the state of meditation (*samādhi*); that he does not dream is because dreams are invoked by such things as volition (*cetana*), conceptual identification (*saṃjñā*), or desire (*kāma*).[136]

The tenet that:

> (27) All Tathāgatas are without defiled factors (*sāsrava dharma*).[137]

supports the claim that, for the Mahāsāṃghikas, Buddhahood is the stage to be attained, as it is only a Buddha who is completely free from afflictions. This further is precursory of the acceptance of the two bodies that in Mahāyāna Buddhism came to be ascribed to the Buddha. This is evidenced in the following:

> (28) The physical body (*rūpakāya*) of the Tathāgata is indeed limitless (*ananta*).[138]

The mere fact that a "physical body" is mentioned (as opposed to an "non-physical" body) presupposes that the Mahāsāṃghikas distinguished multiple aspects in the Buddha's body. At first sight, the claim that the physical body of the Tathāgata is limitless might seem awkward, since also the historical Buddha experienced his *parinirvāṇa.* The remark of Louis de La Vallée Poussin (1913) that even before the time of Aśoka there were sects that regarded the historical Śākyamuni as nothing but a magical double of a real Śākyamuni, a man who had become Buddha a long time ago and who resided in the Tuṣita heaven (i.e., belonging to the realm of sensual passion), may help us to understand this tenet. From the acceptance that the historical Śākyamuni is only a magical double, it is an easy step to accord a kind of eternity to him.[139] Also the above listed statement (24) on the nature of a *bodhisattva* can easily be interpreted in this light. Before going into this problem further, the following two Mahāsāṃghika tenets that relate to the same topic should be given:

> (29) The divine power (*prabhāva*) of the Tathāgata is also limitless.[140]

> (30) The length of life of the Buddhas is also limitless.[141]

That the divine power and the length of life of the Buddhas is limitless, most likely refers to these Buddha-like characteristics, that is, these *dharmas* that make a Buddha "Buddha" (in contradistinction to, for example, an *arhat* who still has doubts). When taking refuge (*śaraṇa*) with the Buddha, one naturally does not take refuge with the *dharma*s that the Buddha shares with worldlings (*pṛthagjana*), but with those *dharma*s that are peculiar to a Buddha. These factors are shared by Śākyamuni Buddha and all other previous (and later) Buddhas.[142] If, indeed, Śākyamuni is only a magical double of a real Śākyamuni who resides in the Tuṣita heaven, one can correctly claim that his physical body is limitless, as other magical doubles are possible.[143] The above three statements (28–30) clearly allude to a later Mahāyānistic interpretation of the Buddha-bodies and the theory of two truths. We can conclude that the Buddha-notion of the Mahāsāṃghikas is not the historical Buddha, which is nothing but the *nirmāṇakāya*, created by a "real" Buddha (his *dharmakāya*) residing in the Tuṣita heaven.[144] In this docetic interpretation of the Buddha, we can see an early germ of the later *trikāya*-concept.[145] Maybe we also have to see statement (30) as an expression of the idea that the Buddha lived on. Connected with the Buddhist shrines, this could mean that it was thought that the Buddha lived on, dwelling in his shrine (*caitya*).[146] We will return to this in section four: "Buddhas, and *Stūpa* Cult."

On the (historical) Buddha's proclaiming of the doctrine we read:

> (31) All the speeches of the Tathāgata are the turning of the wheel of the doctrine (*dharmacakraṃ pravartayanti*).[147]
>
> (32) The Buddha expounds all the doctrines (*dharma*) with a single utterance.[148]
>
> (33) Everything that has been preached by the World-honoured One is in conformity with the truth (*ayathārtha*).[149]
>
> (34) The *sūtra*s proclaimed by the Buddha are all perfect in themselves.[150]

That these opinions gradually became linked to the concept of the supermundaneaity of the Buddha, may possibly be evident in the following statement, that the *Sbc* attributes to the Bahuśrutīyas:

> (35) The teachings of the Buddha on the following five themes are the supermundane teachings (*lokottaraśāsana*) because the teachings on these five themes lead a man to the attainment of the path of emancipation: (1) impermanence (*anityatā*), (2) suffering (*duḥkha*), (3) emptiness (*śūnyatā*), (4) selflessness (*anātmatā*), (5) the peace (*śānta*) of *nirvāṇa*. The teachings of the Tathagata on the themes other than the above are the mundane teachings.[151]

Related to this, is the account in Paramārtha's commentary on Vasumitra's treatise that *Yājñavalkya, awakening from a long *samādhi*, declared that the Mahāsāṃghika school only proclaimed the superficial meaning of the Buddha's doctrine. Thereupon, he himself went over to the proclamation of both the superficial and the profound meaning (including the teaching of the greater vehicle). This is reported to have evoked a schism within the Mahāsāṃghikas, leading to the Bahuśrutīyas.[152] As statement (34) is further the only divergence mentioned between the Bahuśrutīyas and the Mahāsāṃghikas, it is not impossible that this doctrinal matter indeed caused a first schism within the Mahāsāṃghika community.[153] We further have to mention the *Nbv* here, that claims that 137 years after the demise of the Master, Māra invoked a great discord in the community because of five propositions. These propositions are then said to have been praised by Nāga and Sthiramati who taught that "One returns to others in turn; ignorance; doubt; perfect knowledge; and that the path is liberation in itself."[154] Because of these positions—which immediately recall of the five points of Mahādeva—the community is said to have been divided into Sthaviras and Mahāsāṃghikas. Later, after two hundred years had passed, from within the Mahāsāṃghikas, the Ekavyāvahārikas, and Kukkuṭikas are said to have issued. The fundamental position on which the Ekavyāvahārikas based their doctrine is the idea that "The Buddha is supermundane (*lokkottara*)."[155]

We can summarize the above as follows. After the Mahāsāṃghikas and Sthaviravādins had, to all likelihood, split on monastic grounds, within these Mahāsāṃghika circles, the interpretation of the doctrine—the Abhidharma—further developed. In this way, the discussion on the status of an *arhat* that already existed in the early community, became formulated as the "five points of Mahādeva." These "five points" were given as cause of the first schism in the Buddhist community in some historical accounts.[156] As the *arhat* was accepted to be fallible, this issue must have encroached on the interpretation of the concepts of *bodhisattva* and Buddha. This explains why the opinions on the nature of a Buddha and a *bodhisattva* are the positions that were listed as the most important doctrinal tenets in the later historical accounts, and are treated as the first item of the Krishna schools in the *Sbc*.

These concepts of a Buddha and a *bodhisattva* are, in the *Nbv*, the first item dealt with for the Ekavyāvahārikas.[157] Also in Vasumitra's *Sbc*, these are the first tenets listed for the Caityaśailas, Aparaśailas, and Uttaraśailas.[158] The *Sbc* only attributes two of all the above mentioned doctrinal positions to the Caityaśailas, the Aparaśailas, and the Uttaraśailas: the "five points of Mahādeva,"[159] and the opinion that

(36) *Bodhisattva*s are not free from the bad states (*durgati*).[160]

It is remarkable how here, and this in complete analogy with what was claimed in statement (18) concerning the susceptibility of an *arhat* to falling back, not all Chinese versions of Vasumitra's treatise accord. In the oldest version, we read that "*bodhisattvas* are free from bad states of existence."[161] The two more recent Chinese translations claim the opposite. This may reflect the gradual process of attributing supermundane characteristics only to the Buddha, to the disfavor of *arhats* and *bodhisattvas*.[162] While the northern Mahāsāṃghika schools retained a much more divinized concept of a *bodhisattva* and of a Buddha, and hence gradually came to see enlightenment as a "sudden event," the Mahāsāṃghika schools in the Krishna valley region appear to have given a much more human description of a *bodhisattva*.[163] They exalted the Buddha only.

This reinterpretation of the concepts of the *bodhisattva* and the Buddha, and other strong similarities between Mahāyāna and "Mahāsāṃghika," have made some scholars claim that Mahāyāna rose from within the Mahāsāṃghika school.[164] However, to quote Akira Hirakawa, "It would be premature to conclude that the Mahāyāna is a development from the Mahāsāṃghika, simply because the latter advocated a number of progressive ideas."[165] Certain progressive ideas also existed within other Śrāvakayāna groups.[166] The scrutiny of the *stūpa* cult as it was prevalent among the southern Mahāsāṃghika schools, given below, sheds more light on this issue.

Buddhas, and *Stūpa* Cult

One of the supermundane characteristics of the Buddha is the idea that the Buddha lives on (statement 30). This idea may very well have inspired *caitya* worship that became so prevalent in Andhra[167]. Examination of epigraphical data has revealed that among the Aparamahāvinaseliyas, indeed, *caitya* worship was a dominant practice, and that this practice was at least supervised by learned monks.[168] This draws the attention to the element "*caitya*" in the name Caityaśaila. This name either has to be interpreted as "those with a doctrine about shrines," or "those who honor shrines"[169] The *Sbc* attributes the following statement to the Caityaśailas, Aparaśailas, and Uttaraśailas:

> (37) Even if one makes offerings to a *stūpa*[*167] one cannot acquire great fruits (*mahāphala*).[170]

This makes the first interpretation of the above suggested two the most likely one.[171] Such an interpretation is, at first sight, corroborated in the *Mahāsāṃghikavinaya* (*Mishase wufen jieben*).[172] Here, giving (*dāna*) is claimed not to evoke great fruit, but only some happiness.

The (*Mishase wufen jieben*) further lists the four occasions on which it is allowed for monks to bring offerings to *stūpa*s and *caitya*s,[173] and contains a description of how shrines are built at the four sides of a *stūpa*, and how an image of the Buddha is carved.[174] Akira Hirakawa explained that this phenomenon "probably arose as a religious necessity to meet the demands of the faithful who believed in an eternal Buddha through the medium of the *stūpa*."[175] The argument thus is that worship of the Buddha was a lay practice, and that the origin of the Mahāyāna has to be linked to this *stūpa* worship. It is then supposed that the popularity of *stūpa* worship among the laity, probably forced the *Nikāya saṇgha* to adopt the practice in order to keep the followers tied to the *saṇgha*.[176]

However, after stating that "the land of the *saṇgha* and the land of the *stūpa* must not encroach on each other," the *Mahāsāṃghikavinaya* further says that if the *karmadāna*, because of hardships in the *saṇgha*, sells goods belonging to the *stūpa* and offers it to the *saṇgha*, he has committed the offense of stealing and is guilty of a *pārājika*.[177] The *saṇgha* was not permitted to consume or to use the property owned by the *stūpa*, and at the same time the *stūpa*s could not be renovated or fixed by using materials owned by the *saṇgha*.[178] The mere fact that this is taken up in the *Vinaya* and is connected to the category of *pārājika* offenses is a very likely proof of the fact that, indeed, monks were engaged in practices of *stūpa/caitya* worship. Interpreting the Nagarjunikonda inscriptions that belong to the Aparamahāvanaseliyas, Gregory Schopen comes to the conclusion that the inscriptions "seem to indicate that their redactor did not think of the *dhātu* or 'relic' as a piece or a part of the Buddha," but as "something that contained or enclosed the Buddha himself."[179] If we connect this idea with such concepts as that the Buddha's body was thought to stay on forever (statement [28]), and that the length of his life is limitless (statement [30]), this relic cannot have been taken as something representing the dead Buddha. It may further be remembered here, that the deified body of the Buddha, was, in the *Śalistambha Sūtra*, referred to as the *dharmaśarīra*.[180] To paraphrase Gregory Schopen, it thus appears that the Mahācetiya at Nagarjunikonda was conceived of as a structure housing the living presence of the Buddha, and that any worship of "it" would actually be of *him*.[181]

This interpretation is sustained by the following position that, in *Kathāvatthu* XVII, 1, is attributed to the Andhakas:

(38) The *ārhat* has accumulation of merit.[182]

A similar statement is *Kathāvatthu* VII, 5, attributed to the Rājagiriyas and to the Siddhārthikas:

(39) One accumulates merit (*puṇya*) [by giving that] consists of joy (*paribhogamaya*).[183]

What has to be understood under "joy," is explained in *Kathāvatthu* VII, 6, a statement equally attributed to the Rājagiriyas and to the Siddhārthikas:

(40) That what is given here sustains elsewhere.[184]

According to Buddhaghoṣa, "elsewhere" means "the deceased."[185] In the Indian social context, renunciation of worldly life is likely to have left monks/nuns with feelings of anxiety regarding their relatives. The idea of "transference of merit" and *stūpa* cult can be perfectly interpreted in this context.[186] It is, in this respect, telling that ideas of "transference of merit" and *stūpa* worship were not restricted to Mahāsāṃghika circles only.[187] It is further not improbable that Buddha worship was gradually expanded to worship of the community (*saṇgha*), the third element of the *triśaraṇa*. This may be evidenced in the following statement that *Bhavya (*Nbv*) attributes to the Bahuśrutīyas:

(41) The community (*saṇgha*) is supermundane (*lokottara*).[188]

The Mahāsāṃghika doctrine as it is transmitted in textual form shows to parallel the actual practice of Mahāsāṃghika monks and nuns as it is revealed by epigraphical evidence. *Stūpa* worship in the sense as described by Gregory Schopen—that is, that any worship of "it" would actually be of *him*—implies that the Buddha is conceived of as someone who possesses supermundane capacities. Such supermundane characteristics are enumerated in the *Sbc*. As the stage of the *bodhisattva* immediately precedes the one of the Buddha, also to this *bodhisattva* at least some supermundane characteristics are ascribed. The latter tendency was stronger among the northern Mahāsāṃghika schools, who had a much more divinized concept of a *bodhisattva* than the southern schools had. As the attainment of enlightenment is an individual mental process, *stūpa* worship as prevalent in the Krishna valley region is likely to have to be interpreted in the light of "transference of merit."

Conclusion

An analysis of epigraphical and textual records, and of the doctrinal viewpoints attributed to the different Mahāsāṃghika groups shows that, to all probability, the Mahāsāṃghikas originated on monastic grounds. In a later phase, different subgroups issued from within these Mahāsāṃghikas. To all probability, it was the so-called five points of Mahādeva that demote the position of an *arhat* that triggered this further fragmentation within the Mahāsāṃghikas. In fact, the quality of arhatship had been the subject of scholarly discussion already in other early schools. This implies that the "five points" were not the doctrinal issue most peculiar for the Mahāsāṃghikas. Much more innovative was the Mahāsāṃghika interpretation of the *bodhisattva* and the Buddha, to whom supermundane characteristics were ascribed. The fact that the Mahāsāṃghika groups in the Krishna valley region appear to have had a much more human interpretation of the *bodhisattva* than the northern groups had—bodhisattvaship being the outcome of a gradual process of interiorization of the individual adept—explains why, in the South, the outerworldly characteristics became attributed to the Buddha only. *Stūpa* worship was hereby conceived of as worship of the supermundane Buddha himself, that is, of the Buddha in his doctrinal body. Epigraphical evidence reveals that worship of the Buddha had the aim to transfer merit in this life.

Notes

1. For some reflections on the traditional view of the primacy of literary sources over epigraphical evidence: see G. Schopen, *Bones, Stones, and Buddhist Monks. Collected Papers on the Archaeology, Epigraphy, and Texts of Monastic Buddhism in India* (Honolulu: University of Hawaii Press, 1997), pp. 1–9. On the use of epigraphical sources to testify the spread of Buddhist schools, in contradistinction to their origin, see P. Kieffer-Pülz, "Die buddhistische Gemeinde," in H. Bechert et al., *Der Buddhismus I. Der indische Buddhismus und seine Verzweigungen* (Stuttgart: Kohlhammer, 2000), p. 292.

2. For a general overview and description of the Nagarjunikonda and Amaravati sites: see J. Burgess, *The Buddhist Stupas of Amaravati and Jaggayyapeta in the Krishna District, Madras Presidency, Surveyed in 1882*. Archaeological Survey of Southern India (London: Trübner & Co.), 1887; A. Foucher, "Les Sculptures d'Amarāvatī," *Revue des Arts Asiatiques* V/1, 1928, pp. 9–24; A. H. Longhurst, "The Buddhist Antiquities of Nāgārjunikoṇḍa, Madras Presidency," *Memoirs of the Archaeological Survey of India* 54, 1938; C. Sivaramamurti, "Amarāvatī Sculptures in the Madras Government Museum," *Bulletin of the Madras Government Museum*, 1942.

3. The inscription concerned is "*Mahī[śā]saka*," on a pillar in Nagarjunikonda from the year 11 of Ehuvula Santamula II of the Ikṣvākus (end of third century AD). See *Epigraphia Indica* XX, pp. 24–25. The Mahīśāsaka community will be the subject of a separate study.

4. Two inscriptions "*Bahusutīya*" are found on a pillar in Nagarjunikonda. The first dates from the reign of Māṭharīputra Vīrapurusadatta (ca. 250–275), the second is dated in the second year of Ehuvula Śāntamūla II of the Ikṣvākus (end of third century AD). See *Epigraphia Indica* XX, p. 24, and XXI, pp. 61–62, respectively.

5. An inscription "*Cetikiya*," found in Amaravati, dates from the reign of Vāsiṣṭhīputra Pulomā (ca. 130–159). See H. Lüders, *A List of Brahmi Inscriptions from the Earliest Times to About A.D. 400 with the Exception of Those of Aśoka*. Varanasi: Indological Book House, 1973, no. 1248. Undated references to the Caitikas are "*Cetika*" on a tile from Amaravati (C. Sivaramamurti, "Sculptures," no. 33), "*Cetiyavamdaka*" (H. Lüders, *Inscriptions*, no. 1223), "*Cetiavadaka*" (H. Lüders, *Inscriptions*, no. 1263), "*Cetika of Rajagiri*" (H. Lüders, *Inscriptions*, no. 1250), and "*Mahāvanasala*" (H. Lüders, *Inscriptions*, no. 1272). In Amaravati, there further is an inscription "*Jadikiya*" (H. Lüders, *Inscriptions*, no. 1244), an inscription "*[Se]liya*" (H. Lüders, *Inscriptions* no. 1270; E. Hultzsch, "Amarāvatī-Inschriften," *ZDMG* XXXVII, 1883, p. 554), and an inscription "*Mahāvanaseliya*" (H. Lüders, *Inscriptions*, no. 1230). With respect to the "Mahāvanaseliya," G. Bühler, "Correspondence," *JRAS*, 1892, p. 597, claimed that the term "Mahāvanasāliya" that repeatedly occurs in the Amaravati inscriptions as an epithet of teachers, may refer to a Buddhist school. See also note #7.

6. The name "*Puvasell[i]ya*" is mentioned on a pillar in Dharanikota, probably dating from Vāsiṣṭhīputra Pulomā (ca. 130–159) (*Epigraphia Indica* XXIV, pp. 256–260; *Annual Report on South Indian Epigraphy for the Year Ending 31 March 1923*. Madras: Government Press, 1924, p. 97). "*Puvaseliya*" is further mentioned on a pillar in Alluru (undated) (N. Dutt, "The Mahāsāṃghika School of Buddhism," *University of Calcutta: Journal of the Department of Letters* VII, 1922, p. 125).

7. We have two inscriptions "*Aparamahāvinaseliya*," both on a pillar in Nagarjunikonda, from the year 6 of Māṭharīputra Vīrapuruṣadatta of the Ikṣvākus (ca. 250–275) (*Epigraphia Indica* XX, p. 17 and pp. 19–20). We further find "*Aparamahavinaseliya*" in a temple in Nagarjunikonda, from the year 18 of the same king (*Epigraphia Indica* XX, pp. 21–22). The Aparamahāvinaseliya are also referred to as "*Ayirahaṃgha*" and as "*Ayirahagha*," that is, "Holy Community" (*Epigraphia Indica* XX, pp. 15–17 and pp. 19–20 respectively) on inscriptions found in Nagarjunikonda, that have to be dated in the sixth year of Māṭharīputra Vīrapuruṣadatta of the Ikṣvākus (ca. 250–275). According to E. Lamotte, *Histoire du bouddhisme indien, des origines à l'ère Śaka*. Louvain: Bibliothèque du Muséon, 43, 1958, p. 582, "Āryasaṃgha" is the title that the Mahāsāṃghikas of the region of Guntur assumed in the first centuries of the Christian era. See also note #5.

8. Hereby, the term "sect" (*nikāya*) only refers to differences of ordination lineage (*upasampadā*), and the term "school" to groups that are identified according to doctrinal position. See H. Bechert, "Aśoka's 'Schismenedikt' und der Begriff Sanghabheda," *WZKSO* V, 1961; H. Bechert, "Notes on the Formation of Buddhist Sects and the Origins of Mahāyāna," in L. Alsdorf and F. M. Müller (eds.), *German Scholars on India. Contributions to Indian Studies* (Varanasi: Chowkhamba Sanskrit Series Office), 1973, pp. 8–10; P. Kieffer-Pülz, "Die buddhistische Gemeinde," p. 288.

9. E. Lamotte, *Histoire*, pp. 301–302, dates Vasumitra 400 years after the Buddha's *parinirvāṇa*. J. Masuda, "Origin and Doctrines of Early Indian Buddhist Schools: A Translation of the Hsüan-Chwang Version of Vasumitra's Treatise I-pu tsung-lun lun. Translated with Annotations," *AM* 2, 1925, p. 8, situates Vasumitra in the first century AD. On the dates of the three Chinese versions of the *Samayabhedoparacanacakra—Yibuzong lun lun* (T.2031), *Shiba bu lun* (T.2032), and *Buzhiyi lun* (T.2033), see J. Masuda, ibid., pp. 5–6; E. Lamotte, ibid., p. 302; B. Wang, "Buddhist Nikāyas through Ancient Chinese Eyes," *Untersuchungen zur buddhistischen Literatur.* Sanskrit-Wörterbuch der buddhistischen Texte aus den Turfanfunden, Beiheft 5. Göttingen: Vandenhoeck & Ruprecht, 1994, p. 171 and pp. 175–176. On the problem of Vasumitra's authorship: see L. S. Cousins, "The 'Five Points' and the Origins of the Buddhist Schools," in T. Skorupski (ed.), *The Buddhist Forum.* London: School of Oriental and African Studies, University of London, 1991, vol. 2, p. 28, where he proposes a date from the third to fourth century AD. On the problem of the attribution of the *Shiba bu lun* to Paramārtha or Kumārajīva: see J. Masuda, "Early Indian Buddhist Schools. A Translation from the Hsüan-Chwang Version of Vasumitra's Treatise," *University of Calcutta: Journal of the Department of Letters* I, 1920, p. 1; J. Masuda, ibid., 1925, pp. 5–6.

10. On the identity of the Ekavyāvahārikas and the Lokottaravādins: see A. Bareau, *Les sectes bouddhiques du petit véhicule* (Paris: Publications de l'Ecole Française d'Extrême-Orient 38), 1955, p. 75; L. S. Cousins, "The 'Five Points,' " p. 49, explains the name Ekavyāvahārika as that the "One-utterancers" "held the belief that Buddhas have only one kind of utterance, i.e. a transcendent utterance. Hence too their alternative name of Lokottaravādins 'those whose doctrine is transcendent' or 'those who affirm the transcendent speaking (of the Buddha).' " With this position, L. S. Cousins claims that they were opposed to the Kukkuṭikas, according to whom the Buddha had two kinds of speech: transcendent and ordinary, the latter when speaking about ordinary things. See on this subject statements (32) through (35) below. See also G. Roth, "Particular Features of the Language of the Ārya-Mahāsāṃghika-Lokottaravādins and Their Importance for Early Buddhist Tradition," in H. Bechert (ed.), *Die Sprache der ältesten buddhistischen Überlieferung. The Language of the Earliest Buddhist Tradition* (Göttingen: Vandenhoeck & Ruprecht, 1980), p. 79. As to geographical presence, we know that the Lokottaravādins resided in the North, more precisely in the region of Bamiyan. See E. Windisch, "Die Komposition des Mahāvastu. Ein Beitrag zur Quellenkunde des Buddhismus," *Abhandlungen der Philologisch—historischen Klasse der Königlich Sächsischen Gesellschaft der Wissenschaften* XXVII, 1909, p. 469; *Da Tang xiyu ji* T.2087, p. 873b13 (trans. S. Beal, *Si-yu-ki. Buddhist Records of the Western World. Translated from the Chinese of Hiuen Tsiang (A.D. 629).* Delhi: Motilal Banarsidass, 1994, Pt. I, p. 50; Th. Watters, *On Yuan Chwang's Travels in India.* Oriental Translation Fund. New Series, vol. XIV. London: Royal Asiatic Society, 1904–1905, vol. I, pp. 116–120). See also notes #11 and #51.

11. For the discussion on the names "Gokulika," "Kukkuḷaka," "Kukkuṭika," "Kaukkuṭika": see A. Bareau, *Sectes*, p. 79. According to L. S. Cousins, "The 'Five Points,' " p. 49, this name most probably originated from the name of the Kukkuṭārāma in Pataliputra, a monastery associated in some sources with the

Mahāsāṃghikas. Their precise place of residence is not known. On the cause of this first schism within the Mahāsāṃghika school, P. Demiéville, "L'origine des sectes bouddhiques d'après Paramārtha," *MCB* I, 1931–32, pp. 21–22, p. 41, note b, claims that it was caused by the Ekavyāvahārika and Lokottaravāda acceptance of Mahāyāna *sūtra*s as the authentic word of the Buddha, while the Kukkuṭikas are supposed to have only recognized the authority of the Abhidharma.

12. According to Paramārtha (557–669), in his commentary on Vasumitra's *Sbc* (*Sanlun xuanyi jian you ji* T.2300, p. 460c6 ff.), this school was founded by *Yājñavalkya. Having seen that the Mahāsāṃghikas were only developing the superficial meaning of the scriptures, not the profound meaning, *Yājñavalkya is said to have established a new school that proclaimed the profound doctrine. See P. Demiéville, "Origine," p. 22, p. 47; Kuiji, *Yibuzong lun lun shuji*, 17a1–9. See also note #152.

13. According to A. Bareau, *Sectes*, p. 84, the name 'Prajñaptivādin' probably refers to their doctrine that everything is mere nominal (*prajñapti*). On their residing in the Himalaya mountains: see P. Demiéville, "Origine," pp. 49–50.

14. T.2031, p. 15a26–b8. The same chronology is found in T.2032, p. 18a14–23 and in T.2033, p. 20a26–b7. This chronology of the schools and sects that have issued from the Mahāsāṃghikas parallels the one presented in *Dīp* V30–54 (B.C. Law (ed.), "The Chronicle of the Island of Ceylon or the Dipavamsa. A Historical Poem of the 4th century A.D.," *The Ceylon Historical Journal* 1957–1958, no's. 1–4, pp. 41–43; trans. pp. 162–164).

15. T.2031, p. 15a20. See also T.2032, p. 18a17–20 and T.2033, p. 20b2–4. According to E. Lamotte, "Buddhist Controversy over the Five Propositions," *IHQ* XXXII, 1956, p. 150, Xuanzang had this information from the **Abhidharmamahāvibhāṣaśāstra* (*Apidamo dapiposha lun*, T.1545, pp. 510c23–512a19). Paramārtha (T.2300, pp. 455b3–456c16) and his pupil Jizang (549–623) in his *Sanlun xuanyi* T.1852, p. 8b22–c13, reproduced the account of the *Vibhāṣa*. This version of the account is again taken up by Xuanzang in T.2087, p. 886b11–22. (trans. S. Beal, *Si-yu-ki*, Pt. I, pp. 150–151; Th. Watters, *Travels*, vol. I, pp. 267–269). See also P. Demiéville, "A propos du concile de Vaiśāli," *TP* 40, 1951, pp. 267–269, note #2. According to the *Chu sanzang ji ji* T.2145, p. 19c26, the adherents of Mahādeva would have called themselves Mahāsāṃghikas. See in this respect A. Schiefner (trans.), *Tāranātha's Geschichte des Buddhismus in Indien—aus dem Tibetischen übersetzt.* St. Petersburg: Kaiserlichen Akademie der Wissenschaften, Eggers & Co., 1868, p. 293; L. de La Vallée Poussin, "The 'Five Points' of Mahādeva and the Kathāvatthu,' *JRAS* 1910, p. 415, note #1. For the life of Mahādeva: see P. Demiéville, ibid., pp. 262–269; E. Frauwallner, "Die buddhistischen Konzile," *ZDMG* 102, 1952, pp. 87–88; A. Bareau, *Les premiers conciles bouddhiques*. Paris: Presses Universitaires de France, 1955, p. 98. For the discussion on the existence of two Mahādevas: see N. Dutt, *Early Monastic Buddhism*. Calcutta: Calcutta Oriental Series no. 30, 1945, vol. 2, p. 120; P. Demiévillle, ibid., pp. 267–269, note #2.

16. A. Bareau, "Les origines du Śāriputrābhidharmaśāstra," *Le Muséon* LXIII, 1–2, 1950, p. 70, dates the compilation of the work between the third century BC and the first century BC to the 1st century AD. A. Bareau, *Sectes*, p. 21, dates the existing version of the *Śriputraparipṛcchāsūtra* ca. AD 300. The affiliation of the *Śāriputraparipṛcchāsūtra* is still a matter of scholarly debate. A.

Bareau, *Sectes*, p. 17; J. Nattier and Ch. S. Prebish, "Mahāsāṃghika Origins: The Beginnings of Buddhist Sectarianism," *HR* 16, 1976/77, p. 249; L. S. Cousins, "The 'Five Points,'" p. 28; and B. Wang, "Buddhist Nikāyas," p. 170, ascribe the text to the Mahāsāṃghikas. The text was translated into Chinese during the Eastern Jin Dynasty (317–420).

17. *Shelifu wen jing* T.1465, p. 900c6–10.

18. See A. Bareau, *Sectes*, p. 22; E. Lamotte, *Histoire*, pp. 592–593.

19. A. Schiefner (trans.), *Geschichte*, p. 271.

20. A. Bareau, *Sectes*, p. 23.

21. E. Lamotte, *Histoire*, p. 592, calls them "Mūlamahāsāṃghikas."

22. A. Bareau, *Sectes*, p. 23, A. Bareau, "Trois traités sur les sectes bouddhiques attribués à Vasumitra, Bhavya et Vinītadeva. IIe Partie," *JA* 244, 1956, p. 171, and E. Lamotte, *Histoire*, pp. 592–593, call them "Siddhārthikas."

23. See A. Schiefner (trans), *Geschichte*, p. 271.

24. See trans. Ktv, pp. xxii–xxiv and p. 104.

25. Rājagirika inscriptions are: (1) "*Rājagirinivāsika*" (H. Lüders, *Inscriptions*, no. 1250), and (2) "*Rājagiri*" (H. Lüders, *Inscriptions*, no. 1225), both on an undated sculpture at Amaravati.

26. A Siddhartika inscription is: "*Sidhata*" (H. Lüders, *Inscriptions*, no. 1281; C. Sivaramamurti, "Sculptures," no. 102) on an undated sculpture at Amaravati. See also note #22.

27. For further chronologies of the origination of the Mahāsāṃghikas and their offshoots: see Vinītadeva's *Samayabhedoparacanacakrenikāyabhedopadarśanasaṃgraha* (henceforth *Sbcs*) (trans. A. Bareau, "Trois traités. pt. II," pp. 192–200), *Mañjuśrīparipṛcchāsūtra (Wenshushili wen jing)* T.468, p. 501a29–b12; Yijing, *Nanhai jigui neifa zhuan* T.2125, p. 205a26 ff. (trans. J. Takakusu, *A Record of the Buddhist Religion as Practised in India and the Malay Archipelago (A.D. 671–695)*. Delhi: Munshiram Manoharlal, 1966, pp. xxiii–xxiv, pp. 7–20); "*San lun yi juan*" (trans. S. Julien, "Listes diverses des noms des dix-huit écoles schismatiques qui sont sorties du Bouddhisme," *JA* XIV, 1859, pp. 330–331, pp. 334–335, pp. 336–338, pp. 341–342, pp. 343–345), and the *Varṣāgrapṛcchāsūtra* (See W. W. Rockhill, *The Life of the Buddha and the Early History of His Order. Derived from Tibetan Works in the Bkah-hgyur and Bstanhgyur, followed by notices on the early history of Tibet and Khoten*. London: Trübner, 1884. Reprint Asian Educational Services, Delhi, 1992, p. 183). See further also A. Bareau, *Sectes*, pp. 19–27.

28. For epigraphical evidence on the Mahāsāṃgikas in Mathura, see M. Shizutani, "Matorā to Daishōbu," *IBK* XIII/1, 1965. We have an inscription "*Mahasaghia*" that is dated in the first century AD, that is, almost one and a half centuries prior to our inscriptions in the Krishna valley region (S. Konow (ed.), *Kharoshṭhī Inscriptions—with the Exception of Those of Aśoka, Corpus Inscriptionum Indicarum. vol. II, part 1* (Varanasi: Indological Book House, 1969, pp. 48–49).

29. For linguistic evidence on the spread of the Mahāsāṃghikas, see G. Roth, "Particular Features," p. 85.

30. AB: *Anno Buddhae*, dating from the *parinirvāṇa* of the Buddha. From inscriptional evidence, we know that the Bahuśrutīyas resided in the North, more precisely close to Peshawar. See S. Konow (ed.), *Inscriptions*, pp. 120–122.

31. A. Bareau, *Sectes*, p. 32. See also note #10.

32. A. Bareau, *Sectes*, pp. 32–33, further specifies the date of the origin of the Caitikas and Uttaraśailas as "the end of the second, beginning of the 3rd century after the Buddha's *nirvāṇa*." E. Lamotte, *Histoire*, p. 586, claims that the split of Mahāsāṃghikas into Caityaśailas was on the matter of ordination. Hereby, the partisans of Mahādeva II (see also note #15) are claimed to have gone to the mountainous region (probably Andhra country), where they formed the Caityaśailas, which soon divided into Easterners (Pūrvaśaila) and Westerners (Uttaraśaila). He further suggests the first century of the common era for the moment of arising of the Pūrvaśailas and Aparaśailas.

33. T.2031, p. 15a15–23; T.2032, p. 18a9–14, p. 18a17 ff.; T.2033, p. 20a15–25, p. 20b2 ff.; *Nbv*, list 3; T.1545, pp. 510c23–512a19; T.1852, p. 8b22–c13.

34. The "ten points" are only given in the accounts that belong to the Sthaviravāda tradition: *Dīp* V, 16 (trans. H. Oldenberg, *The Dīpavaṃsa: An Ancient Buddhist Historical Record*. London: Williams and Norgate, 1879, p. 35); *Mhv* IV, 9 (trans. W. Geiger, *The Mahāvaṃsa or the Great Chronicle of Ceylon*. Pali Text Society. Oxford: Oxford University Press, 1912, pp. 19 ff.). On the tenth of the "ten points," the *Mahāsāṃghikavinaya* and the *Pāli Vinaya* agree: the monks of Vaiśāli were accepting monetary donations, the precept-keeper (*vinayadhara*) objected to this, and this gave rise to a controversy. See *Pāli Vinaya*: H. Oldenberg (ed.), *Vinayapiṭakaṃ, Vol. II. Cullavagga*. London: Luzac & Co. Ltd., 1964, pp. 294–298; I. B. Horner (trans.), *The Book of the Discipline (vinaya-piṭaka)*. London: Luzac & Co. Ltd., 1963, vol. V, pp. 407–414; *Mohesengqi lü* T.1425, p. 231a29–b22. See also *Mahīśāsakavinaya* (*Mishasebu hexi wufen lü*) T.1421, p. 192a27 ff.; *Dharmaguptakavinaya* (*Sifen lü*) T.1428, pp. 968c19–969c3; *Daśādhyāyavinaya* (*Shisong lü*) T.1435, p. 450a28–29; [*Mūlasarvāstivada*]*Vinayakṣudrakavastu* (*Genben shuoyiqieyoubu pinaiye zashi*) T.1451, pp. 411c4–413c26 ff. Also T.1465, pp. 900b20–28, mentions disciplinary grounds as the cause of this schism, but does not call this "the ten points."

35. The first list of *Bhavya (*Nbv*) mentions "various points of controversy" as cause of the schism, without further specification; the second list of *Bhavya lists eighteen schools, but does not give reasons for the schisms that provoked their origin. See A. Bareau, "Trois traités. pt. II," p. 168.

36. J. Nattier and Ch.S. Prebish, "Origins," p. 239.

37. See T.1425, pp. 493a28–c22. See also M. Hofinger, *Étude sur le concile de Vaiśālī*. Louvain: Bibliothèque du Muséon, 1946, p. 173; E. Frauwallner, *The Earliest Vinaya and the Beginnings of Buddhist Literature*. Roma: Serie Orientale Roma VIII, 1956, pp. 9–10; Ch. S. Prebish, "A Review of Scholarship on the Buddhist Councils," *JAS* XXXIII, no. 2, 1974, p. 252.

38. It thus becomes very likely that the dogmatic questions that tradition relates to a third Buddhist council, were the causes of further schisms within the Mahāsāṃghika school. See N. Dutt, "The Mahāsāṃghika School of Buddhism," pp. 121–122; J. Nattier and Ch. S. Prebish, "Origins," p. 238; P. Kieffer-Pülz, "Die buddhistische Gemeinde," p. 293. It may also be remembered here that Kuiji, in his *Dacheng fayuanyi lin zhang* T.1861, p. 270c8 ff. records that Vāṣpa, not Mahādeva, was the leader of the Mahāsāṃghikas.

39. T.2031, pp. 15c17–18; T.2032, pp. 18b25–27; T.2033, pp. 20c20–21. Thesis 27 of Vasumitra (*Sbc*); theses 13 and 15 of *Bhavya (*Nbv*); thesis 16 of Vinītadeva

(*Sbcs*).(*) *Ktv* II, 1, II, 2, II, 3, II, 4, and II, 5 (trans. Ktv, pp. 111–123) ascribe this position to the Pūrvaśailas (and Aparaśailas). See also note #159.

(*) In what follows, we follow the numbering of J. Masuda, "Origins and Doctrines," 1925.

40. *Fenbie gongde lun* T.1507, pp. 32c9–10. This work was translated between AD 25 and 220. See E. Lamotte, "Buddhist Controversy," p. 156.

41. See J. Nattier and Ch. S. Prebish, "Origins," p. 257.

42. This is, for example, seen in statement (24) and note #128.

43. Paragraph 47 of the *Śālistamba Sūtra* predicts such a complete Buddhahood: "Whosoever [. . .] understands conditioned arising perfectly [. . .] 'He will become a perfect, complete Buddha!' " See N. Ross Reat, *The Śālistamba Sūtra*. Delhi: Motilal Banarsidass, 1993, p. 10, p. 72. In "The Historical Buddha and His Teaching," in K. Potter (ed.), *Encyclopedia of Indian Philosophies. Volume VII: Abhidharma Buddhism to 150 A.D.* Delhi: Motilal Banarsidass, 1996, p. 27, N. Ross Reat claims that the *The Śālistambha Sūtra* may be a Mahāsāṃghika work.

44. T.1852, pp. 8b18–19. See also note #11.

45. T.2300, pp. 456a25–b23. As remarked by André Bareau, *Sectes*, p. 32, the time elapsed between the first schism and the further fragmentation of the Mahāsāṃghikas, at most half a century later, is most likely too short to have made such a textual evolution possible.

46. For this attribution: see T.2300, pp. 460c3–22. See also A. Bareau, "Les sectes bouddhiques du Petit Véhicule et leurs Abhidharmapiṭaka," *BEFEO*, 1951, p. 1; E. H. Johnston (trans.), *The Buddhacarita, Or Acts of the Buddha*. Reprint Delhi: Oriental Books Reprint Corporation, 1972, pp. xxxi–xxxv.

47. See É. Sénart (ed.), *Le Mahāvastu. Texte Sanscrit Publié pour la première fois et accompagné d'introductions et d'un commentaire*. Paris: Imprimerie Nationale, vol. 1, 1882, p. 2. The work was edited by É. Sénart under the above mentioned title (1882–1897), and translated by J. Jones as *The Mahāvastu*. 3 vols. London: Luzac, 1949–56.

48. N. A. Sastri (ed.), *Satyasiddhiśāstra of Harivarman*. Baroda: Oriental Institute, vol. 1, 1975, p. i, claims that he was a native of Kashmir. According to A. K. Warder, *Indian Buddhism*. Delhi: Motilal Banarsidass, 1980/2, p. 293, note #2, he wrote near Pataliputra.

49. See N. A. Sastri (ed.), *Satyasiddhiśāstra*, p. vii, who gives AD 412 as date of translation into Chinese.

50. J. Jones (trans.), *The Mahāvastu*, vol. 1, p. xi.

51. See J. Jones (trans.), *The Mahāvastu*, vol. 1, p. xii; E. Windisch, "Komposition," pp. 473–474 and pp. 476 ff. See also H. Oldenberg, "Buddhistische Studien," *ZDMG* LII, 1898, p. 644; H. Oldenberg, "Studien zur Mahāvastu," *Nachrichten von der königlichen Gesellschaft der Wissenschaften zu Göttingen. Philologisch-historische Klasse*, 1912, pp. 141–142 and p. 152. N. Ross Reat, *The Śālistamba Sūtra*, p. 2, remarks that most of the content of the *Mahāvastu* is mythological and therefore uninformative regarding the nature of their early doctrine.

52. Edited by N. A. Jayawickrama as *Kathāvatthu*. London: Routledge & Kegan Paul, 1979, and translated by B. C. Law as *The Debates Commentary (Kathāvatthuppakarana-Aṭṭhakathā)* (London: Luzac & Company, 1940).

53. See A. Bareau, *Dhammasaṅgaṇi. Traduction Annotée.* Thèse complémentaire présentée à la Faculté des Lettres de l'Université de Paris pour le Doctorat Es-Lettres. Paris, 1951, p. 32.

54. See trans. Ktv, p. xxxiii. See also L. de La Vallée Poussin, "Le Vijñānakaya et le Kathāvatthu," *Bulletins de la classe des lettres.* Académie Royale de Belgique 5e Série, T.VIII, 1922, no. 11, p. 520; E. Frauwallner, "Abhidharma-Studien IV. Der Abhidharma der anderen Schulen," *WZKSO* XVI, 1972, p. 124. L.S. Cousins, "The 'Five Points,' " p. 45, argues that "the *Kathāvatthu* was expanded and reshaped precisely at this time (= second century BC) in response to ideas coming from" the Mahāsāṃghikas.

55. See *Shelifu apitan lun* T.1548, pp. 525b1–3; *Gao seng zhuan,* T.2059, pp. 329c2–8; T.2145, pp. 71a7–11.

56. This conclusion is mainly sustained by observations related to the structure of the work. Also some doctrinal issues make a Dharmaguptaka affiliation likely. See A. Bareau, "Origines," pp. 84–85, p. 94; A. Bareau, "Sectes bouddhiques," p. 1; E. Frauwallner, "Der Abhidharma der anderen Schulen," p. 133; L. Schmithausen, "Beiträge zur Schulzugehörigkeit und Textgeschichte kanonischer und postkanonischer buddhistischen Materialen," in H. Bechert (ed.), *Zur Schulzugehörigkeit von Werken der Hīnayāna-Literatur*. Göttingen: Vandenhoeck & Ruprecht, Pt. 2, 1987, p. 318; K. Matsuda, "Three Fragments Related to the Śāriputra-Abhidharma*," in J. Braarvig (ed.), *Manuscripts in the Schøyen Collection.* Vol. II. Oslo: Hermes Publishing, 2002, p. 246.

57. T.2031, pp. 17a26–27; T.2032, pp. 19c5–6; T.2033, pp. 22b15–16. See also A. Bareau, *L'absolu en philosophie bouddhique. Evolution de la notion d'asamskrta.* Paris: Centre de documentation universitaire, 1951, p. 264 and p. 266.

58. See A. Bareau, "Origines," pp. 76–77, notes #50 ff.

59. See C. Willemen, B. Dessein, C. Cox, *Sarvāstivāda Buddhist Scholasticism,* Handbuch der Orientalistik. Zweite Abteilung, Indien, no. 11. Leiden: E. J. Brill, 1998, pp. 231–233.

60. According to *Kaiyuan shi jiao lu,* T.2154, pp. 521b14–17, the **Abhidharmavibhāṣaśāstra* (T.1546) was translated by Buddhavarman and Daotai between AD 437 and 439. These dates are contradicted by the preface to this Chinese translation (T.1546, p. 1a7 ff., p. 414c22 ff.), according to which the translation was done between AD 425–427. See also T.2145, p. 73c28 ff.; T.2154, p. 620c1–11. On these two sets of dates: see K. Kawamura, *Abidatsumaronsho no Shiryōteki Kenkyū.* Kyōto: Nihon Gakujutsu Shinkōkai, 1974, p. 131, note #6.

61. That is, *caksurvijñāna, śrotravijñāna, ghrāṇavijñāna, jihvāvijñāna, sprastavyavijñāna.*

62. T.2031, p. 15c12; T.2032, p. 18b22; T.2033, p. 20c15. Thesis 22 of Vasumitra (*Sbc*); thesis 11 of Vinītadeva (*Sbcs*). *Ktv* X, 3 (trans. Ktv, pp. 245–246) attributes this thesis to the Mahāsāṃghikas only. See further also Kuiji, 221-8-3, 28a3–7; J. Masuda, "Origin and Doctrines," p. 22, note #1. In thesis 11 of *Bhavya (*Nbv*), "six" forms of consciousness are mentioned. See in this respect M. Walleser, *Die Sekten des alten Buddhismus,* Heidelberg: Carl Winter's Universitätsbuchhandlung, 1927, p. 33. See also note #65.

63. See trans. Ktv, p. 245.

64. AN, vol. 1, p. 113. Cf. *Ekottarāgama Zengyi ahan jing*, T.125, pp. 603c22–28. See further trans. Ktv, p. 246; N. Dutt, "Doctrines of the Mahasanghika School of Buddhism" *IHQ* XIII, 1937, pp. 574–576.

65. T.2031, p. 15c12–13; T.2032, p. 18b22; T.2033, p. 20c15. Thesis 23 of Vasumitra (*Sbc*); thesis 12 of Vinītadeva (*Sbcs*). See also *Ktv* VIII, 7 (trans. Ktv, pp. 218–220); Kuiji, 221-8-3, 28a8–b1.

66. T.2031, pp. 15c27–28; T.2032, p. 18c5; T.2033, p. 21a1. Thesis 41 of Vasumitra (*Sbc*); thesis 18 of *Bhavya (*Nbv*); thesis 32 of Vinītadeva (*Sbcs*). See also *Ktv* III, 3 (trans. Ktv, pp. 144–145); Kuiji, 221-8-3, 31a13–32a1. T.1548, pp. 697b18–22, explains that with worldlings, the mind is defiled, but not with noble persons. This may explain why *Bhavya mentions six forms of consciousness (see note #62). This is related to the Mahāyāna doctrine that mind is essentially and originally pure but becomes impure by adventitious afflictions. This pure mind is identical with the *dharmakāya* of the Buddha. See on this P. S. Jaini, "The Sautrāntika Theory of bīja," *BSOAS* XXII, 2, 1959, p. 249. On the early notions of "*rūpakāya*" and "*dharmakāya*," see K. Régamey, *Three Chapters from the Samādhirājasūtra*. The Warsaw Society of Sciences and Letters 1. Warsaw: Publications of the Oriental Commission, 1938, pp. 23–24.

67. See *Ktv* VIII, 7 (trans. Ktv, p. 219); J. Masuda, "Origin and Doctrines," pp. 22–23, note #2.

68. See SN, *Nidānavaggo*, 1 (SN, vol. 2, p. 1).

69. *Ktv* VIII, 8, XVI, 9 (trans. Ktv, pp. 220–221, pp. 309–310) ascribe the existence of form in the realm of formlessness to the Andhakas.

70. See also AN LXIII, 3 (*Mahāvagga*) (AN, vol. 3, p. 411).

71. See on this: C. Cox, "On the Possibility of a Nonexistent Object of Consciousness: Sarvāstivādin and Dārṣṭāntika Theories," *JIABS* 11/1, 1988, p. 34.

72. T.2031, p. 15c13–15; T.2032, p. 18b23; T.2033, p. 20c15–16. Thesis 24 of Vasumitra (*Sbc*); thesis 13 of Vinītadeva (*Sbcs*). See also Kuiji, 221-8-3, 28b2–5.

73. See J. Masuda, "Origin and Doctrines," p. 23, note #1.

74. T.1545, pp. 47b1–3 and b26–27. See also J. Masuda, "Origin and Doctrines," p. 33, note #2. This is also discussed in T.1546, pp. 35b4–5.

75. T.2031, p. 16a7; T.2032, p. 18c10; T.2033, p. 21a10. Thesis 3 of Vasumitra (*Sbc*). See also Kuiji, 221-8-3, 33b3–5.

76. T.2031, p. 16a10; T.2032, p. 18c11–12; T.2033, p. 21a12–13. Thesis 8 of Vasumitra (*Sbc*); thesis 31 of Vinītadeva (*Sbcs*). See also Kuiji, 221-8-3, 34a4–17.

77. See A. Bareau, *Sectes*, p. 75 and p. 79 respectively.

78. See G. Roth (ed.), *Bhikṣuṇī-Vinaya. Manual of Discipline for Buddhist Nuns*. Patna: K. P. Jayaswal Research Institute, 1970, p. xiii; S. Lévi, "Note sur des Manuscrits Sanscrits provenant de Bamiyan (Afghanistan) et de Gilgit (Cachemire)," *JA* 220, 1932, p. 5. See also note #10.

79. On the Mahāsāṃghika doctrine that there is only one mind that adapts itself to the various sense organs and objects, see J. Masuda, "Origin and Doctrines," pp. 34–35, note #4.

80. T.1545, pp. 96a27–29. This is also discussed in T.1546, pp. 80a3–5.

81. T.2031, pp. 16a9–10; T.2032, pp. 18c11; T.2033, pp. 21a11–12. Thesis 7 of Vasumitra (*Sbc*).

82. See Kuiji, op. cit., 34a1–3.

83. See AN II, 36–37. Cp. *Saṃyuktāgama* (*Za'ahan jing*) T.99, pp. 28b9–15.

84. See E. Lamotte, "Passions and Impregnations of the Passions in Buddhism," in L. S. Cousins et al. (eds.), *Buddhist Studies in Honour of I. B. Horner*. Dordrecht: D. Reidel Publishing Company, 1974, pp. 91–92.

85. On the notion "*kāritra*," see L. de La Vallée Poussin, "Documents d'Abhidharma—La Controverse de Temps; les deux, les quatre, les trois Vérités," *MCB* V, 1936–1937, p. 131; E. Frauwallner, "Abhidharma-Studien. V. Der Sarvāstivādaḥ. Eine entwicklungsgeschichtliche Studie," *WZKSO* XVII, 1973, pp. 104–109.

86. T.2031, p. 16a1–2; T.2032, p. 18c7; T.2033, p. 21a4. Thesis 44 of Vasumitra (*Sbc*); thesis 20 of *Bhavya (*Nbv*). See also Kuiji, 221-8-3, 32a12–14.

87. T.2031, p. 16a8; T.2033, p. 21a11. Thesis 5 of Vasumitra (*Sbc*); thesis 29 of Vinītadeva (*Sbcs*). See also *Ktv* XV, 11 (trans. Ktv, pp. 300–302); Kuiji, 221-8-3, 33b10–13; J. Masuda, "Origin and Doctrines," pp. 33–34, note #4.

88. T.1646, pp. 258c10–11.

89. T.1646, pp. 258c11–18.

90. T.2031, p. 15c22; T.2032, p. 18c1; T.2033, p. 20c25. Thesis 36 of Vasumitra (*Sbc*). See also Kuiji, 221-8-3, 30b6–9.

91. T.2031, pp. 15c29–16a1; T.2032, p. 18c6; T.2033, pp. 21a2–4. Thesis 43 of Vasumitra (*Sbc*); thesis 19 of *Bhavya (*Nbv*); thesis 33 of Vinītadeva (*Sbcs*). In *Ktv* XI, 1 (trans. Ktv, pp. 253–255), this opinion is attributed to the Mahāsāṃghikas. See also Kuiji, 221-8-3, 32a7–11; *Ktv* XIV, 5 and XIV, 6 (trans. Ktv, pp. 253–255 and pp. 287–288); J. Masuda, "Origin and Doctrines," pp. 30–31, note #3; N. Dutt, "Doctrines," pp. 569–571.

92. T.2031, p. 15c28–29; T.2032, p. 18c5–6; T.2033, p. 21a2. Thesis 42 of Vasumitra (*Sbc*); thesis 18 of *Bhavya (*Nbv*). See also Kuiji, 221-8-3, 32a2–6; *Ktv* IX, 4 (trans. Ktv: pp. 234–236); J. Masuda, "Origin and Doctrines," p. 30, note #2; and *Ktv* XIV, 5 (trans. Ktv, pp. 498–499).

93. See note #86.

94. T.2031, p. 16a8–9; T.2032, pp. 18c10–11; T.2033, p. 21a11. Thesis 6 of Vasumitra (*Sbc*); thesis 30 of Vinītadeva (*Sbcs*). Thesis 30 of Vinītadeva (*Sbcs*) states that "germs and sprouts develop simultaneously." See Kuiji, 221-8-3, 33b14–17.

95. T.2031, p. 16a7–8; T.2032, p. 18c10; T.2033, p. 21a10–11. Thesis 4 of Vasumitra (*Sbc*); thesis 28 of Vinītadeva (*Sbcs*). See also Kuiji, 221-8-3, 33b6–9.

96. T.2031, p. 16a3; T.2033, p. 21a5. Thesis 46 of Vasumitra (*Sbc*); thesis 34 of Vinītadeva (*Sbcs*). See also Kuiji, 221-8-3, 32b10–13; J. Masuda, "Origin and Doctrines," pp. 31–32, note #3. According to Buddhaghoṣa's commentary to *Ktv* VIII, 2 (trans. Ktv, pp. 212–213), the Pūrvaśailas accepted the existence of intermediate existence.

97. T.2031, pp. 15c18–19; T.2032, p. 18b27; T.2033, p. 20c22. Thesis 31 of Vasumitra (*Sbc*). See also Kuiji, 221-8-3, 29b8–10.

98 T.1545, p. 14a5–8. This is also discussed in T.1546, p. 9b11–12.

99. T.2031, pp. 15c20–21; T.2032, pp. 18b27–28; T.2033, pp. 20c22–23. Thesis 33b of Vasumitra (*Sbc*); thesis 19 of Vinītadeva (*Sbcs*). See also Kuiji, 221-8-3, 30a7–11; J. Masuda, "Origin and Doctrines," pp. 25–26, note #3.

100. That is, *anityatā, duḥkha, śūnyatā, anātmaka; hetu, samudaya, prabhava, pratyaya; nirodha, śānta, praṇīta, niḥsaraṇa; mārga, nyāya, pratipatti, nairyāṇika.*

101. That is, the antidote (*pratipakṣa*) for the contaminants to be abandoned through the vision of suffering of the realm of sensual passion.

102. T.2031, pp. 15c22–23; T.2033, p. 20c25. Thesis 37 of Vasumitra (*Sbc*); thesis 16 of *Bhavya (*Nbv*). See also Kuiji, 221-8-3, 30b10–13; J. Masuda, "Origin and Doctrines," pp. 27–28, note #3.

103. T.2032, p. 18c1.

104. Trans. Ktv, pp. 130–134. It thus appears that some Mahāsāṃghika groups, among which the Andhakas, were more conservative in their opinion on higher realization of the truths than some other Mahāsāṃghika groups were.

105. T.2031, p. 16a4–5. Thesis 1 of Vasumitra (*Sbc*). See also *Ktv* I, 4, II, 9 (trans. Ktv, pp. 76–80, pp. 130–134); Kuiji, 221-8-3, 33a3–12.

106. T.2031, p. 15c20; T.2033, p. 20c14–15. Thesis 33a of Vasumitra (*Sbc*); thesis 18 of Vinītadeva (*Sbcs*). See also Kuiji, 221-8-3, 29b14–30a6; J. Masuda, "Origin and Doctrines," p. 25, note #2.

107. Trans. Ktv, pp. 146–148.

108. On the identity of the one who goes to the fruit of the streamwinner and the "eighth person": see trans. Ktv, p. 147; Kuiji, 221-8-3, 29b15; J. Masuda, "Origin and Doctrines," p. 25, note #2.

109. T.2031, p. 15c15–16; T.2032, p. 18b24–25; T.2033, p. 20c16–17. Thesis 25 of Vasumitra (*Sbc*); thesis 14 of *Bhavya (*Nbv*); thesis 14 of Vinītadeva (*Sbcs*). See also *Ktv* II, 5, XVIII, 8 (trans. Ktv, pp. 120–123, pp. 331–332); Kuiji, 221-8-3, 28b9–29a4.

110. T.2031, p. 15c23–24; T.2032, p. 18c1–2; T.2033, p. 20c25–26. Thesis 38 of Vasumitra (*Sbc*); thesis 21 of Vinītadeva (*Sbcs*). See also Kuiji, 221-8-3, 30b14–31a1. Meant are: *pitṛghāta, mātṛghāta, arhadvadha, saṃghabheda,* and *tathāgatasyāntike dustacittarudhirotpādāna.*

111. T.2031, pp. 15c21–22. Thesis 34 of Vasumitra (*Sbc*); thesis 20 of Vinītadeva (*Sbcs*). See also Kuiji, 221-8-3, 30a12–17.

112. T.2032, pp. 18c28–29.

113. T.2033, pp. 20c23–24.

114. Both the Buddha and whoever reached liberation are called *arhat*. See A. Bareau, "Les controverses relatives à la nature de l'arhant dans le Bouddhisme ancien," *IIJ* 1, 1957, pp. 241–250; J. Bronkhorst, "Die buddhistische Lehre," in H. Bechert et al. (ed.), *Der Buddhismus I. Der indische Buddhismus und seine Verzweigungen.* Stuttgart: Kohlhammer, 2000, p. 127.

115. The Buddha, for example, was described as having "all-knowledge," while the *arhat* did not have this. See P. S. Jaini, "On the ignorance of the Arhat," in R. E. Buswell and R. M. Gimello (eds.), *Paths to Liberation. The Mārga and Its Transformations in Buddhist Thought.* Honolulu: University of Hawaii, 1992, p. 135, p. 143, note #1. See also H. Bechert, "Zur Frühgeschichte des Mahāyāna-Buddhismus," *ZDMG* 113/3, 1964, p. 532; J. Bronkhorst, "Die buddhistische Lehre," pp. 127–128.

116. A. Bareau, "Trois traités sur les sectes bouddiques dues à Vasumitra, Bhavya et Vinītadeva. Première Partie," *JA* 1–2, 1954, p. 242, enumerates the five

points of Mahādeva as the twenty-eighth thesis. In *Bhavya's *Nbv*, this point is listed as the thirteenth of twenty-one theses attributed to the Ekavyāvahārikas.

117. For the Bahuśrutīyas: T.2031, pp. 16a14–15; T.2032, p. 18c15–17; T.2033, p. 21a16–18. Thesis 3 of Vasumitra (*Sbc*); Thesis 2 of Vinītadeva (*Sbcs*). See also Kuiji, 221-8-3, 34b18–35a2. In *Bhavya's *Nbv*, these five points are, for the Bahuśrutīyas, reduced to one: the *arhat* obtains the dispensation (*upadeśa*) with the help of others. For the Caityaśailas, Aparaśailas, and Uttaraśailas: T.2031, pp. 16a23–24; T.2032, pp. 18c24–25; T.2033, pp. 21a26–28. Thesis 3 of Vasumitra (*Sbc*). See also Kuiji, 221-8-3, 36b3–5.

118. U. Wogihara (ed.), *Sphuṭārthābhidharmakośavyākhyā of Yaśomitra*. Tōkyō: Sankibō Buddhist Book Store, 1971, vol. 1, p. 7; P. S. Jaini, "On the ignorance of the Arhat," pp. 136–137. See also T.2031, pp. 15c4–5; T.2032, pp. 18b16–17; T.2033, pp. 20c4–5 (thesis 13 of Vasumitra (*Sbc*); thesis 5 of Vinītadeva (*Sbcs*). See also Kuiji, 221-8-3, 25b11–17; *Ktv* V, 9 (trans. Ktv, p. 183). Cf. T.1546, p. 239b6, b19, c2); and T.2031, p. 15c5; T.2032, p. 18b17; T.2033, p. 20c5–6 (thesis 14 of Vasumitra (*Sbc*); thesis 5 of Vinītadeva (*Sbcs*). See also Kuiji, 221-8-3, 25b18–26a5. Cf. T.1546, pp. 239c12–23).

119. Trans, Ktv, pp. 114–119.

120. It is very likely that when Xuanzang claims that an *arhat* is not subject to falling back (statement 18), he only refers to those types of *arhat* to whom this quality applies. In this respect, L. S. Cousins, "The 'Five Points,' " p. 37, remarks that the word used for doubt is *kaṅkhā*, a word that is less technical than *vicikicchā*. Such an interpretation is also evident in the **Satyasiddhiśāstra*. See N. A. Sastri (ed.): *Satyasiddhiśāstra*, pp. 288 ff. See also N. Dutt, "Doctrines," pp. 560–563.

121. T.2031, pp. 15c6–8; T.2032, pp. 18b18–19; T.2033, pp. 20c7–9. Thesis 16 of Vasumitra (*Sbc*); thesis 6 of *Bhavya (*Nbv*); thesis 9 of Vinītadeva (*Sbcs*). In *Ktv* XIV, 2 (trans. Ktv, pp. 283–285), this thesis is ascribed to the Pubbaseliyas and the Aparaseliyas. See also Kuiji, 221-8-3, 26b2–15. T.2032, pp. 18b18–19 has: "Bodhisattvas do not love their mother's womb."

122. T.2031, p. 15c8; T.2032, p. 18b19; T.2033, p. 20c9. Thesis 17 of Vasumitra (*Sbc*); thesis 7 of *Bhavya (*Nbv*). See also Kuiji, 221-8-3, 26b16–27a6.

123. T.2031, p. 15c9; T.2032, p. 18b19–20; T.2033, p. 20c9–10. Thesis 18 of Vasumitra (*Sbc*); thesis 7 of *Bhavya (*Nbv*). See also Kuiji, 221-8-3, 27a7–17.

124. T. 2031, p. 15c6, p. 15c8: "yiqie," p. 15c7: "jie"; T.2032, p. 18b19: "yiqie"; and T.2033, p. 20c7, p. 20c10: "yiqie," p. 20c10: "jie."

125. T.2031, p. 15c9–10; T.2032, p. 18b20; T.2033, p. 20c10–11. Thesis 19 of Vasumitra (*Sbc*); thesis 8 of *Bhavya (*Nbv*); thesis 8 of Vinītadeva (*Sbcs*). See also Kuiji, 221-8-3, 27a18–b3.

126. N. Dutt, "Doctrines," p. 560 claims that, for the Mahāsāṃghikas, it is so that from the moment an individual develops *bodhicitta*, he becomes a *bodhisattva* and is destined to become a Buddha. He follows a career which is different from that of a *śrāvaka*.

127. Trans. Ktv, pp. 228–229.

128. T.2031, pp. 15c10–11; T.2032, pp. 18b20–21, T.2033, pp. 20c11–13. Thesis 20 of Vasumitra (*Sbc*); thesis 9 of *Bhavya (*Nbv*). See also *Ktv* XXIII, 3 (trans. Ktv, pp. 366–367); Kuiji, 221-8-3, 27b4–13.

129. T.2031, p. 15b27; T.2032, p. 18b11–12; T.2033, p. 20b27. Thesis 1 of Vasumitra (*Sbc*); thesis 1 of *Bhavya (*Nbv*) for the Ekavyāvahārikas; thesis 1 of Vinītadeva (*Sbcs*) for the Lokottaravādins. In the *Ktv* XVIII, 1 (trans. Ktv, p. 323), this thesis is attributed to the Vetullakas. According to Buddhaghoṣa's commentary (see Ktv, p. 323), "Some, like the Vetulyakas [. . .] hold that the Exalted One, when born in the heaven of Delight, dwelt there while visiting this world only in a shape specially created." On these Vetulyakas, not much is known. A. Bareau, *Sectes*, p. 254, claims that their doctrine had its roots in an Andhaka-Mahīśāsaka-Dharmaguptaka syncretism. See also Kuiji, 221-8-3, 23a5–13. See also notes #133 and #134, and further E. Windisch, "Buddha's Geburt und die Lehre von der Seelenwanderung," *Abhandlungen der Philologisch-historischen Klasse der Königlich Sächsischen Gesellschaft der Wissenschaften* XXVI, 1908, p. 142; E. Windisch, "Komposition," p. 470.

130. T.2031, p. 15b27: "yiqie," p. 15b27, c5: "zhu; T.2032, p. 18b11: "yiqie"; T.2033, p. 20b27: "yiqie."

131. See E. Lamotte, "Passions," pp. 94 ff.

132. See L. de La Vallée Poussin, "The three bodies of a Buddha (*trikāya*)," *JRAS* XXXVIII, 1906, p. 949. See also note #145.

133. See AN (*Catukkanipāta* 4, *Cakkavagga*, 36) (AN, vol. 2, p. 39) and SN (*Khandhasamyuttam*, *Khajjaniyavagga*, 94) (SN, vol. 3, p. 140). Cp. T.99, pp. 28a29–b8.

134. E. Lamotte, "Passions," p. 95, remarks that the Mahāsāṃghika list of unique factors of the Buddha (*āveṇikadharma*) is the same as the Mahāyāna list.

135. T.2031, p. 15c2; T.2032, p. 18b15; T.2033, p. 20c2. Thesis 10 of Vasumitra (*Sbc*). See also Kuiji, 221-8-3, 25a7–12.

136. See Kuiji, 221-8-3, 25a8–9; J. Masuda, "Origin and Doctrines," p. 20, note #3.

137. T.2031, p. 15b27; T.2033, p. 20b27. Thesis 2 of Vasumitra (*Sbc*); theses 2 and 5 in *Bhavya (*Nbv*). See also *Ktv* XVIII, 1 (trans. Ktv, pp. 323–324); Kuiji, 221-8-3, 23a14–18; N. Dutt, "Doctrines," p. 551, note #4. T.2032, p. 18b12 has: "All tathāgatas are without worldly factors."

138. T.2031, p. 15b29; T.2032, p. 18b13–14; T.2033, p. 20b29. Thesis 6 of Vasumitra (*Sbc*); thesis 3 of Vinītadeva (*Nbv*). See also Kuiji, 221-8-3, 24a12–b5. Related to this is the opinion that the Buddhas exist as substance (*dravya*), an opinion ascribed to the Lokottaravādins by Vinītadeva (*Sbcs*).

139. L. de La Vallée Poussin, "Note sur les Corps du Bouddha," *Le Muséon* XIV, 1913, p. 259.

140. T.2031, pp. 15b29–c1; T.2032, pp. 18b14; T.2033, pp. 20b29–c1. Thesis 7 of Vasumitra (*Sbc*). See also Kuiji, 221-8-3, 24b6–11. Cf. T.1646, pp. 239b29–c10. See also *Ktv* XI, 5 (trans. Ktv, pp. 258–260).

141. T.2031, p. 15c1; T.2032, p. 18b14; T.2033, p. 20c1. Thesis 8 of Vasumitra (*Sbc*); thesis 3 of Vinītadeva (*Sbcs*). See also Kuiji, 221-8-3, 24b12–16; N. Dutt, *Aspects of Mahāyāna Buddhism and Its relation to Hīnayāna*. London: Luzac & Co., 1930, p. 31, note #2.

142. See L. de La Vallée Poussin, "Note sur les Corps du Bouddha," p. 267 and pp. 268–269: "On ne prend pas refuge dans le *rūpakāya*, car celui-ci

n'est pas modifiée par l'acquisition de la qualité "de Bouddha." See also MN, vol. 1, pp. 247–249.

143. See Kuiji, 221-8-3, 24b13–15.

144. See L. de La Vallée Poussin, "The three bodies," pp. 945–946.

145. N. Ross Reat, *The Śālistamba Sūtra*, p. 32, draws our attention to the fact that in this text, the deified Buddha is referred to as *dharmaśarīra*. This passage is dated back to the period of the council of Vaishali (N. Ross Reat, ibid., p. 4).

146. See G. Schopen, *Bones, Stones, Monks*, p. 158. See also the connection of inscriptions with the Ayira-haṃgha, described by G. Schopen, ibid., p. 159. See also A. Bareau, "La construction et le culte des stupa d'après les *Vinayapiṭaka*," *BEFEO* 52, 1962, pp. 268–269.

147. T.2031, p. 15b27–28; T.2032, p. 18b12–13; T.2033, p. 20b28. Thesis 3 of Vasumitra (*Sbc*); thesis 3 of *Bhavya (*Nbv*); thesis 7 of Vinītadeva (*Sbcs*). See also Kuiji, 221-8-3, 23b1–16.

148. T.2031, p. 15b28; T.2032, p. 18b13; T.2033, p. 20b28–29. Thesis 4 of Vasumitra (*Sbc*). See also Kuiji, 221-8-3, 23b17–24a3. See also note #10.

149. T.2031, p. 15b28–29; T.2032, p. 18b13; T.2033, p. 20b29. Thesis 5 of Vasumitra (*Sbc*); thesis 4 of *Bhavya (*Nbv*). See also Kuiji, 221-8-3, 24a4–11.

150. T.2031, p. 15c24; T.2032, pp. 18c2–3; T.2033, pp. 20c26–27. Thesis 39 of Vasumitra (*Sbc*). See also Kuiji, 221-8-3, 31a2–7; J. Masuda, "Origin and Doctrines," p. 28, note #2. This may refer to a remark, to be read in *Da Bannieban jing* T.7, p. 195c5 ff., where the Buddha himself alludes to "imperfect *sūtras*." See also J. Masuda, "Origin and Doctrines," p. 28, note #2.

151. T.2031, p. 16a12–14; T.2032, pp. 18c14–15; T.2033, pp. 21a15–17. Theses 1 and 2 of Vasumitra (*Sbc*) for the Bahuśrutīyas (see A. Bareau, "Trois traités. Pt. I," p. 236). See also thesis 1 of Vinītadeva (*Sbcs*), where "suffering" is replaced with "path" (see A. Bareau, "Trois traités. Pt. II," p. 198). See also Kuiji, 221-8-3, 34b6–15.

152. T.2300, p. 460c6–26. See also P. Demiéville, "Origine," p. 48, note b. See also notes #11 and #12.

153. See A. Bareau, *Sectes*, p. 82; A. Warder, *Indian Buddhism*, p. 278.

154. A. Bareau, "Trois traités. Pt. II," pp. 172–173.

155. A. Bareau, "Trois traités. Pt. II," p. 173. To all above given items on the Buddha, the Lokottaravādins add two more: "The words of the Buddhas manifest their essence (*garbha*)" (thesis 4 of *Bhavya), and "The Buddhas exist as substance (*dravya*)" (thesis 2 of Vinītadeva).

156. See L. S. Cousins, "The 'Five Points,' " pp. 37–47, pp. 52–54. See also A. Wayman, "The Mahāsāṃghika and the Tathāgatagarbha (Buddhist Doctrinal History, Study 1)," *JIABS* 1/1, 1978, p. 35.

157. A. Bareau, "Trois traités. Pt. II," p. 173.

158. T.2031, p. 16a22.

159. T.2031, p. 16a23; T.2032, pp. 18c24–25; T.2033, pp. 21a26–28. Thesis 3 of Vasumitra (*Sbc*). *Ktv* II, 1, II, 2, II, 3, II, 4, II, 5 (trans. Ktv, pp. 111–123).

160. T.2031, p. 16a22; T.2033, p. 21a25. Thesis 1 of Vasumitra (*Sbc*). See also note #128.

161. T.2032, pp. 18c23–24.

162. See P. Harrison, "Who Gets to Ride in the Great Vehicle? Self-Image and Identity Among the Followers of the Early Mahāyāna," *JIABS* 10/1, 1987, p. 80.

163. See J. Nattier and Ch. S. Prebish, "Origins," pp. 259 ff.

164. See, among others, N. Dutt, *Aspects of Mahāyāna Buddhism*, p. 41; N. Dutt, "Notes on the Nāgārjunikoṇḍa Inscriptions," *IHQ* VII, 1931, pp. 633–653; L. de La Vallée Poussin, "Notes et bibliographie bouddhiques," *MCB* I, 1931–32, p. 382; P. S. Sastri, "The Rise and Growth of Buddhism in Andhra," *IHQ* XXXI, 1955, pp. 72–73. See also P. Demiéville, "Origine," p. 19, pp. 23–24; E. Lamotte, "Sur la formation du Mahāyāna," in F. Weller et al. (eds.), *Asiatica. Festschrift Weller. Zum 65. Geburtstag gewidmet van seinen Freunden, Kollegen und Schülern* (Leipzig: Otto Harrassowitz, 1954), pp. 386–388.

165. A. Hirakawa, "The Rise of Mahāyāna Buddhism and Its Relationship to the Worship of Stupas," *Memoirs of the Research Department of the Toyo Bunko* 22, 1963, p. 57.

166. It may be reminded here, that also in Theravāda philosophy elements of "Mahāyānism" are to be discerned. See H. Bechert, "Notes on the Formation of Buddhist Sects," pp. 12–13 and pp. 16–17; H. Bechert, "Mahāyāna Literature in Sri Lanka: the Early Phase," in L. Lancaster (ed.), *Prajñāpāramitā and Related Systems. Studies in Honor of Edward Conze*. Berkeley: Regents of the University of California, 1977. We can also refer to the so-called Sthavira-Mahāyāna referred to by Xuanzang in T.2087, p. 934a15 (trans. S. Beal *Si-yu-ki*, Pt. II, p. 247; Th. Watters, *Travels*, vol. 2, p. 138). See also H. Bechert, "Buddha-Feld und Verdienstübertragung: Mahāyāna-Ideen im Theravāda-Buddhismus Ceylons," *Bulletin de la Classe des Lettres et des Sciences Morales et Politiques*. Académie Royale de Belgique, 5e Série, Tome LXII, 1976, pp. 36–37, p. 47; B. Wang, "Buddhist Nikāyas," pp. 177–178; H. Bechert, "Frühgeschichte," p. 535; G. Schopen, "Mahāyāna in Indian Inscriptions," *IIJ* 21, 1979; R.S. Cohen, "Discontented Categories: Hīnayāna and Mahāyāna in Indian Buddhist History," *Journal of the American Academy of Religion* LXIII, 1, 1995, pp. 7–9, pp. 16–19; P. Harrison, "Searching for the Origins of the Mahāyāna: What Are We Looking For?" *EB* New Series XXVIII/1, 1995, pp. 56–57.

167. G. Schopen, *Bones, Stones, Monks*, pp. 159–160 claims that "one of the most notable characteristics of the Aparamahāvinaseliya inscriptions at Nagarjunikonda is the complete avoidance of the term *stūpa*. [. . .] The Buddhist "shrines" are always called *cetiyas*." The Chinese translators of the *Sbc*, however, have invariably translated "*stūpa*": T.2031, p. 16a22; T.2032, p. 18c24; T.2033, p. 21a25.

168. G. Schopen, *Bones, Stones, Monks*, pp. 148–160. See also notes #5 and #7.

169. See L. S. Cousins, "The 'Five Points,' " p. 50.

170. T.2031, p. 16a22–23; T.2032, p. 18c24; T.2033, p. 21a25–26. Thesis 2 of Vasumitra (*Sbc*); thesis 2 of Vinītadeva (*Sbcs*). See also Kuiji, 221-8-3, 36a16–20.

171. See L. S. Cousins, "The 'Five Points,' " p. 50.

172. T.1425, p. 498c7–9. See also A. Bareau, "La construction et le culte des stūpa," p. 249.

173. T.1425, p. 498b26–28. See also A. Bareau, "La construction et le culte des stūpa," p. 250.

174. T.1425, p. 498a18ff.

175. A. Hirakawa, "Mahāyāna Buddhism," p. 93.

176. A. Hirakawa, "Mahāyāna Buddhism," p. 104. See also A. Wayman, "The Mahāsāṃghika and the Tathāgatagarbha," p. 42. G. Schopen, *Bones, Stones, Monks*, p. 148 opposes this idea. See also A. Wayman and E. Rosen, "The Rise of Mahāyāna and Inscriptional Evidence at Nāgārjunikoṇḍa," *The Indian Journal of Buddhist Studies* 2/1, 1990, pp. 59–60.

177. T.1425, p. 498a12ff.

178. T.1425, p. 251c22–27. See also A. Hirakawa, "Mahāyāna Buddhism," p. 99.

179. G. Schopen, *Bones, Stones, Monks*, p. 158.

180. See note #145.

181. G. Schopen, *Bones, Stones, Monks*, p. 160. There even is argument that the rise of Mahāyāna diminished the importance of *stūpa* worship to the favour of sacred texts. See D. McMahan, "Orality, Writing, and Authority in South Asian Buddhism: Visionary Literature and the Struggle for Legitimacy in the Mahāyāna," *HR* 37, 1998, p. 273.

182. Trans. Ktv, p. 312.

183. Trans. Ktv, pp. 200–203. See also V. V. Gokhale, "What Is Avijñaptirūpa (Conceiled Form of Activity)?" *New Indian Antiquary* I, 1938/1, pp. 72–73. The position of *Ktv* VII, 4 (trans. Ktv, pp. 198–200) is related to this: "Giving (*dāna*) is a mental factor (*caitasika dharma*)." Also this position is attributed to the Rājagiriyas and to the Siddhārthikas.

184. Trans. Ktv, pp. 203–205.

185. See further AN, vol. V, pp. 269–279; and H. Bechert, "Buddha-Feld," p. 39 and p. 41; L. de La Vallée Poussin, *L'Inde aux temps des Mauryas et des Barbares, Grecs, Scythes, Parthes et Yue-tchi.* Paris: E. De Boccard, 1930, p. 149.

186. See for this: G. Schopen, *Bones, Stones, Monks*, pp. 251–253.

187. See P. Harrison, "Searching for the Origins of the Mahāyāna," pp. 61–62; G. Schopen, *Bones, Stones, Monks*, p. 159; A. Wayman and E. Rosen, "The Rise of Mahāyāna Buddhism," p. 56. See also note #166. On the idea of "transference of merit" in Pali sources, see G. P. Malalasekera, " 'Transference of Merit' in Ceylonese Buddhism," *PEW* 17, 1967, pp. 85–90; R. Gombrich, " 'Merit transference' in Sinhalese Buddhism: A Case Study of the Interaction Between Doctrine and Practice,' *HR* 11, 1972, pp. 203–219; J. P. McDermott, "Sādhīna Jātaka: A Case Against the Transfer of Merit," *JAOS* 94, 1974, pp. 385–387; H. Bechert, "Buddha-Field and Transfer of Merit in a Theravāda Source," *IIJ* 35, 1992, pp. 101–105.

188. See A. Bareau, "Trois traités. Pt. II," p. 175.

CHAPTER 3

Amaravati as Lens

Envisioning Buddhism in the Ruins of the Great Stūpa

JACOB N. KINNARD

> [T]he Tope at Amaravati has been so completely destroyed that a traveler might ride over the mounds in which it is buried without suspecting what they covered. . . .
>
> —James Fergussn, *Tree and Serpent Worship*

The ruined *stūpa* at Amaravati has been one of the most analyzed structures in the history of Buddhism: the stone slabs, columns, and friezes that were recovered from the site have for well over a century been celebrated by scholars as the high point of Buddhist art and architecture, the "jewel in the crown of early Indian art" that, in the words of a popular survey of the Buddhist art of India, exhibits a "suave richness never surpassed even by the finest Gupta works."[1] Along with the *stūpa*s at Sanci and Bharhut, there has been no more influential Buddhist structure. The basic visual vocabulary of Buddhism is expressed very early on at Amaravati, and expressed with striking clarity and coherence.

Indeed, the sculptural motifs and forms of Amaravati's great *stūpa* fundamentally influenced the development of Buddhist iconography at other sites in India, presenting a basic visual lexicon that would for centuries inform and guide Buddhist artisans in their production of sculpture and architecture. Furthermore, these sculptures also presented a visual blueprint for a range of ritual performance that established a model of Buddhist practice that would be replicated for centuries in India and elsewhere in the Buddhist world. Finally, there is the important second-order issue of how the early scholarly interpretations of Amaravati's art, beginning in the mid-nineteenth century, shaped—or perhaps misshaped would be more precise—our basic scholarly conceptions of the development of Buddhist artistic motifs, as well as of Buddhist practice itself.

In this chapter, I want first to provide a brief orienting history of Amaravati, one that focuses in particular on the discovery of the great *stūpa* in the early nineteenth century. I will then move to a discussion of how the early interpreters of the sculpture excavated at Amaravati established what amounted to a hegemonic understanding of early Buddhist artistic and religious practice, one that fundamentally privileged narrative over ritual. Finally, I will then briefly discuss the influence that Amaravati had within the Buddhist world, and suggest that one of the most important aspects of Amaravati's influence, and one that has been all but overlooked, is the degree to which the early sculptures of Amaravati not only established forms of Buddhist ritual practice that were centered on the person and body of the Buddha, but also, in their emphasis on the places associated with the events in his life, helped create, indirectly, perhaps, the need to preserve the actual sites themselves.

A Mysterious Structure Discovered

The ruins of the great temple of Amaravati were discovered by accident at the end of the eighteenth century, when a local ruler, the Rajah of Chintapalle, Vassareddy Nayudu, began to establish a new palace and town near the Saiva Ameresvara temple.[2] In need of building materials, Nayudu had limestone slabs moved from the nearby remains of what was then known as Dipaldinne, "the hill of lights," a sprawling ruin near the banks of the Krishna River. In the process, dozens of Buddhist sculptures were uncovered—stone slabs, reliefs, pillars—many of which were reused in the building of Nayudu's palace. In 1797 Colonel Colin Mackenzie, then a surveyor for the British East India Company, learned of the discovery of the images, and visited the site shortly afterward. On initial inspection he found what he called a "mysterious structure," a "great low mound, the upper part of which rose in a turreted shape to the height of twenty feet."[3] Scattered about were various pieces of sculpture, fragments of carved stone work and pillars, and large limestone slabs. Mackenzie stayed only briefly during this initial visit, making a few sketches, but was at any rate there long enough to recognize that this was a major archeological find.

Mackenzie was not able to return to Amaravati until 1816, by which time he had been appointed Surveyor General of India; he and his assistants stayed for six months (his staff stayed on until 1818), making sketches and excavating stone images.[4] By this time, though, many of the images that had originally been uncovered had already been taken away from the site. According to his report, Nayudu was apparently convinced that there was treasure buried at the site and he had "virtually disemboweled it,"[5] subsequently carting away anything that could be used in the construction of the palace and the steps of the Śivaganga tank. Mackenzie laments that in the process the reliefs on the slabs had been largely rubbed off; the mound itself, the remains of the Amaravati Mahācaitya, was now almost completely gone; and the center of the great *stūpa* had been dug out to be used as a water tank. There were, however, still a great many images and stone reliefs lying about.

Mackenzie had eleven of these images removed and sent to Calcutta; two remained there, at the Indian Museum, and nine were later sent to London to the collection of the East India Company. Although there continued to be sporadic minor excavations at the site over the next two decades, no major work was done at Amaravati again until 1845, when Sir Walter Elliot of the Madras Civil Service set about excavating a part of the *stūpa*. Elliot eventually removed seventy-nine pieces—sculptures and parts of the railings which, collectively, would eventually become know as the "Elliot Marbles" when they finally found a home in the British Museum—and these were taken to Madras and essentially neglected until they were sent off to London in 1859. Again, the images were more or less forgotten until James Fergusson, while assembling an exhibition of photographs for the 1867 Paris Universal Exhibition in London, went searching for castings to be included in the exhibition. He learned, while examining four of the sculptures that Mackenzie had unearthed at Amaravati, that there was "a large collection of marbles from the same monument . . . stored in the coach-houses of the establishment."[6] A year later, Fergusson published his sprawling *Tree and Serpent Worship*, which included reproductions of all of these images. This strange and rather obscure volume, as we shall see, proved to be tremendously influential in the understanding of early Buddhist art and ritual practice.

On its face, this is certainly not a unique series of events in the history of British archaeology in India—an accidental discovery, incomplete excavations, images lost, stolen, neglected, reused—and the images that were found at this sight were not, at least initially, viewed as extraordinary, as evinced by their consistent neglect. This moment marks, however, one of the most important points in the West's interest and understanding of Buddhism, rivaled in significance by Hodgson's manuscript discovery in Nepal (which provided one of the first substantial collections of Buddhist texts in Sanskrit and really led to the textual study of Buddhism by Western scholars). The images that were discovered here became some of the most written about objects in the Buddhist world, and along with the images from Sanci and Bharhut they formed the evidential basis for one of the most replicated ideas about Buddhism: that early Buddhism was an aniconic tradition that prohibited the physical representation of its founder and that categorically eschewed idolatry and ritual.

Amaravati and the Aniconic Buddha

The remains of the great *stūpa* that is known usually simply as "Amaravati" are located near the banks of the Krishna River, in Guntur District, near the ruins of the ancient city of Dharanikota, which had been a significant regional center from perhaps as early as the fifth century BCE.[7] Like the later Nagarjunakonda, Amaravati no doubt owes much of its fame and significance to its proximity to the Krishna and its river traffic, which brought not only commercial traffic, but also pilgrims from other parts of Andhra, other regions of India, and elsewhere in South and Southeast Asia.[8]

The very early history of the Amaravati *stūpa* and Buddhist activity at the site has been a matter of some speculation and debate, much of it centered on the question of the dating of the earliest activities at the site; Robert Knox has characterized this discourse as the "manipulation of shadowy information from ancient historical texts" which "obscures the broader historical significance of the monument."[9] Leaving the details of this often complicated debate aside,[10] then, it is safe, at any rate, based on sculptural fragments and various inscriptions, to say that Buddhist activity at the site began sometime during the Mauryan period (fourth through second centuries BCE)—it has been suggested that Amaravati might have been directly supported by Aśoka himself, although this seems unlikely, or at the very least unsubstantiated. At any rate, the earliest sculptural remains from Amaravati resemble those from the contemporary structures at Bharhut and Sanci, in that they present a basic, albeit fragmentary, narrative of the Buddha's life.[11] Certainly it is likely that there was a shared iconographic lexicon in India during this early period; and given Amaravati's proximity to the Krishna, allowing access to both river and ocean travel, the similarities in both content and style between Amaravati and Bharhut and Sanci may be well more than coincidence.

In the sculpture of the very early period, the Buddha is not represented at Amaravati. Instead, we see those objects that are typically associated with his presence: the empty throne, the footprints, the *dharmacakra,* and the Bodhi tree. Because of this apparent absence of the physical form of the Buddha, a basic and pervasive assumption about the early art of Amaravati has been that it, like that found at Bharhut and Sanci, was the product of an aniconic artistic and ritual ideology; in other words, that those responsible for the images intentionally omitted the figure of the Buddha, substituting for his physical form an array of symbolic representations. Perhaps the most prominent of the early popularizers of this theory was Alfred Foucher.

In his highly influential essay, "The Beginnings of Buddhist Art," Foucher writes: "When we find the stone-carvers of India in full activity, we observe that they are very industriously engaged in carrying out the strange undertaking of representing the life of Buddha without Buddha."[12] Foucher was so confident in his conception of Buddhist art as aniconic that he declared that his interpretation of this "strange undertaking" would be the standard "of which every history of Buddhist art will have at the outset to render account."[13] He had not underestimated the influence of his theory, for as Susan Huntington has pointed out, "So deeply embedded within a matrix of long-standing views of Buddhist doctrinal, institutional, and sectarian history is the aniconic interpretation of early Buddhist art that any erosion of the theory threatens to crumble the foundations upon which decades of scholarship have been built."[14] Although I do not want to further prolong this already tired discussion, I think it important to acknowledge Huntington's important critique of Foucher and his interpretive lineage. She boldly proposes a very different *modus operandi*: rather than read into the early images an ideology that is nowhere unambiguously expressed in any Buddhist texts, and rather than look for such texts to explain the images, we ought instead to look at the images themselves. When we do so, Huntington asserts, we see that such images are not, in fact, narratives of the Buddha's life—that is, essentially instructive "texts" to be read by the contemporary viewer—but rather are very often commemorations of post-*nirvāṇa* events, commemorations of ongoing ritual practices and the places associated with these events and practices. "I contend," writes Huntington, "that at least some of the so-called aniconic scenes depict sacred locations of Buddhism being visited by laypersons, most likely some time after the Buddha had lived."[15]

Let me emphasize that this is an extremely important observation, one that is relevant not only to our understanding of the actual sculptures from Amaravati, but also to their influence on both the sculptural traditions that later developed elsewhere in India—particularly in the Northeast during the Pāla period (eighth through twelfth centuries)—as well as the ritual and devotional context in which such sculptures functioned. For what we see at Amaravati is not simply sculpture as narrative, as has been so often assumed, but sculpture as both a record of ritual activity as well as a kind of blueprint for its continued performance. In other words, following Huntington, I want to suggest that Amaravati's sculpture is best seen as what Clifford Geertz has famously called a model of and a model for ritual behavior. This has important implications. What we see in much of the sculpture at Amaravati is not, in fact, the sculptural narration of events in the Buddha's life—as has been their standard interpretation since the sculpture first came to light in the 1880s—but precisely what Huntington suggests: the commemoration and celebration of postdeath ritual activity, devotion directed toward the Buddha's physical remains, the *dharmacakra*, the throne, the footprints, and the Bodhi tree. Furthermore, because these rituals were indelibly tied to the actual places that the Buddha had visited, the places where these events actually took place, these very early sculptures seem also to have served for later Buddhists as a kind of imperative to preserve—and in some cases resurrect—these physical sites centuries after the sculptures were produced.[16]

Mackenzie was the first Westerner to write about Amaravati's sculpture; preliminary extracts from his journal were first published in 1807, as well as an article in 1823.[17] Over the next half century, a variety of short articles were published on the site: Elliot began to write about Amaravati and its sculpture beginning in the 1840s, and Robert Sewell made several reports in the 1870s and 1880s.[18] These were largely the works of archaeologists, mostly concerned with issues of dating and provenance and the attempt to piece together a model of the monument as a whole. It was James Fergusson, though, who really first attempted to analyze the sculptures, in his *Tree and Serpent Worship*, a landmark—albeit a largely neglected one—in the study of Indian art and archaeology. It was also Fergusson who "rescued" the sculptures that Mackenzie and Elliot had shipped to England—they were lying neglected, exposed to the elements, for decades—having been, by his own account, smitten with them when he first saw them in the 1840s. He thus set out to write a book about Amaravati and Sanci, one that would not be "a mere description of the two Topes," which would have relegated it (the book) "to the small and I fear diminishing body of enthusiasts who are supposed to delight in grubbing in the despised local antiquities of India."[19] Rather, what Fergusson undertook was a study that would place these images into the larger context not only of Indian religion, but world religion and art: what he produced, *Tree and Serpent Worship*, is a behemoth of a work, a massive, overly ambitious, essentializing, and ultimately fascinating book.

Fergusson considered himself to be something of an archaeologist, although he was not formally trained as such, and he is throughout the book obsessed with dating, an obsession that tends to move him completely away from any consideration of the original function and context of the images. This emphasis on dating, as I have already noted, is a basic component of nearly everything that has been written on Amaravati. Nonetheless, Fergusson does attempt to understand the images as narratives—he uses language such as the "story told in the lower bas-relief" or the "story of the left-hand pillar" throughout the work—and when possible, he looks to the available texts, especially the *Lalitavistara*, for guidance, again marking the beginning of a trend in scholarship on Indian art that persists to this day, linking image and text in such a way that the text is always given priority over the image.[20] Nowhere in his massive work does Fergusson consider the possibility that the images uncovered at Amaravati might have been situated in a ritual context, might have been not only the commemoration of rituals, but also ritual objects themselves. Significantly, in a book published only seven years after *Tree and Serpent Worship*, James Burgess does.

Burgess's *The Buddhist Stūpas of Amarāvatī and Jaggayyapeta*, published in 1882, is the first truly interpretive work devoted Amaravati.[21] It is in this book that we see the first real development of the aniconic thesis, although, significantly, Burgess in fact recognizes, albeit fleetingly, the possibility that the symbols that appear in the images at Amaravati might actually have been the actual objects of devotion in the scenes depicted, as opposed to symbolic stand-ins for the unrepresentable, and therefore absent, Buddha. For instance, Burgess analyzes a fragment from the outer railing that depicts, in its center, several figures kneeling in veneration before the Bodhi tree and two footprints on what he sees as an altar: "Three men are seated on each side, wearing the Andhra turban, and two on each side below, in a horizontal position, are paying worship to it."[22] It is, to be sure, only a passing observation, but Burgess seems to recognize, without second thought, that the object of veneration is not the Buddha, aniconically represented by the tree and footprints, but rather the pillar itself; in other words, that this image does not present a visual narrative of the Buddha's life, but a visual record of ritual activity that took place after his death. Burgess does not further develop the point, although throughout the text he makes several other allusions to this sort of representation of ritual veneration.[23]

The question might reasonably be asked, then: Why, if it was recognized as early as the 1880s, was this ritual dimension of the images from Amaravati ignored? The answer is complex, of course. In part, it may be simply that since Burgess himself did not make much of this interpretation it was overlooked by subsequent scholars; furthermore, Burgess emphasized what he saw as a marked shift in iconography that he says took place late in what he calls the Middle Phase of Amaravati's scultpural development, in which the Buddha begins to enter the picture, and he sees this shift, significantly as "a theological, or rather a religious, question which scarcely admits an answer in the present state of knowledge of early Buddhism."[24]

More to the point, though, this recognition, fleeting as it is, of the ritual dimension of Buddhism, as recorded in some of the earliest extant sculptural remains from India, ran contrary to the prevailing understanding of Buddhism as a nonritualistic religion. Indeed, the very idea of the aniconic thesis is intimately connected to the basic Orientalist construction of Buddhism, in that it is at the root of the understanding of Buddhism as a distinctly textual tradition, a kind of virtual religion—to use the contemporary parlance—that in the eyes of its Western interpreters existed more in the realm of ideas expressed in *sūtras* than in practices acted out in rituals.[25] There was, as has been well-documented, a serious political dimension to this portrayal of Buddhism, which I will leave unremarked here; more germane to my purposes, this interpretive construct, this very limited lens through which Buddhist art was viewed in the nineteenth century, has continued to distort the western understanding of early Buddhist art. For when we turn to the actual sculptures produced and used at Amaravati what we see, over and over again, is evidence that contradicts this understanding of Buddhism: scene after scene of ritual devotion to objects associated with the Buddha. These scenes, and particularly the physical objects that are venerated, emphasize at once his absence from the physical world—his pastness, as signified by such motifs as the empty throne and the footprints—as well as his continued presence—as signified by the devotees who are depicted venerating him even in his physical absence.[26]

Mimetic Images

The first image that I want to consider here is a railing pillar very similar to that discussed by Burgess (see above), an image that is now housed in the British Museum collection (fig. 3.1).[27] There can be little doubt that this image, as Knox points out, is "concerned with events associated with the Enlightenment."[28] At the center of the pillar, the main image presents a small Bodhi tree, a pedestal with two footprints, and a group of worshipers, all of whom appear to be women, some bearing offerings. At the bottom of the pillar is a similar scene, with two men offering what

Figure 3.1. Limestone Railing Pillar © The Trustees of the British Museum

appears to be a length of cloth to the footprints. At the top of the pillar there is a river depicted, along with several footprints (in what is perhaps sand or mud), as well as a tree with a hand emerging from it: the river here is no doubt the Phalgu, along the banks of which Śākyamuni began his meditations; the footprints are self evident, perhaps, but further tie the scene to Bodhgaya and its environs; Knox, following Sivaramamurti, suggests that the hand is that of a *vanadevatā*, a forest spirit, who offers it to assist the Buddha in crossing the river.[29] Aside from this rather puzzling detail, the top register seems visually rather straightforward. What, however, are we to make of the other two scenes?

Knox, following C. Sivaramamurti, suggests that the central scene is the well-known episode of the laywoman Sujātā offering food to the near-death Bodhisattva.[30] Sivaramamurti, however, recounts the story of Sujātā in the context of his interpretation of another Amaravati image,[31] one that is really quite different from that discussed by Knox. In that image, we see the Buddha himself, seated, displaying what appears to be the *abhayamudrā*, the gesture of "no fear" (the arm is broke above the wrist, so it is impossible to tell, exactly, but this would be the expected *mudrā*), with several women, some making offerings of what appears to be food, others simply bowing in reverence. Even here, though, it is not clear to me that this is in fact an image of the Sujātā episode; in the textual narrative, after all, Sujātā is alone. This image could just as plausibly be a depiction of general (or generic) worship of the Buddha by his followers. In the image that Knox interprets as the Sujātā episode, though, the offerings are not made to the Buddha, but to the footprints. Certainly it is possible that the footprints were intended to represent the living Buddha, but it seems more likely (or at least more self-evident) that this scene represents precisely what it seems, on its face, to represent: the veneration of images of the Buddha's footprints, a most physical index of his absence, a common visual theme in the Buddhist art of India and a ritual practice that continues to the present day, especially in and around Bodhgaya.[32] Furthermore, as in the image analyzed by Sivaramamurti, there are nearly two dozen women depicted making multiple offerings, not just the lone figure of Sujātā. I would suggest, then, that this image presents a kind of ritual snapshot, an image of both actual and ideal practice. In other words, this is an image of what has been done—offerings to the footprints—and what should continue to be done. Thus one of the pernicious effects of the persistence of the aniconic thesis is the insistence on an overdetermined analysis that not only sees the function of the image as narrative, but must also find a correlation between text and image, despite the fact that in many case it is quite possible that it was in fact not the text that informed the image, but the image that came first.[33] A particularly glaring example of this sort of overdetermined analysis can be seen in the various interpretations of a fragment from one of Amaravati's *stūpa* railings that depicts an empty throne surrounded by worshipers. Fergusson was the first to write analytically about this image—although Mackenzie briefly made note of it—and he seems puzzled as to what it might represent, and thus describes it simply as representing "a Hindu chief. He has the Chaori, but no umbrella, and is followed by one of his wives on the left hand."[34] Burgess, likewise, did not attempt to tie a very similar image to a particular text or narrative, and, like Fergusson, leaves it more or less at that.[35] Thus both of these scholars, writing before the aniconic thesis had been clearly articulated, assume that the image represents precisely what it seems to represent, even if it is a bit of a mystery.

Fifty years later, however, Sivaramamurti writes about another image that presents a similar scene, but he makes what can only be said to be an interpretative leap, and links the image to a specific textual narrative, the visit of Ajātasutta (Skt. Ajātaśātru) and his wife to the Buddha, recounted in the *Aṅguttara Nikāya*.[36] Although he does not give any rationale for this interpretation, he seems simply to have found a textual narrative that can be grafted onto the visual image and then does precisely that, ignoring, in so doing, the visual details of the image itself as well as the narrative details of the textually expressed episode. Knox, subsequently, when he writes the updated catalog of the British Museum collection, then simply labels the image: "The visit to the Buddha of the parricide Ajātaśātru, king of Magadha, with his women and male attendants," and cites only Sivaramamurti as a source.[37]

The image about which Sivaramamurti writes is, however, very different from the one in the British Museum that Knox labels. It is, for one thing, far more elaborate, with elephants and riders, and dozens of worshipers. More important, though, in Sivaramamurti's image the Buddha himself is depicted, whereas in the British Museum piece he is absent. Certainly it is possible that the artisans responsible for the image in the British Museum took the Ajātasattu story as their inspiration, and it is, likewise, possible that the Ajātasutta story was the model for the image about which Sivaramamurti writes, although as I think I have made clear, it is just as likely that these are images that present generic scenes of worship (the images themselves, unlike many of those found at Sanci and Bharhut, were not labeled by the artisans who made them). On the face of it, though, what we see are two very different images that represent two very different things: the one (Sivaramamurti's image) a scene with the living Buddha venerated; the other (Knox's image) with no Buddha depicted and the empty throne worshiped.

Sometimes the throne in the images from Amaravati is neither occupied by the Buddha nor empty; sometimes it has on it a *stūpa*. In such cases, there can be little question that the scene is meant to represent—or commemorate—a post-*nirvāṇa* practice or event, in that the *stūpa* is, de facto, dependent on the Buddha's death, and hence his physical absence from the world, for its very existence. Significantly, none of those who have pushed the aniconic interpretation in relation to Amaravati (Sivaramamurti, Barrett, Knox) has anything particular to say about this variety of image, perhaps because it so clearly seems to represent precisely what it does, in fact, represent—the placement and veneration of a reliquary on the *vajrāsana*, the seat of enlightenment—and thus it needs no external (e.g., textual) verification. Fergusson perhaps provides the minimalist, Ockham's razor standard here: "The action is simple. A casket containing a relic is placed on the throne under an elaborate canopy, and is being worshipped by the Nāga Rājā and his people."[38] Of course the "action" is not simple, and there is in fact much that can be analyzed here, not the least of which is the complex set of philosophical and ritual issues involved in the substitution of the relics for the Buddha.[39] Apparently, though, because there is no obvious textual parallel, those scholars most committed to a image-as-text analysis, with the basic assumption of the aniconic thesis, had nothing to say because such an image does not, in fact, support such a position.

Clearly, then, the artisans and patrons who were responsible for the images at Amaravati were interested in more than narrative: in some cases, they represented scenes from the Buddha's life with the Buddha himself represented; in others, they represented the Buddha's absence with the empty throne, and often represented the throne itself as an object of veneration; and in still other images, they represented the relics being worshiped in place of the Buddha. I want to suggest, as clearly as possible, that such iconographic variety is indicative of the different functions these images would have had in their various contexts at Amaravati—as narratives, as objects of veneration, and as what I have called ritually mimetic images intended to provide a guide to proper worship. Furthermore, I want to argue, such different contextual functions were neither contradictory nor exclusive. Indeed, as I have elsewhere argued, it is the very nature of such images to be multivalent.[40]

There is a dome slab that is now in the British Museum which presents three scenes that is illustrative in this regard: at the bottom of the piece is the empty throne and tree scene, with worshipers; in the middle is another throne, above which is the *dharmacakra*, surrounded by various worshipers; and at the very top of the piece is a *stūpa* being venerated (fig. 3.2).[41] Knox, following Barrett's 1954 catalog, says that these

Figure 3.2. Limestone Dome Slab © The Trustees of the British Museum

three scenes respectively represent the enlightenment, first sermon, and death. Of course each of these scenes is related to these events, but that is clearly not what they would have visually presented to the contemporary viewer/participant: these are all images that are about the absence of the Buddha in the world, scenes that take place after his death, scenes of the veneration of objects and places associated with events in his life, but they are not scenes that depict the events themselves.[42] Certainly, it is possible that such images would have presented the opportunity for narrative of the events themselves and further doctrinal discussion. But fundamentally these are images about ritual.

In the same vein, there is an image now in the Madras State Museum that illustrates my point precisely.[43] On a single slab there are two scenes, separated by a border of flowers and other ornaments. The two scenes are nearly identical, except for one important detail. The scene on the right presents the Buddha in the *dharmacakrapravartana mudrā*, preaching his first sermon at Sarnath; he is flanked by four figures, with two *devatā*s floating about his head. The scene on the left is identical in all regards, except that in place of the preaching Buddha, we find the *dharmacakra*. The fact that these two different modes of presenting what seems to be the same basic motif is striking, and strongly suggests that the agents responsible for this image wanted the viewer/participant to see both images at the same time and to apprehend not simply two different versions of the same moment in the Buddha's life, one iconically presented, the other aniconically. Rather, it seems they intended that their combined visual message be simultaneously absorbed. And what is it? That there is a basic equivalence between the Buddha teaching and the *dharmacakra*; indeed, the latter, as the emblem of his teachings, replaces the Buddha after his death, as the Buddha so poignantly tells Ānanda in the *Dīgha Nikāya*. Such an image, then, at once conveys the narrative, makes an essential doctrinal point about the continued presence of the Buddha in the teachings, and provides a visual guide to the ritual veneration of the wheel itself.

There is a final image from Amaravati that, I think, is worth discussing in this regard, a very complex image that throws something of a wrench into the works of my analysis (fig. 3.3).[44] This image, a dome slab, has to do with the Buddha's birth, a common theme at Amaravati, and presents four different scenes. This is how Knox interprets them: the dream of Māyā; the presentation of the dream to Śuddhodana and its interpretation by his advisors; the birth of Siddhārtha; and the presentation of the baby to the Śākya clan's *ṛṣi*, the *yakṣa* Śākyavardhana.[45] The problem is, there is no baby! Rather, according to Knox, the "baby is shown aniconically, in symbolic form, but is an integral part of the

Figure 3.3. Limestone Dome Slab © The Trustees of the British Museum

narrative structure of these reliefs."[46] Fergusson, for his part, candidly admits that he simply does not know what to make of this image, although he says that what Knox later calls the birth really represents the time before the birth. At any rate, he writes: "It is not quite clear what the fourth compartment is intended to represent, as it is not to be found in any edition of the legend I am acquainted with."[47] He contends that perhaps the cloth is intended as evidence of the birth, and is not, as Knox suggests, carried by Māyā herself—unlikely, of course, given that she has just given birth, and will soon die—but by an attendant. At any rate, this is a puzzling image, in that the baby is not represented and seems to be replaced by the cloth, although the image is clearly presenting scenes in which the Buddha would have been present. Furthermore, to add to the complex puzzle of this stelae, on the cloth are two tiny footprints: these could, certainly, be intended to represent the *bodhisattva*; they could also be intended to present the steps that he is said to have taken immediately after his birth But why are they on the cloth? And why is the baby not represented?

Is what we see here evidence of an aniconic ideology? Perhaps. It may also, however, be an anomaly, a mystery, or be caught up somehow in the significance of the cloth (recall that there is another image at Amaravati, see above, that involves the offering of cloth). It certainly is puzzling that the baby does not appear in this image, since the scenes presented are obviously contemporary to his infancy. To jump to the aniconic conclusion, however, seems at the very least unwarranted, at once too complex (assuming a doctrinal ideology nowhere stated) and too simple (assuming that the image functions as straightforward narrative).

I have intentionally avoided the very complex topic of the dating of Amaravati's scultpure here, largely because I do not believe that causal arguments can be made based on the posited date of a particular piece—that is, the typical argument that the early sculpture, that produced before the second century CE, was the product of an aniconic ideology. Nonetheless, it may well be that some sort of ideological or theological or ritual shift took place sometime around the second century. For instance, there is a spectacular dome slab now in the British museum that was carved on both sides, each at a different time.[48] On one side is a scene that, based on stylistic similarities to other images, particularly those from Bharhut and Sanci, would seem to date to the first century BCE: it presents the *vajrāsana* under the Bodhi tree, without the Buddha, but with two footprints in front of it, being worshiped by several devotees, above which hover several *kinnara*s. On the other side, however, is a far more elaborate image, a carved *stūpa* with tremendous detail, and which appears to date to the second or third century CE. Here, the Buddha appears in several guises. Because these two images were carved on a large slab that would have made up part of the dome of the great temple, only one side could possibly have been visible; in other words, the first side was carved and then, later, the stone was reused, with a very different image presented.

Again, it is possible that this is evidence of a new iconicism at Amaravati, a new ideology governing the production and use of images, one that now admitted the representation of the Buddha. Certainly by the second century CE the Buddha is commonly represented at Amaravati. Again, I do not think that this presents proof that an ideological shift took place. Indeed, as much as he is, indeed, represented, the so-called aniconic indexes—empty throne, footprints, *dharmackra*, and so on—continue to be represented in the later scultpure. Rather, it may well be that the function of these images was simply different, reflecting a shift in ritual practice and philosophical discourse, a shift that would have been consistent with a general emphasis, evinced particularly in the contemporary Mahāyāna texts that were circulating in South India, on the person of the Buddha and on his continued presence in the world. However, and this is crucial, simply because the Buddha appears at this point does not, logically or otherwise, lead to the conclusion that when his form was absent in the earlier sculpture, it was absent because of a prohibition, an aniconic ideology. New buddhalogical ideas were in the air—one need think only of the complex articulation of the different *kāyas* ("bodies") worked out in a variety of texts—and it is perhaps the case that what we see in these images is a visual articulation of some of these ideas.[49] This is, of course, speculative; in the end, however, it is no more speculative than the aniconicism thesis itself, for as Burgess noted well over a century ago, in a remark that is still strikingly relevant to the whole issue today, whatever may have led to the shift in the mode of representing the Buddha, it is a mystery that, still, "scarcely admits an answer in the present state of knowledge of early Buddhism."

Physical and Visual Pilgrimage

The influence that Amaravati had on Buddhist art in other parts of the Indian subcontinent has typically been discussed in stylistic terms. Thus, for instance, Anamika Roy has recently written that "Amaravati art found its expression again in the art of Nagarjunikonda," and goes on to describe what are mostly stylistic similarities, without delving into causal connections between the two sites; this is a typical interpretive *modus operandi*.[50]

Certainly, one can tease out all manner of stylistic and compositional similarities between Amaravati and other complexes in India, and, as I have already noted, given the close proximity of Nagarjunakonda, the documented travel between various Buddhist centers in India, as well as travel between the Eastern coast and Sri Lanka and Southeast Asia, it is likely that artisans, monks, and pilgrims circulated artistic forms and styles. As Debala Mitra has nicely put it: "Amaravati, however, maintained its sanctity till the fag end of Buddhism in India. Up to the fourteenth century AD, it was attracting pilgrims from Ceylon, where have been found several Buddhist sculptures in the characteristic styles of the early and later schools of Amaravati. The Buddhist architecture of Andradhesa produced a lasting effect on this island."[51]

Amaravati's influence was more than stylistic, however. Indeed, the basic ritual forms expressed—or, perhaps, recorded, as Huntington has suggested—in the so-called aniconic sculptures of Amaravati continued for centuries to be replicated throughout the Buddhist world. Furthermore, not only did the artisans and patrons at Amaravati, as well as at Bharhut, Sanci, and Nagarjunakonda, establish a basic ritual lexicon, they also established, when they did actually represent the Buddha, the basis of what would become a standard set of significant events in the Buddha's life. In the process, they also created the centrality of those places as pilgrims' destinations to be visited and preserved by monks and laypersons. Certainly, Amaravati itself was an important pilgrimage site throughout its history, but it was what we might call a second-order pilgrimage place, in that it was not the site of any events in the actual life of the Buddha; rather, what attracted pilgrims to the *stūpa* and its environs were the representations of other pilgrimage places. Many of Amaravati's images depict multiple events in the Buddha's life, events linked to specific places. The very elaborate dome slab I have discussed above presents an excellent example of this prototypical form. The image depicts an elaborately detailed *stūpa* with various scenes from the Buddha's life: these scenes include a standing Buddha in the center, displaying the *abhayamudrā*, flanked by several much smaller standing and kneeling worshipers; a scene that appears to be the dream of Māyā, as well as the birth of Śākyamuni; the Buddha seated in meditation; the Buddha delivering his first sermon (as indicated by the two small deer who flank him, representing the deer park at Sarnath); and other scenes of teaching and veneration. What is particularly significant about this image in the present context is the arrangement of multiple scenes around a single central image, scenes that, when taken together—as they would have been in the ritual context in which the dome slab was originally situated—can be seen to present the Buddha's entire life story in condensed form—birth, enlightenment, teaching, and death (as signified by the *stūpa* form of the dome itself), plus various paradigmatically significant events.

Again, though, this image, and the many similar to it from Amaravati,[52] is not just a narrative, a stone image that is to be "read" by the worshiper. Rather, this image allows the ritual participant to be, in an important sense, a part of these events, not just in his or her mind, but in time and space—the image, in this sense, makes the events and the people and the places present.[53] And in presenting such scenes together, as part of a single image, the artisans have allowed the worshiper to be a part of the ongoing life of the *Dharma*. By the Gupta period, this had become a standard iconographic form in Buddhism—usually a single image surrounded by four or six scenes from his life, almost always including, at least, the enlightenment, the first sermon, and the *pārinirvāṇa*. By the Pālā period, a standard set of eight scenes was developed, the iconographic form known as the *aṣṭamahāprātihārya*, presenting not only a visual narrative, as it were, of the significant events in the Buddha's life, but also a kind of map of this life, a locatively specific narrative, that is, that presented both event and place.[54] These eight scenes all represented actual places that could be, and were, physically visited by Buddhist pilgrims—famously, of course, by the Chinese pilgrims Faxian (in the fifth century) and Xuanzang (in the eighth), but by countless other pilgrims over the centuries.

In general, empahasis on actual place in Buddhism has been downplayed by those who write about Buddhism, at least, if not also by Buddhists on the ground, and this is in part, perhaps, because Buddhism can happen anywhere—the *Dharma* is, necessarily, portable. As I have attempted to demonstrate here, though, Amaravati helps to establish, along with Bharhut, Sanci, and Nagarjunakonda, an increasingly unvarying set of significant events from the Buddha's life—without exact textual parallels, as a set—that were presented by Buddhist artisans. More to the point, though, a great many of these images were not intended, as I have argued, to narrate at all, but rather to depict Buddhist laypersons worshiping at the particular sites that are marked as significant in the Buddha's life. Importantly, the Buddha must be absent from such images precisely because he is absent from the sites themselves. Thus such images, as Huntington has convincingly argued, were certainly intended to mark the significant sites themselves, but they also served, as well, as what I have referred to as a ritual blueprint for proper participation in these sculptural images. Likewise, as images of the Buddha began to proliferate throughout India, marking what Stephen Beyers has called an iconographic "explosion" coinciding—although not necessarily causally—with the rise of the Mahāyāna.[55]

As the influence of Amaravati's early images spread to other parts of the Buddhist world, the places depicted in these images—Bodhgaya, Sarnath, Lumbini, Shravasti, Rajagriha—themselves became extremely important pilgrimage places, places at which monasteries were built and to which pilgrims made often extremely arduous journeys. Significantly, though, in light of the physical and financial difficulty of visiting the actual places, the images continued to serve as the next best thing to being in the actual place; just as a second-century Buddhist could visit Amaravati and, in a sense, experience the events and the places of the Buddha's life, so too, over the next two millennia, could Buddhists all over the world, from Mandalay to Montreal, continue to make these "virtual pilgrimages" via physical images, images that very much have their roots—in form as well as function—in the great temple of Amaravati.

Notes

1. J. C. Harle, *The Art and Architecture of the Indian Subcontinent* (New Haven: Yale University Press, 1994), pp. 34 and 38.

2. See N. S. Ramaswami, *Amarāvatī: The Art and History of the Stūpa and the Temple* (Hyderbad: Government of Andhra Pradesh, 1975); see also Upinder Singh, "Amarāvatī: The Discovery of the Mahacaitya (1797–1886)," *Society for South Asian Studies Journal* 17 (2001):

3. Major C. Mackenzie, "Extracts of a Journal," *Asiatick Researches* 9 (1807): 272–278, p. 270.

4. Mackenzie records these in his brief 1823 report, "Ruins of Amurvarty, Depauldina, and Durnacotta," *Asiatic Journal* 15 (1823): 464–478; a more complete account of Mackenzie's archaeological expeditions, as well as Mackenzie's journal, appeared in Robert Sewell's *Report on the Amarāvatī Tope* (London: Her Majesty's Stationary Office, 1880). For more on Mackenzie, see Jennifer Howes, "Colin Mackenzie and the Stūpa at Amarāvatī," *SSAS Journal* 18.1 (2002): 53–65; and Nicholas B. Dirks, *Castes of Mind: Colonialism and the Making of Modern India* (Princeton: Princeton University Press, 2001), especially pp. 79–99.

5. Ramaswami, *Amarāvatī*, p. 21.

6. Fergusson, *Tree and Serpent Worship*, p. iii.

7. See Robert Knox, *Amarāvatī: Buddhist Sculpture from the Great Stupa* (London: British Museum Press, 1992), p. 10

8. For evidence of the travel on the Krishna, see K. Raghavachary, "Dharanikota and Its Western Contacts," *Quarterly Review of Historical Studies* 12.3 (1973): 166–170. See also Geri Malandra, *Unfolding a Maṇḍala: The Buddhist Caves at Ellora* (Albany: State University of New York Press, 1993), p. 5, where she notes that there was constant exchange between various Buddhist sites in Southern India. For Andhra's economic contact with the world beyond Asia, see E. H. Warmington, *The Commerce Between the Roman Empire and India* (London: Curzon, 1974). See also H. P. Ray, "Shared Faith: Buddhism and Trading Groups

in Early South Asia (fourth through third century BCE to seventh century CE)," paper given at the Indian Ocean Conference, UCLA, 2002.

9. Knox, *Amarāvatī*, p. 9.

10. Most relevantly, see Vidya Dehejia, "Early Activity at Amarāvatī," *Archives of Asian Art* 22 (1969–70): 41–54; and also I. K. Sarma, "Early Sculptures and Epigraphs from South-East India: New Evidence from Amarāvatī," in F. M. Asher and G. S. Gai, eds., *Indian Epigraphy* (New Delhi: Oxford, 1985), pp. 15–23; and C. Sivaramamurti, *Amarāvatī Sculptures in the Chennai Government Museum* (Chennai: Thiru S. Rangamani, 1998, first published in 1942). I am intentionally avoiding what I see as the obsessive concern with the dating of the remains of Amaravati, precisely because the remains are so very fragmentary, and singling out any given piece for precise dating is not only a decidedly sketchy business, but such an activity tends to obscure the basic fact that the various periods of sculptural activity at Amaravati would have overlapped in situ, and thus all but obscure the ritual and devotional dynamics of this sculpture; see Fergusson, *Tree and Serpent Worship*, especially p. 153, for a particularly blatant, and particularly early, example of this temporal obsession. See also Knox, *Amarāvatī*, pp. 54–56, for a useful reminder that the sculpture that has been recovered from Amaravati would never have simply existed in a single age, but rather been part of a complexly overlapping temporal context, in which images from a span of some 500 years would have coexisted.

11. See Knox, *Amarāvatī*, pp. 12–13, and Dehejia, "Early Activity at Amarāvatī," and also P. R. Srinivasan, "Recently Discovered Early Inscriptions from Amarāvatī and their Significance," *Lalit Kalā* 10 (1961): 59–60. For a general overview of the epigraphic and sculpural remains of the early period, see Anamika Roy, *Amarāvatī Stūpa: A Critical Comparison of Epigraphic, Architectural and Sculptural Evidence* (Delhi: Agam Kala Prakashan, 1994).

12. Alfred Foucher, "The Beginnings of Buddhist Art," in *The Beginnings of Buddhist Art and Other Essays in Indian and Central-Asian Archaeology* (Paris: Paul Geuthner, 1917), p. 4.

13. Ibid., p. 5.

14. Susan L. Huntington, "Early Buddhist Art and the Theory of Aniconism," *Art Journal* 49 (1990): 401–408, p. 401.

15. Ibid., p. 403.

16. Asoka is typically credited with establishing the tradtion of pilgrimage in the Buddhist tradition, with his *dhammayatta* after his conversion; see Romila Thapar, *Aśoka and the Decline of the Mauryas* (Delhi: Oxford University Press, 1997).

17. Mackenzie, "Extracts of a Journal," and "Ruins of Amurvarty, Depauldina, and Durnacotta," *Asiatic Journal* 15 (1823): 464–478; see also Sewell's *Report on the Amarāvatī Tope*.

18. Sir Walter Elliot, "Archaeology of the Krishna District," *Indian Antiquary* 1 (1872): 346–348.

19. Fergusson, *Tree and Serpent Worship*, p. v.

20. See, for instance, pp. 173–174, or p. 181, where he finds it difficult to match the image with the text, and admits that what he sees in the image—what appears to be the temptation of Māra—in the end "is so much unlike Buddhism that we must probably look elsewhere for a solution of the myth. . . ."

21. The full title of this book is *The Buddhist Stupas of Amaravati and Jaggayyapeta in the Krishna District, Madras Presidency* (London: Trubner & Co., 1882); Burgess also published, two years earlier, a more strictly archaeological study, *Notes on the Amarāvatī Stupa* (Archaeological Survey of Southern India, 1882).

22. Burgess, *The Buddhist Stupas*, p. 34.

23. Ibid., pp. 89–90.

24. Ibid., p. 59.

25. See Gregory Schopen, "Archeology and Protestant Presuppostions in the Study of Indian Buddhism," *History of Relgions* 31.1 (1991): 1–23; Philip C. Almond, *The British Discovery of Buddhism* (Cambridge: Cambridge University Press, 1998); as well as the essays in Donald S. Lopez, Jr., *Curators of the Buddha: The Study of Buddhsm Under Colonialism* (Chicago: University of Chicago Press, 1995).

26. See Jacob N. Kinnard, "The Field of the Buddha's Presence," in *Embodying the Dharma: Buddhist Relic Veneration in Asia*, Kevin Trainor and David Germano, eds. (Albany: State University of New York Press, 2004).

27. See Knox, *Amarāvatī*, p. 51, pl. 6; or Barrett, *Sculptures from Amarāvatī in the British Museum* (London: Trustees of the British Museum, 1954), pl. 21 for a better reproduction.

28. Knox, *Amarāvatī*, p. 51.

29. See Knox, *Amarāvatī*, p. 50, and Sivaramamurti, *Amarāvatī Sculptures in the Madras Government Museum* (Madras: Government Press, 1942), for a more extensive discussion of the story, pp. 66–67.

30. Knox, *Amarāvatī*, p. 50; Sivaramamurti, *Amarāvatī Sculptures*, p. 253.

31. Sivaramamurti, *Amarāvatī Sculptures*, pl. 60, figure 2.

32. See Jacob N. Kinnard, "The Polyvalent *Pāda*s of Viṣṇu and the Buddha," *History of Religions* 40.1 (2000): 32–57.

33. See A. K. Norman, *Pali Literature* (Wiesbaden, 1983), for a discussion of the formation of the Pali Canon.

34. Fergusson, *Tree and Serpent*, p. 181, pl. 13.

35. Burgess, *The Buddhist Stupas*, p. 57, pl. 23, fig. 3.

36. Sivaramamurti, *Amarāvatī Sculptures*, pp. 189–190.

37. Knox, *Amarāvatī*, p. 83.

38. Fergusson, *Tree and Serpent Worship*, p. 179, remarking on pl. 62.

39. See Kinnard, "The Field of the Buddha's Presence."

40. See Kinnard, *Imaging Wisdom: Seeing and Knowing in the Art of Indian Buddhism* (Surrey: Curzon, 1999), as well as Kinnard, "Polyvalent *Pādas*."

41. Knox, *Amarāvatī*, pp. 163–164, plate 88.

42. I am, again, indebted to Susan Huntington here, particularly her argument articulated in "Early Buddhist Art and the Theory of Aniconism."

43. Sivaramamurti, *Amaravati Sculptures*, plate 20, figs. 1 and 2, and pp. 167–168.

44. Knox, *Amarāvatī*, plates 60 and 61, pp. 120–121.

45. Knox, *Amarāvatī*, p. 119.

46. Knox, *Amarāvatī*, p. 119; see also Burgess, *Buddhist Stupas*, pl. 7.

47. Fergusson, *Tree and Serpent*, p. 212.

48. Knox, *Amarāvatī*, pl. 72, pp. 139–140, and also pp. 119–120.

49. See Frank E. Reynolds, "The Several Bodies of the Buddha: Reflections on a Neglected Aspect of the Theravāda Tradition," *History of Religions* 16.4 (1977): 374–389.

50. Roy, p. 160. Sees also A. Ray, *Life and Art of Early Andradesha* (Delhi: Agam Kala Prakashan, 1983), and also K. M. Varma, *Amarāvatī and the Beginnings of Stucco Modelling in India* (Santiketan: Proddu, 1985).

51. Debala Mitra, *Buddhist Monuments*, p. 198.

52. See, additionally, Knox, *Amarāvatī*, pls. 69–70, pp. 133–136; pl. 71, pp. 137–138; pl. 78, pp. 151–156; and also the many dome slabs recovered from the ruins of the temple, pp. 163ff.

53. For a more general discussion of images and presence in Buddhism, see Kinnard, "The Field of the Buddha's Presence."

54. See Kinnard, "Reevaluating the Eighth–Ninth Century Pāla Milieu: Icono-Conservatism and the Persistence of Śākyamuni," *Journal of the International Association of Buddhist Studies* 20.1:281–300; and John Huntington, "Pilgrimage as Image: The Cult of the *Aṣṭamahāpratihārya*, Part I," *Orientations* 18.7 (1987): 55–63, and "Part II," *Orientations* 18.8 (1987): 56–68.

55. See Stephan Beyer, "Notes on the Vision Quest in Early Mahāyāna," in *Prajñāpāramitā and Related Systems: Studies in Honour of Edward Conze*, ed. Lewis Lancaster (Berkeley: Berkeley Buddhist Studies Series, 1977), pp. 329–340.

CHAPTER 4

Buddhism in Andhra and Its Influence on Buddhism in Sri Lanka

JOHN CLIFFORD HOLT AND SREE PADMA

Throughout the history of religions, one of the most ubiquitous patterns of religious expression is the mythic articulation of ethnic, class, caste or national origins. Mythic expressions of this nature are often crucial to how a community conceives of its collective identity, how it imagines the beginning of religious tradition, its founder, or even the very cosmogonic origins of the world.[1] In India, perhaps one of the best examples of this mythic pattern comes in the form of *Ṛg Veda* 10.90 where, from the Brahmanical religious perspective, the origins and hierarchical structures of traditional society (and the brahmin position within it) are linked to the veritable creation of society through a divine sacrificial dismemberment of the mythical first person, Puruṣa. In the West, this same pattern of collective mythic consciousness relating social identity to origins is clearly manifested not only biblically in the manner in which the Hebraic identity of Israel is ultimately linked to the ancestral Abraham, Isaac, and Jacob and then back to the first man Adam during the primordial creation of the world, but also ecclesiastically in the way in which various Christian reform groups throughout European and American history have asserted that their forms of religiosity most authentically re-create and are indubitably linked to the original spirit of the religion as it was envisaged by Jesus or his apostles at the beginning of what is now regarded as the "common era" (CE). In the history of Buddhism specifically, there are a variety of mythic examples reflecting this very same pattern wherein a given ethnic society or monastic sect has linked its identity with the origins of the religious tradition. Within the Theravāda Buddhist religious traditions of Sri Lanka, Burma, and Thailand, for example, well-known national mythologies link the beginnings of Sinhalese, Burmese, and Thai ethnic identities to mythic visits of the Buddha to their countries, or with the coming of ancestors who are converted to the *Dharma*.[2] Within those same countries and cultures, the institution of the Theravada monastic *saṇgha* is understood as the direct descendent of the original brethren who followed the Buddha into homelessness.

The ancestors of the Telugu people of Andhra also appealed to this genre of myth during an earlier period of their history in order to articulate their own perceived primordial connection to Buddhist origins. Hsüan-tsang cites a legend current during the seventh century CE that the Buddha himself once visited Andhra.[3] The Pāli *Suttanipāta* of the *Khuddaka Nikāya,* certainly of a much earlier date by many centuries, contains in its final chapter a story about how a brahmin from Shravasti by the name of Bavari who, in search of detachment, had traveled south to live by the banks of the Godavari River where, having fallen ill due to a curse laid on him by a beggar, was advised by a friendly *yakṣa* to travel back to Shravasti to learn about the nature of all *duḥkha* (suffering) from the Buddha. Bavari not only follows her advice, but proceeds along with sixteen of his students to meet the Buddha who in turn preaches a discourse on *parayāna* ("the way to the beyond"). In the process, Bavari and his brahmin students become enlightened as *arahant*s before returning to their native Andhra to establish the *saṇgha*.[4] B. S. L. Hanumantha Rao, cites a different legend of how Mahākātyayāna, one of the Buddha's foremost disciples, converted the then king of the Assakas who subsequently became a *bhikkhu*. From that time onward, according to the legend, Buddhist monks from Andhra were referred to as Andhakas.[5] All three of these instances indicate how Buddhists of Andhra exercised their mythic imaginations to understand how their communities could be considered direct descendents of the earliest Buddhist community in a manner not at all different from how Sinhalas, Burmese, and Thais have imagined their own ancient religious identities.

Indeed, when myths such as these are historicized, the result is a narrative construction congenial to affirmation of religious identity. In the following pages of this chapter, we shall first review some of the important and well-known scholarship on the origins of Buddhist monastic schism in ancient north India and the beginning of rival sectarian claims for legitimacy between the Mahāsāṃghika and Sthāviravādin (of which the later Theravāda is a descendent) Buddhist communities as a prelude to examining the development and legacy of the Mahāsāṃghikas in Andhra as a "proto-Mahāyāna" movement. We shall then relate early evidence of general Mahāyāna influence in Sri Lanka before coming to our central focus, which highlights the specific ways in which the Buddhism of Andhra made a definitive historical impact on the Sri Lankan Buddhist scene as a result of extensive contacts between the Amaravati and Nagarjunakonda communities of Andhra and various parts of Sri Lanka. The implication of our study, given by way of conclusion, is that, contrary to the views expressed as a result of a Sinhalese mythicization of history, the Buddhism of Sri Lanka was historically much more inclusive and definitely far more variegated than many of its modern apologists or often politically inspired mythologists would normally claim. Further, it openly embraced many innovations of cultural religious expression as these had previously developed in regions of south India, chiefly Andhra. That is, the Buddhism of Sri Lanka may be known throughout the Buddhist world for its confessions of doctrinal purity and claims of institutional conservatism (that for 2,500 years it has maintained the original teachings and practice of the Buddha), but the evidence marshaled in our article will demonstrate that the religious culture of its Buddhists during the Lankan Anuradhapura period and beyond was not necessarily so insulated and self-generated, and that much of its inspiration, innovation, and vitality can be traced not only to the conservative tenacity of Theravāda tradition per se, but also to injections of religio-cultural expression from an Andhra impetus, from off-shoot branches of the old Sthāviravādin nemesis and rival, the Mahāsāṃghikas.

Schism in the Saṇgha

The school of Buddhism that came to dominate the religious culture of Andhra during the period from approximately the third century BCE through the third and fourth century CE was the Mahāsāṃghika, often regarded in scholarly circles as one of the forerunners of the later developing Mahāyāna because of their views regarding rules of monastic discipline (*vinaya*), their conceptions of the nature of the Buddha, and their association with a variety of religious practices that may have originally been exclusively the province of the laity.

It is difficult to know with any degree of great certainty exactly how unity within the early north Indian Buddhist *saṇgha* was originally fractured and why separate monastic schools of distinctive sectarian identities were forged. Suggestions in Pāli sources indicate that, even during the lifetime of the Buddha, there may have been schismatic pressures at work within the monkhood. Early *vinaya* ritual traditions, including the *prātimokṣa* and *pavārāna*,[6] created a binding moral effect on the community that also sustained an ethos of egalitarian collectivity and responsibility. However, as a community under its own *samaya* within ancient Indian society,[7] the *saṇgha* was largely a self-regulatory social institution, a semiautonomous association that was bound to witness competing interpretive understandings of what constituted the true teachings and practices leading to the final religious goal. Because of these competing understandings regarding details of the *Dharma* and *vinaya* of the Buddha, a series of monastic councils were convened in the centuries following the Buddha's demise to settle the inevitable disputes that had arisen. We are particularly interested in the issues associated with the so-called Second Great Buddhist Council purportedly held about one hundred years following the death of the Buddha; for a crucial schism between the Sthāviravādins, whose bastion of privilege became Sri Lanka, and the Mahāsāṃghikas ("Great Assembly," who, as we have noted, eventually came to dominate religious culture in Andhra), is said to have been one of its consequences.

A considerable amount of scholarly discussion has focussed on the historicity and substance of the First and Second Great Buddhist Councils.[8] What interests us specifically is the perceptions from each side of the monastic divide regarding the "other." From the Theravāda perspective articulated in the Pāli *Vinaya Cullavagga* and the mytho-historical Sinhalese monastic chronicle, the *Mahāvaṃsa*, the Mahāsāṃghikas were accused by the Sthāviravādins of laxity in regard to keeping the *vinaya* rules of monastic discipline. The Sthāviravādins cited ten points of controversial behavior, some involved with seemingly very minor concerns, as especially indicative of Mahāsāṃghika spiritual carelessness. One of the ten points, for instance, had to do with whether or not storing salt in an animal horn is acceptable. But others, such as whether or not a *bhikkhu* should be in possession of money, are more serious complaints. In any case, the schismatic issue has been framed from the Theravādin side as being one primarily concerned with the integrity of monastic behavior. Theravāda, especially in Sri Lanka but in Burma and Thailand as well, has always staked its claims for purity in relation to strictly upholding monastic discipline. Its understanding of this initial schism functions, therefore, as a kind of mythic social charter for its own conservative self-identity within the Buddhist world as the preservers of the Buddha's original teachings. Further, what is important to keep in mind here is that for the Theravādins, behavioral expression is regarded as a mirror of mental disposition. Ill-disciplined behavior would be understood as evidence of minds that had not yet been fully tamed and had yet to realize the fullness of complete awareness.[9] Thus, from the Theravāda point of view, anachronistic or not, the Mahāsāṃghikas failed in their self-efforts to translate mental discipline into behavioral praxis. In short, they were regarded as spiritually inferior.

From the Mahāsāṃghika point of view, the schism was framed rather differently: it centered on an argument over five theses advanced by a dissident (from the Sthāviravādin point of view) teacher, one Mahādeva, and according to Prebish and Nattier, was also about Mahāsāṃghika objections to Sthāviravādin expansion of the root *Vinaya* text.[10] In any case, the five theses were concerned with the following matters: an *arahant* may entertain doubts on matters of *Dharma*, cannot achieve enlightenment without the aid of a preceptor, may be an *arahant* and yet not know it, may commit behavioral infractions due to unconscious temptations, and may gain insight by means of a sudden shout.[11] Mahādeva's five theses seem to be of a far more theoretical nature than the more concrete disciplinary concerns advanced on the Sthāviravāda side. With the exception of the last thesis, which seems to be a precursor of later Mahāyāna predilections for sudden enlightenment, each of the theses appears to be aimed at the diminution of the Sthāviravāda understanding of how *nibbāṇa* is won through rigorous self-effort. The last of these may, indeed, foreshadow the later Mahāyāna understanding of *tathāgatagarbha*. It is also clear in these theses that Mahādeva wanted to insist on an existential element of unpredictability, of human humility, of the fragility and vulnerability of even those who have advanced to superior stages of the religious life. By implication, the Mahāsāṃghika position seems at once to attack the perceived arrogance of self-realized and self-proclaimed *arahants* representative of the Sthāviravādins, on the one hand, and also imply the need for some self-transcendent powers of assistance in the quest for religious realization on the other. That is, Mahādeva argues at once for the possibility of realizing what is already inherent (*tathāgatagarbha*) and also the possible need to reach beyond one's own self and one's own rigorous self-effort to experience the final *summum bonum* by means of otherworldly intervention. Implicit in Mahādeva's Mahāsāṃghika theses is the raison d'être for *bodhisattvas* and their *lokottara* (transmundane) soteriological significance as well as the assertion that one may already be enlightened. Both of these positions are later fully formulated in Mahāyāna.

The substance of these basic differences between Mahāsāṃghika and Sthāviravādin, defended from a thoroughly rehearsed Theravāda *Abhidhamma* perspective, is articulated at length in the *Kathāvatthu*[12] purportedly within the proceedings of the so-called Third Great Buddhist Council held during the time of Aśoka in the third century BCE at Pataliputra in north India. We are not so concerned with the exact details of doctrine discussed in this importance text for the moment. We will discuss the ramifications of the doctrinal split for Sri Lankan Buddhism later. What we wish to stress now is that the *Kathāvatthu* and the *Mahāvaṃsa*[13] both reemphasize that the Mahāsāṃghikas are said to have held the heretical positions that were defeated in this debate. The *Kathāvatthu* mentions that by this time the Mahāsāṃghikas had migrated south to Andhra and had settled down at Amaravati and Nagarjunakonda,[14] which later became their centers of power and support. It further lists the various Mahāsāṃghika sects, as does the *Mahāvaṃsa*, which collectively came to be known as Andhakas (to indicate their geographical locales) and Caityakas (to indicate the centrality they accorded *stūpa* veneration in the religious life).

Mahāsāṃghika Buddhism in Andhra

Inscriptions found and deciphered at Amaravati and Nagarjunkonda tend to support the generalities mentioned in the *Kathāvatthu* and the Sri Lankan chronicles.[15] These inscriptions indicate that the Mahāsāṃghikas, possibly as early as Aśoka's time (some would contend by the time of the Second Great Buddhist Council), possessed their own *Tripiṭaka*,[16] and had established other monastic centers to the north at Pataliputra, Mathura, Karli, and Vaishali as well.[17]

The subsequent development of Mahāsāṃghika Buddhism in Andhra would seem to be marked by a growing popularization of lay participation in cultic practice and a further cosmological reassessment of the nature of the Buddha. With regard to the former, the making and transference of merit through the erection, decoration, and worship of *caitya*s seems to have emerged as the primary form of religious activity among the laity, especially the royal and business classes, and also among the monks. Coomaraswamy, as well as Sree Padma, have argued that the unusually widespread proliferation of *caitya*s in Andhra during this early period was due to a cultural synthesis taking place between Buddhism and the religious customs prevalent among the *Yakṣa*s or other protohistoric peoples of Andhra.[18] In support of this thesis, it should be noted that a very large number of *Yakṣa*s carrying garlands and depicted as mythic figures were sculpted at Amaravati, thus marking the participation of these tribal peoples in the cult of Buddhism.[19] But what is of greater significance to us is the large number of inscriptions in Andhra that record the gifts of donors, the merit from which was dedicated for the afterlife benefit of familial relations as well as for the entire world.[20] The building of *stūpa*s and the practice of merit transfer seemed to have become the hallmarks of popular Buddhism in early Andhra.

The Buddhist practice of merit transference has its roots in ancient Brahmanical rites for the dead. That its principle was subsequently absorbed into Buddhist tradition, including the later Theravāda, is clearly indicated in the popular sermons told to the laity by monks recorded in the Pāli *Petavatthu*.[21] Its spiritual ethos is totally consistent with the later emergent Mahāyāna *bodhisattva* ethic: to give selflessly of oneself by eschewing immediate spiritual reward for the ultimate benefit of others. That is, the altruism for which Mahāyāna came to be so well-known could be an abstract generalization of the earlier practice of merit-transfer.

The religious valorization of altruism and the emerging emphasis on securing supramundane assistance was stressed through a developing ontology of compassion (*karuṇā*) in the canonical writings of the Mahāsāṃghikas in Andhra. These qualities of the Buddha reveal a *lokottara* ("beyond this world") as well as a this-worldly cosmological and soteriological significance. Two brief examples from the Mahāsāṃghika's *Mahāvastu* will suffice to illustrate these propensities. These examples, though innocent of the fully developed Mahāyāna *bodhisattva* notion per se, contain the seed of concepts later associated with the most widely propitiated of all Mahāyāna *bodhisattvas*, Avalokiteśvara, best known for the manner in which he surveys the *saṃsāra*ic world of suffering out of compassion for humanity in general and his devotees in particular.

There are two sections of the *Mahāvastu* entitled *Avalokita Sūtra*. The first is fundamentally a sermon about how the Buddha conquered Māra (the personification of death). Nanda, a celestial *deva* (divinity), requests the Buddha to preach this sermon for the benefit and well-being of both *deva*s and humans alike. The key to the title of the *sūtra* lies in a twice-repeated passage translated by Jones as follows:

> When monks, the Bodhisattva from this shore *surveys* the shore beyond, the antecedent conditions of the survey being actually present, devas who have great power worship the Tathāgata with the highest worship and honour him with the highest honour, while the Suddhavasa devas get eighteen grounds for rejoicing [emphasis ours].[22]

The second *sūtra* (with the same title) is far more thoroughly developed and therefore contains a much richer source of symbolism. The key to its title comes at the beginning of the text when a monk named Visuddhimati says to the Buddha: "Let the Exalted One disclose what he saw, when as a *bodhisattva*, he had come to the *bodhi* throne and for the benefit and welfare of the entire world, made his *survey*"[23] [emphasis ours]. In a footnote to this passage, Jones argues that the use of the term *avalokitam* here, which he has translated as "survey," was subsequently incorporated into the name of Bodhisattva Avalokiteśvara.[24] But what is central to this discussion is that the action undertaken to effect the end of the religious goal, the overcoming of suffering, is initiated by the Buddha, rather than by the self-effort of some human being. It reveals a theocentric soteriological worldview.

As interesting, however, is the following passage from the same *sūtra* which characterizes the Buddha in a manner anticipating the character of later cosmic Mahāyāna *bodhisattvas*. In this passage, Māra's son is describing the Buddha to Māra in a way that seems to prefigure specifically the later developed character of Avalokiteśvara:

> When this peerless, virtuous man was born, the earth with its rocks shook six times. The ten quarters of the world were all lit up. Celestial musical instruments gave forth music without anyone playing them.
>
> Devas held up celestial sun shads, and the Buddha-field was overspread with banners and flags. Throngs of gods and hosts of devas waved their garments. Noble men became alert.
>
> He will become the eye of the whole world, a light dispelling darkness. He will scatter the darkness of those who are in misery. Do not in thy feeble understanding, nurture distrust for him.
>
> For he will become a shelter for the whole world, a protection, an island, a refuge, and a rest. Those men and devas who put not their trust in him pass to the terrible hells of Avīci.
>
> He is without a peer in the world, worthy of offerings. He is ever benevolent and compassionate to the world. When all men and women realize this they will become blessed here in all the world.
>
> But he who nurtures a mind distrustful of him who is endowed with merit, who has shed his passions, the Sakyan lion, verily, there will be no prosperous state for him.[25]

This passage is remarkable for many reasons. It emphasizes the altruism and compassion of the Buddha. The symbolism of lightness, an essential motif associated with *deva*s (*deva*, it should be recalled, literally means "shining one"), now seems to have become directly associated with the Buddha. While speculative, this passage also seems to refer to the conceptual (but perhaps not cultic) beginnings of a more *bhakti*-oriented Buddhism and popular Mahāyāna.

The profile of the Buddha here is somewhat, although not entirely at odds with the later Theravāda conception of the Buddha who passes into *nibbāṇa* beyond the realms of *saṃsāra*. Rather, it would seem to be something of a "proto-Mahāyāna" view of the Buddha with its emphasis on the ever-compassionate *bodhisattva* figure set on rescuing the devoted from conditions of suffering in the rebirths of *saṃsāra*. That such a passage would be conceived by the Mahāsāṃghikas and incorporated into their canonical text is an indication of the extent to which their emerging transcendental *lokottara* view of the Buddha, in opposition to a view of Gotama the Buddha as a paradigmatic teacher and monk (the later dominant orthodox Theravādin perception), had become thoroughly rooted in their "buddhology" and cosmology by this early time. This is not to argue unequivocally that supramundane aspects were not part of the Buddha's profile in Theravāda Pāli literature.

At the time that the Buddha was being so regarded by the Mahāsāṃghika communities in Andhra, a concomitant shift was occurring in the manner in which the Buddha was being represented within the context of cultic veneration. The *bodhi* tree, the throne, the dharma wheel and footprints of the Buddha, symbols invoked for the veneration of the Buddha's presence at the ancient sites of Bharhut, Bodh Gaya, and Sanci, were gradually being replaced at Amaravati by consecrated Buddha figures in various poses of preaching, teaching or mediating.[26] A literary work of the Śātavāhana period, the *Gāthāsaptasati* also makes explicit reference to the idea of *bhakti* and self-surrender while consecrating an image.[27] The *Gandavyūha* also identifies Andhra as the land of *bodhisattva* worship par excellence.[28] What we are interested in determining is the extent to which these Mahāsāṃghika developments, which seem to have been at the forefront of an emerging Mahāyāna also occurring in northwest Gandhara, made any impact on Buddhist traditions developing simultaneously in Sri Lanka. Before making that assessment, it is necessary to review briefly the early phases of Mahāyāna presence in Sri Lanka.

The "Proto-Mahāyāna" Presence in Sri Lanka

Inscriptions at Sri Parvata in Andhra indicate the presence of three monastic establishments during the later Amaravati period belonging to the Sinhalese Theravāda, two of which were affiliated with the Mahāvihāra monastery, the bastion of Theravāda conservatism in Anuradhapura, Sri Lanka.[29] The Mahāvihāravāsins may have sponsored vigorous missionaries at this time. They are said to have been successful in conversion efforts in places as diverse as Kashmir, Gandhara, China, Cilata, Tosala, Aparanata, Vanga, Vanavasa, and Yavana. In addition to coming into interaction with other Buddhist communities through missionary activities, Buddhists from Sri Lanka also came into contact with emergent Mahāyāna notions when undertaking pilgrimages from Sri Lanka to the other holy and famous Buddhist sites in India. These instances of interaction are reflective of the later phases of the long history of contact between these two Buddhist cultural centers.

Even as early as the first century BCE, schismatic pressures in Sri Lanka would seem to imply the presence of Mahāsāṃghika or "proto-Mahāyāna" influence in Anuradhapura. We use the term "imply" advisedly in referring to these early instances, for it is difficult to prove directly and without a doubt Andhra's influence until we consider artistic and archaeological evidence from the third century CE, the material to which we shall turn in the next section of this article.

The *Mahāvaṃsa* asserts that during the reign of the Sri Lankan king Vaṭṭagāmaṇi (103–102 and 89–77 BCE) after the successful resistance of a military invasion from south India, the first written Pāli versions of the *Tripiṭaka* were commissioned. At the same time, Vaṭṭagāmaṇi constructed and gifted the Abhayagiri monastery in Anuradhapura to one Mahātissa, a loyal *bhikkhu* supporter who had played a major role in helping to expel south Indian invaders. When this same monk was charged with infractions of the *vinaya* rules by rival monks from the Mahāvihāra, a number of Mahāvihāra monks, in protest, crossed over to join Mahātissa at the Abhayagiri fraternity. Thus, what was later to become an historic rivalry[30] throughout the history of Buddhism in Sri Lanka seems to have first originated, from the Theravāda perspective, over matters of interpretation with regard to monastic discipline, the same interpretation provided on the Theravāda side regarding the original split with the Mahāsāṃghikas at the Second Great Buddhist Council.

Toward the end of Vaṭṭagāmaṇi's rule, a south Indian monk named Dhammaruci arrived in Anuradhapura with a company of followers and, finding themselves unwelcome at the Mahāvihāra fraternity because of their affiliation with the *Vajjiputtaka* sect, took up residence at Abhayagiri and began to propound their non-Theravādin views on *Dharma*. It is difficult to determine with certainty if these were specifically early Mahāyāna perspectives on *Dharma* or not, but the fact that they were considered illegitimate by the Mahāvihāra Theravādins suggests just such an implication.[31] The two monasteries again clashed publicly during the reign of Bhātikabhaya (19 BCE–CE 9). Again, the dispute is said to have been over matters of interpreting *vinaya*, but more significant is the fact that in the public debate that ensued, the Abhayagiri monks relied on canonical texts written in Sanskrit rather than Pāli, thereby indicating another important growing distinction between the two fraternities, and one that at least circumstantially suggests a Mahāyāna presence, or the possible presence of Mahāsāṃghika texts.

The first fairly certain indications of Mahāyāna teachings present at the Abhayagiri monastery occurs during the reign of Vohārika Tissa (CE 214–236) when the king appointed his minister Kapila, according to the *Nikāya Sangrahāya*,[32] to decide whether or not the Mahāvihāra's claim that the Sanskrit *Vaitulyapiṭaka sūtra*s being used at the Abhayagiri were truly the teachings of the Buddha. Kapila found in favor of the Mahāvihāra monks, the Vaitulya *sūtra*s were burned, and the Vaitulya (meaning "dissenting") monks were disrobed and banished.

The controversy over Vetulla (Pāli for Sanskrit Vaitulya) teachings surfaced again, and rather dramatically, during the reign of Goṭhakābhaya (ca. CE 255). That Mahāyāna-oriented conceptions were present not only among the ranks of the monastic community but among the laity and kings as well, despite the suppression of the Vaitulyas under Vohārika Tissa, seems evident from the *Mahāvaṃsa*'s account of Goṭhakābhaya's predecessor, King Sirisanghabodhi, whose short reign of kingship (CE 251–253) is characterized in such a way that it is clear that kings were now beginning to interpret the significance of their own reigns by means of comparisons to the *bodhisattva* concept.[33] But Goṭhakābaya, who had been but a treasurer under Sirisanghabodhi, was more sympathetic to the Theravāda worldview and the political pressures exerted by the Mahāvihāra. Following Sirisangabodhi's reign, he pillaged the Abhayagiri monastery and banished sixty of its monks to south India. A monk-poet by the name of Sanghamitta from the famous Kāveripāṭṭaṇam monastery took up their cause, traveled from south India to Anuradhapura, gained the king's favor, and subsequently became the king's *rājaguru* (royal preceptor).[34] It is particularly important to note that the oldest surviving sculpted Sinhalese Buddha images probably date to the reign of this king and "are reminiscent of the South Indian Amaravati School."[35] Upon the ascension to the throne of Mahāsena (CE 276–303) Sanghamitta succeeded in convincing the new king that the Theravāda Mahāvihāra *bhikkhu*s did not teach the true *vinaya*. Consequently, the king issued a decree prohibiting the giving of alms to the Mahāvihāra community, a decree that led to the Theravādin monastery's abandonment and temporary destruction.

Along its boundaries, he began the construction of the Jetavāna monastery with its massive *stūpa* within which gold plates containing Mahāyāna *prājñāpāramitā* texts have recently been discovered.

That the interpretation of *dharma* and *vinaya* of the Vaitulya monks in Anuradhapura was a development of "proto-Mahāyāna" or Mahāsāṃghika origins seems a reasonable inference. The eminent fifth century CE orthodox commentator of the Theravāda Mahāvihāra, Buddhaghoṣa, characterized the teachings of the Vetullaka sect as *mahāśūññavāda* ("the path of great emptiness"). Two centuries earlier in Andhra, Nāgārjuna had formulated his philosophical arguments equating *nirvāṇa* with *saṃsāra* on the basis of the existential and cosmological significance of *śūnyata*. Elaborating on their teachings in his commentary on the *Kathāvatthu* (which, it should be recalled, had originally equated the supramundane views of the Buddha advanced by the Mahāsāṃghika Andhakas with the Vaitulyas), Buddhaghoṣa explains that the Vetullakas held a docetic view of the Buddha; that is, they believed that the Buddha is utterly transcendent and appeared in human form as Siddhattha Gotama only to make known the truth of *Dharma*. This "buddhology," of course, is similar to the views advanced by the earlier Mahāsāṃghikas who had propounded the view that their were two natures of the Buddha: one eternal and transcendent (*lokottara*) and the other temporal.

From Presence to Impact: Andhra's Influence on Sri Lanka

In the previous section, we noted evidence drawn chiefly from Sinhalese sources regarding the presence of "proto-Mahāyāna" conceptions in Sri Lanka in the earlier phases of Buddhist monastic history. That presence was discussed chiefly within the context of how Theravāda monastic sources describe conflicts with "heretical" monks over matters of orthodoxy and orthpraxy. In this section, we will discuss other forms of evidence that seem to indicate how the religious practices and artistic traditions of the Mahāsāṃghikas cultivated in Andhra Pradesh made a formative impact on Buddhist tradition throughout Sri Lanka.

While the building and veneration of *stūpa*s is a practice known to have been in vogue at least since the second century BCE reign of the Sinhalese hero and warrior king Duṭṭhagāmṇi, the practice must have been certainly enhanced and legitimated further by the emphasis on the practice and ideology of merit-making and merit-transfer so heavily emphasized in Andhra Buddhism. Indeed, the ability to construct *stūpa*s for the glorification of the Buddha became a measure of the Sinhalese king's own spiritual and material well-being throughout the remainder of the history of kingship in Sinhalese Sri Lanka. While we have noted that merit-making and merit-transfer were probably also practiced in Theravāda circles from an early date, the later profusion of *caitya* building may very well have been stimulated by contact with the Andhra *Caityakas*, though there is no way to prove this directly.

Of more direct and concrete significance is the manner in which the Buddha became depicted in sculptural representation in Sri Lanka. By the third and fourth centuries CE, Theravādins were erecting images of the Buddha in preaching, teaching and meditating poses. By the seventh and eighth centuries, these images had become enormous in size. Those surviving at Aukana, Sasseruva, and numerous other later sites are typical examples reflecting an understanding of the Buddha as superhuman in conception, cosmic in being.

Ulrich von Schroeder has argued that the earliest surviving images of the Buddha found in Anuradhapura date to the third century CE. His conclusion is further corroborated and detailed by many other scholars who also point to an unmistakable Andhra inspiration for these images. Coomaraswamy, for instance, observed that

> The most characteristic Buddha images of Anuradhapura are what would be called in India the Gupta style. The design very closely recalls the (Pre-Gupta) Amaravati standing figures and at the same time shows an approach to a later type in the transparent clinging drapery.[36]

Vogel's assessment lends further support:

> In their general style, and particularly in the treatment of drapery with its schematic folds, these images exhibit a close relationship to the Buddha type of Amaravati.[37]

Benjamin Rowland argued that the inspiration for both Buddhist sculpture and architecture came especially from the later part of (third century CE and after) Amaravati school. In referring to the earliest standing Buddha images at Anuradhapura cited by von Schroeder, Rowland states:

> It needs but a glance to see in them a Sinhalese adaptation of the type of Buddha fashioned at Amaravati. Although some seated Buddhas from Anuradhapura are related to later Andhra models, the Indian prototype for this statue has to be sought in such Kushan images from Katra . . . and has to be dated not later than the 3rd century AD.[38]

Senarat Paranivitana was so struck by the parallels between Buddhist sculptures in Andhra and Sri Lanka that he said:

> The earliest type of Buddha image known in Ceylon is that of the Andhra school . . . The evidence of the influence of Andhra art on that of early Ceylon is so overwhelming, that it may even be suggested that a branch of that school was established in Ceylon.[39]

Though, as we have just seen, the predominant view in scholarly circles asserts that the earliest Buddha images in Sri Lanka were decidedly influenced by the art flourishing in Amaravati and elsewhere in Andhra, many Sinhalese Buddhist scholars (perhaps captive to the collective mythic consciousness we cited in our introduction), argue to the contrary. Ven. Walpola Rahula, in regard to the *Mahāvaṃsa*'s claim that Devānampiya Tissa (the Sinhalese king converted by Asoka's missionary son Mahinda in the third century BCE) had a stone image of the Buddha placed in the Thūparāma at Anuradhapura, states that:

> If we accept this statement, Ceylon had the earliest Buddha image in the world. Merely because we do not find Buddha images among the early sculptures at Bharhut and Sanchi, it is not logical to conclude that there were no Buddha images made in the 3rd century B.C. anywhere else either.[40]

Von Schroeder has cited a series of incredible statements made by D. T. Devendra in his *The Buddha Image and Ceylon* in which it is asserted fallaciously that there was no aniconic phase of Buddhist art in Sri Lanka, that Buddha images were part and parcel of the religion since the time of its introduction to the land, that the Sinhalese were the first to ever use the image of the Buddha ceremoniously, and the first to ever create Buddha images in the round.[41] Siri Gunasinghe, another Sinhalese Buddhist apologetic scholar, went so far as to argue that monks from Ceylon introduced the cult of the Buddha image to south India in the second century CE.[42] The culture critic, novelist, sometime anthropologist, and still revered Sinhalese Buddhist nationalist, Martin Wickramasinghe, popularized the view that Sri Lanka was home to the first Buddha images ever created and that their production in India had been more of a commercial than a spiritual matter.[43]

In fact, not only was Andhra the stylistic inspiration for Buddha images created in Sri Lanka, but numerous archaeological finds prove that images in the round and other forms of sculpted carving were frequently imported directly from Andhra for ritual use in Buddhist monasteries, including those coming under the administrative aegis of the Mahāvihāravāsins. These artistic creations were carved on or out of a type of green-hued limestone found only in the Amaravati and Nagarjunkonda regions of Andhra. Specifically, von Schroder cites as evidence: a limestone Mahāmerugala *valhalkada* pillar from a fifth century CE relic chamber in the Rāmakal Dāgaba near Sigiriya in the Matale district of central Sri Lanka;[44] imported limestone slabs forming part of a *bodhigāra* near Kurunegala (midway between modern Colombo and Anuradhapura) depicting the miracle at Shravasti and the dream of Queen Mahāmāya, which are also very similar in style to limestone slab carvings excavated at Amaravati and now preserved in the British Museum;[45] limestone carvings from the Jetavāna monastic complex in Anuradhapura that resemble sculptures exhumed at Nagarjunkonda;[46] three imported standing Buddha figures made of limestone found at Anuradhapura, Trincomalee, and Kuccaveli (30 miles north of Trincomalee);[47] and, five imported limestone seated Buddhas at Trincomalee, Polonnaruva, and Panduvas Nuvara.[48] Von Schroeder also cites numerous instances where comparisons between pieces created in Andhra of limestone and in Sri Lanka out of dolomite marble bear out striking stylistic affinities reinforcing the view that Sinhalese artists modeled their work on Andhra prototypes. For examples, to illustrate this point, he has documented and photographed three *buddhapāda*s from Mullaitivu (extreme northeast coast), Jetavāna (Anuradhapura), and Trincomalee that compare closely in style with a *buddhapāda* found in the Guntur District in Andhra,[49] a sculpture of a *yakṣini* at Jetavāna in Anuradhapura imported from Amaravati that probably functioned as a model for Sinhalese creations,[50] five very early representations of Mucalinda figures from Kantale (between Anuradhapura and Trincomalee), Seruvila (just south of Trincomalee), and Mahintale (just east of Anuradhapura), all of which are obviously inspired by prototypes at Amaravati.[51] He has also provided evidence of Andhra's great influence with regard to the rendering of *nāgarāja*[52] Padmanidhi and Sankanidhi (attendants of Kuvera or Jambhala) figures,[53] as well as moonstones.[54] Through copious photographic presentations of the evidence, he illustrates how all of these artistic creations were clearly derived stylistically from Andhra prototypes. Von Schroeder's evidence is thorough and conclusive. It is abundantly clear that Buddhist Sri Lanka's material religious culture of the first millennium CE owes much of its inspiration to Andhra creations.

At this point, it needs to be emphasized that by noting the artistic influence of Andhra on Sri Lanka, we also mean to imply a philosophical impact on conceptions of the Buddha and *bodhisattva* as well. In discussing the general relationships between art, religious thought, symbols, and society, Kenneth Clark has put the matter abstractly in this way:

> In the relationship of art and society the importance of an accepted iconography cannot be overly stated. Without it, the network of beliefs and customs which hold a society together may never take shape as art. *If an iconography contains a number of sufficiently powerful symbols, it can positively alter a philosophical system.* The points of dogma for which no satisfactory image can be created tend to be dropped and popular religious expression and episodes which have scarcely occupied the attention of theologians tend to grow in importance if they produce a compelling image [emphasis ours].[55]

The appearance of anthropomorphic images of the Buddha were both a catalyst for and a symbol of changing conceptions of the Buddha. Even in the polemical Theravāda Pāli chronicles, the *Dīpavaṃsa* and *Mahāvaṃsa* composed in the fourth and fifth centuries CE, and in measured contrast to the earlier Pāli *Nikāyas*, the Buddha is imagined in ever more spectacular ways stressing his supramundane abilities and character. Earlier we mentioned the massive Buddha figures from the seventh and eighth centuries sculpted at Aukana and Sasseruva. These figures signal the beginnings of the tradition of making enormous figures to indicate not only the cosmic character of the Buddha, but his heroic nature as well. By the Polonnaruva period, enormity had become standardized and huge statues or sculptures of the Buddha continue to be fashioned to the present day.

In addition to how the development of iconic representation signals a changing conception of the Buddha, an almost equally powerful influence on the Theravāda in Sri Lanka can be seen in the evolving development of the notion of the *bodhisattva*. In centuries subsequent to the impact of Andhra Buddhism and its Mahāyāna proclivities, many Sri Lankan kings, ostensibly Theravādin in their sympathies, understood themselves to be "buddhas-in-the-making." King Buddhadāsa (CE 340–368) is described as having "lived openly before the people the life that bodisattvas lead,"[56] King Dhatusena (CE 459–477) had a sculpture made of the Bodhisattva Maitreya in which the *bodhisattva* was fashioned in "the complete equipment of a king,"[57] in a tenth-century inscription, King Mahinda IV proclaimed that "none but bodhisattvas would become kings of a prosperous Lanka,"[58] and in the twelfth-century Nissanka Malla recorded the inscription that "the appearance of an impartial king should be welcomed as the appearance of a buddha."[59] It is also worth noting that the ten *pāramitās* (spiritual perfections) constituting the *bodhisattva* path also seem to have been associated with the ten royal duties incumbent on a king. In describing the piety of Upatissa II (CE 522), the *Culavaṃsa* refers to the practise of both within the same sentence, thereby fusing the ideals of kingship and bodhisattvahood: "Shunning the ten sinful actions, he practiced the ten meritorious works; the King fulfilled the ten royal duties and the ten paramitas."[60] The conflation of kingship and *bodhisttva* did not end with the Anuradhapura period. The *Nikāya Sangrahāya* states that Vijayabāhu IV (CE 1270–1272) was popularly known as "Bosat Vijayabāhu"[61] while the fifteen-century Parakramabāhu VI of Kotte was referred to as "Bosat Parakramabāhu" in an inscription.[62] While there is no doubt that the *bodhisattva* concept is also present in Theravāda Pāli literature, especially with reference to the Buddha's previous incarnations in the *Jātakas* and to its presence in the Maitreya cult, its application to kingship and its later association with deities in Sri Lanka would seem to point to Mahāyāna inspirations. With regard to how the *bodhisattva* concept was later associated with deities, all of the major national guardian deities incorporated into the hierarchical pantheon of Sinhala Buddhist traditions including Vishnu, Pattini, Saman, Skandha, Vibhiṣana, and Nātha came to be regarded eventually as *bodhisattvas*. The last is of particular significance because his original identification has been clearly established as the Mahāyāna Bodhisattva Avalokiteśvara. As Nātha, this *bodhisattva*/god became the guardian deity of the late medieval Kandyan Kingdom and later also became associated with future Bodhisattva Maitreya. The nature and conception of divinity in Buddhist Sri Lanka, therefore, was clearly abetted by the *bodhisattva* concept originally derived from Andhra.

Conclusion

In this chapter, we have attempted to sketch out in general outline the legacy of influence ultimately emanating from the Mahāsāṃghika Andhra context for aspects of Buddhism in Sri Lanka. What we have endeavored to make clear is that the emergent Theravāda Buddhist tradition of Sri Lanka has absorbed much more from Mahāsāṃghika sources in Andhra and other parts of south India than its contemporary apologists would normally admit. The practice of merit-transfer, the construction and veneration of *stūpas*, but especially the erection, stylization, and consecration of Buddha images, traditional conceptions of Buddhist kingship, and the manner in which divinity is understood, are all aspects of Sinhala Buddhist tradition that owe all or part of their impetus to development of religion amid the Mahāsāṃghika Andhra community.

No religious tradition exists in a historical vacuum, no matter how an evolved community may later mythicize its history to proclaim an unadulterated relationship to the origins of the religion. The Buddhist tradition of Sri Lanka certainly has a long, rich, and textured past. But its longevity and vitality has been due as much to the ways in which it has reacted inclusively and creatively to religio-cultural innovations originating elsewhere on the Indian subcontinent as much as it has been due to its often self-professed conserving ethos. The history of Buddhism in Sri Lanka is thus one of both continuity and change, of transformation as well as preservation.

Notes

1. Excellent sources for locating a rich variety of examples can be found in Charles Long, *Alpha: The Myths of Creation* (New York: Braziller, 1962) and Barbara Sproul, *Primal Myths: Creating the World* (New York: Harper and Row, 1979).

2. See, for example, the myths of the Buddha's three visits to Sri Lanka, the coming of the primordial Sinhalese king Vijaya prophesied by the dying Buddha to establish a community that would preserve his *dhamma*, and the succesful conversions by Aśoka's missionary son Mahinda as these stories are mythically framed as history by the fifth century CE monk Mahānāma in the opening chapters of *The Mahāvaṃsa or the Great Chronicle of Ceylon*. Wilhelm Geiger et al., ed. and trans. (London: Luzac and Co. for the Pāli Text Society, 1964).

3. See Thomas Watters, *On Yuan Chwang's Travels in India 629–645,* 2 vols., ed. by T. W. Rhys Davids and S. W. Bushell (London: Royal Asiatic Society, 1904–1905; reprint Delhi, 1961), p. 209.

4. See H. Saddhatissa, trans., *The Sutta-Nipata* (London: Curzon Press, Ltd., 1985), pp. 114–133.

5. B. S. L. Hanumantha Rao, *Religion in Andhra* (Hyderabad: Government of Andhra Pradesh, 1993), p. 55.

6. The *prātimokṣa* was a collective rite of the *saṇgha* transacted every two weeks in which each item of the the monastic code of discipline was collectively recited to ensure that individual monks systematically examined the intentions of their personal actions. Ritually it became a statement of the *saṇgha*'s continuing pure *śila* (moral behavior). The *pavārana* functioned in much the same way during the three-month period of *vassa* (rain retreat) except that, in this instance, monks were "invited" to scrutinize each other's behavior. For a further discussion, see John Clifford Holt, "Ritual Expression in the Vinayapitaka," *History of Religions* 18 (1978): 41–53.

7. In underscoring the relative autonomy of the early Buddhist *saṇgha*, Sukumar Dutt, *Buddhist Monks and Monasteries in India* (London: George Allen and Unwin, 1962), pp. 80–81, has stated that "the conception of society in the political philosophy of ancient India was that of an aggregate composed of units

of diverse kinds—learned bodies, village communities, religious corporations, and so on. Each was regarded as subject to its own system of law, called *Samaya* (Conventional Law) in ancient Indian Jurisprudence. With regard to these units of society, it was the king's constitutional duty to see that none of them suffered from internal or external disruption and that the system of conventional law of each was not transgressed. Among these societal units, the Buddhist *saṇgha* became one, an "association group" functioning under a system of law of its own." For the *saṇgha*, this *samaya* was *vinaya*.

8. The Pāli Theravāda account of the First Great Buddhist Council is found in chapter 11 of the *Cullavagga*, the concluding portion of the *vinaya* narrative, see I. B. Horner, ed. and trans., *The Book of the Discipline (Vinaya-piṭaka)*, 5 vols. (London: Pali Text Society, 1938–52) 5: 393–406 and the *Mahāvaṃsa*, pp. 14–25. Many traditional Buddhist scholars, especially those sympathetic to the Theravādin tradition, accept the historicity of these accounts and they are frequently referred to as sanctified authority. See, for instance, Goukaldas De, *Democracy in the Early Buddhist Sangha* (Calcutta: University of Calcutta, 1955), p. 4ff. Other scholars, primarily European, suggest otherwise. R. O. Franke, for instance, flatly denied the historicity of both the *Cullavagga* account of First Great Buddhist Council and its account of the Second. See his "The Buddhist Councils at Rajagaha and Vesali as Alleged in Cullavagga XI, XII," *Journal of the Pāli Text Society* 8 (1908): 68. Louis de la Vallee Poussin, "The Buddhist Councils," *Indian Antiquary* 37 (1908): 17–18, conceded that while the *Cullavagga* accounts could not be regarded as historical documents, episodes within the account, particularly those associated Ānanda's attaining of enlightenment, seem to be of high antiquity nonetheless. Jean Przyluski, in his *Le Concile de Rajagṛha* (Paris: Paul Geunther, 1926–28), argued that the meaning of the First Council must be interpreted allegorically as expressing the early *saṇgha*'s concern for purity. That the account of the First Council was actually inspired a century later by the issues germane to the Second Great Buddhist Council was suggested by Erich Frauwallner, *The Earliest Vinaya and the Beginnings of Buddhist Literature* (Roma: Institut Italiano per il Medio ed Estremo Oriente, 1956), pp. 153–154, and also by Andre Bareau, *Les premiers conciles bouddhiques* (Paris: Presses Universitaires, 1955), p. 28.

9. We are referring here to the importance of the Theravāda understanding action, or *kamma* classically stated in the *Anguttara Nikāya* and elsewhere: *Cetanaham bhikkhave kammam vadami; cetayitva kammam karoti kayena vacaya manasa* ("O bhkkhus, it is volition that I call *kamma*. Having willed, one acts through body, speech and mind.") See F. L. Woodward and E. M. Hare, eds. and trans., *The Book of Gradual Sayings (Anguttara Nikāya)*, 5 vols. (London: Oxford University Press, 1930–36) 3: 295.

10. Charles Prebish and Janice Nattier. "Mahāsāṃghika Origins: The Beginnings of Buddhist Sectarianism," *History of Religions* 16 (Feb., 1977): 237–272. Prebish, "The Pratimoksa Expansion in the Rise of Indian Buddhist Sectarianism," to be published in *The Pacific World* (2007) has further pointed how the Pāli Theravāda *Vinaya* contains an additional five *saikṣa dharma*s in comparison to the Mahāsāṃghika *Vinaya*, a very likely cause of debate and eventual acrimony.

11. Louis de la Vallee Poussin, "The Five Points of Mahādeva and the Kāthavatthu," *Journal of the Royal Asiatic Society (Bombay Branch)* 1910, pp. 413–423 and Charles Prebish and Janice Nattier, "Mahāsāṃghika Origins: The Beginnings of Buddhist Sectarianism," *History of Religions* 16 (1977): 237–272.

12. See Shwe Zan Aung and C. A. F. Rhys Davids, eds. and trans., *The Kathavatthu: Points of Controversy or Subjects of Discourse* (London: Pali Text Society, 1915).

13. *Mahāvaṃsa*, p. 26.

14. Cited in Nalinaksha Dutt, *Buddhist Sects in India* (Calcutta: Mukhopadhyay, 1970), pp. 70–71. See also *Epigrapha Indica* 20: 64, and Etienne Lamotte, *History of Indian Buddhism* (Louvain-Paris, Peeters Press, 1988), p. 348.

15. See Sree Padma's chapter in this volume for further details.

16. James Burgess, *The Buddhist Stupas of Amaravati and Jaggayyapeta* (Varanasi: Indological Book House, 1970; originally published in London, 1887), p. 162, and Nalinaksha Dutt, "Notes on the Nagarjunakonda Inscriptions," *Indian Historical Quarterly* 7 (1931): 640.

17. *Epigrapha Indica* 15: 262; 19: 68; 30: 183–184; see also Lamotte, *History of Indian Buddhism*, pp. 348–350.

18. Ananda K. Coomaraswamy, *The Yakshas*, 2 vols. (Washington: Smithsonian, 1928–31), 1: 17–24.

19. Burgess, *The Buddhist Stupa at Amaravati*, p. 22.

20. Burgess, *Notes on the Amaravati Stupa* (Varanasi: Prithivi Prakashan, 1972; originally published in Madras, 1882), p. 53. See also *Luder's List*, no. 1239.

21. John Clifford Holt, "Assisting the Dead by Venerating the Living: Merit Transfer in Early Buddhism," *Numen* 27 (1981): 1–28; see also Richard Gombrich, "Merit Transfer in Sinhalese Buddhism: A Case Study in the Interaction between Doctrine and Practice," *History of Religions* 11 (1971): 203–219, and G. P. Malalasekere, "Transference of Merit in Ceylonese Buddhism," *Philosophy East and West* 17 (1967): 85–90.

22. J. J. Jones, ed. and trans., *The Mahāvastu*, 3 vols. (*Sacred Books of the Buddhists*, vols. 17–19; London: Luzac and Company, 1956) 2: 245.

23. Ibid., 274.

24. Ibid., note 7.

25. Ibid., 277.

26. C. Sivaramurti, *Amaravati Sculptures in the Madras Government Museum* (Madras: Government Museum, 1942), see plate LXIV, fig. 2, especially. See also Burgess, *The Buddhist Stupa at Amaravati*, plates XXXI and XXXII.

27. *Gathasaptasati* (Bombay: Nirnaya Sagar Press, 1869), iv, 8.

28. According to Nalinaksha Dutt in his "Notes on the Nargajunakonda Inscriptions," p. 639.

29. *Epigrapha Indica* XX, pp. 23–29 and XXXII, p. 247.

30. This intrasangha split between these two fraternities has been sustained in one form or another throughout Theravāda Buddhist history in Sri Lanka, well beyond the Anuradhapura period. Though King Parakramabahu I of Polonnaruva succeeded in unifying the *saṇgha* in the eleventh century CE, the general lines of this original division between Abhayagiri and Mahāvihāra was used to

characterise the split beween the so-called *gamavasis* ("village dwellers") and the *vanavāsis* ("forest dwellers") from at least the fifteenth-century CE reign of Parakramabahu VI of Kotte onward.

31. For a full discussion of this development, see S. Paranavitana, "Mahayanism in Ceylon," *Ceylon Journal of Science,* section G, 2 (1928): 35–71.

32. Fernando, C. M., trans., and Gunawardhana, W. F., trans., *Nikāya Sangrahāya (Being a History of Budddhism in India and Ceylon* (Colombo: H. Cottle, 1908), pp. 12–13.

33. *Mahāvaṃsa,* pp. 261–263; the description of Sirisanghabodhi's short reign of altruistic self-sacrifice on behalf of his people includes his epithet *mahāsattva* ("great being"), a term almost always used to designate *bodhisattvas* in Sanskrit literature. So influential was Sirisanghabodhi's profile of compassionate kingship that every second Sinhala king from the seventh through the twelth century included Sirisanghabodhi's name in his official title, while *every* king from the thirteenth through sixteenth century incorporated his name formally.

34. T. N. Ramachandran, "The Nagapattinam and Other Buddhist Bronzes in the Madras Museum," *Bulletin of the Madras Government Museum,* n.s. 7 (1954), p. 4.

35. Ulrich von Schroeder, *Buddhist Sculptures of Sri Lanka* (Hong Kong, Visual Dharma Publications, 1990), p. 118. Von Schroeder also notes that in the immediate vicinity where three of these images were excavated in the Abhayagiri complex fragments of imported limestone reliefs unmistakeably of Andhra origins were also found.

36. A. K., Coomaraswamy, *Arts and Crafts of Indian and Ceylon* (London: T. N. Foulis, 1913), p. 51.

37. J. Ph. Vogel, *Buddhist Art in India, Ceylon and Java* (Oxford, UK: The Clarendon Press, 1935), pp. 84–85.

38. Benjamin Rowland, *The Art and Architecture of India: Buddhist, Hindu and Jain* (London: Penguin Books, 1953), pp. 209–223.

39. Senarat Paranavitana, *Art of the Ancient Sinhalese* (Colombo: Lake House, 1971), p. 13.

40. Walpola Rahula, *History of Buddhism in Ceylon: The Anuradhapura Period (3rd C. BC–10th C. AD)* (Colombo: M. D. Gunasena, 1956), pp. 122–124.

41. Cited in von Schroeder, *Buddhist Sculptures in Sri Lanka,* p. 22.

42. Siri Gunasinghe, "Ceylon and the Buddha Image in the Round," *Artibus Asiae* 19 (1956): 258.

43. See Martin Wickramasinghe, "The Development of the Buddha Image in Ceylon, *Buddhist Annual 2511–1967* (1967), p. 51; and *Buddhism and Art* (Colombo, M. D. Gunasena, 1972), pp. 22–23 and 70.

44. Von Schroeder, *Buddhist Sculptures of Sri Lanka,* p. 67, plate 3G.

45. Ibid., p. 76, plates 8D and E.

46. Ibid., pp. 78–79, plates 9A–9D.

47. Ibid., pp. 106–107, plates, 18C, 18E and 18F, and 18A, 18B, and 18C.

48. Ibid., pp. 110–111, plates 20A through 20I.

49. Ibid., pp. 72–73, plates 6B–F.

50. Ibid., p. 78, plates 9A and 9D.

51. Ibid., pp. 130–131, plates 31A, 31F through 31H.

52. Ibid., p. 340, plates 100A and 100B for comparison.

53. Ibid., pp. 330–331, plates 94 A and 94B compared to plates 94C through 94F.

54. Ibid., pp. 353–355, plates 105A compared to plates 105B through 105E

55. Kenneth Clark, *Monuments of Vision* (London: John Murray Publishers, 1981), p. 68.

56. Wilhelm Geiger, ed. and trans., *Cūlavaṃsa (Being the More Recent Part of the Mahavamsa)*, 2 vols. (Colombo: Ceylon Government Information Dept., 1953; Pali Text Society Translation Series 18 and 20), 1: 10.

57. Ibid., 36.

58. *Epigraphia Zeylanica*, 7 vols. (London: Oxford University Press, 1904–), 3:234.

59. Ibid., 2: 113.

60. *Cūlavaṃsa* 1: 17.

61. *Nikāya Sanghrāhaya*, p. 24.

62. Epigrapha Zeylanica, 3: 67.

CHAPTER 5

Candrakīrti on the Medieval Military Culture of South India

KAREN C. LANG

Candrakīrti (ca. 550–650 CE) wrote commentaries on the works of Nāgārjuna and Āryadeva, in the late sixth to early seventh century, when royal patronage of Brahmiṇ and Jain temples eclipsed the generous support once given to Buddhists and their institutions. In his commentary on Āryadeva's *Catuḥśataka,* Candrakīrti refutes Brahmanical and Jain beliefs and practices and presents a vigorous defense of Buddhism, perhaps, to counteract the declining support Buddhism received in court circles. In the fourth chapter, he attacks the entrenched military culture that plagued medieval South India, as the Cālukya dynasty kings and their rivals, the Pallavas and Pāṇḍyas, struggled for supremacy. In a literary debate with an unnamed royal adversary, Candrakīrti defends the Buddhist values of compassion and nonviolence.

We have little historically reliable information about Candrakīrti's life. Most scholars assume that Candrakīrti was active sometime between 550 and 650 CE because in his works he criticizes other Buddhist authors, Dharmapāla, Vasubandhu, Dignāga, and Bhāvaviveka, who lived in the sixth century or earlier.[1] According to the sixteenth-century religious history (*chos 'byung*) of Tārānātha,[2] Candrakīrti was born in South India and entered a monastery, where he mastered all the Buddhist scriptures. Tārānātha places Candrakīrti's birth in Samanta during the reign of King Harṣa's son, a date that is too late since the father's reign ended in 647 CE. The location of Candrakīrti's birthplace in South India, however, is more promising. Samanta ("flatlands") most likely refers to the delta formed by the Krishna River and the Godavari, the river Candrakīrti refers to as "the dark daughter of the southern ocean."

Numerous Buddhist institutions once flourished in the fertile region of the Krishna and Godavari river valleys, now modern Andhra Pradesh. Buddhism had the support of Sātavāhana dynasty kings and the female members of the succeeding Ikṣvākus dynasty. Donors' inscriptions at Buddhist sites indicate support for these Buddhist institutions continued into the early medieval period. Two-way monastic travel back and forth between South India and Sri Lanka maintained the Buddhist connection between these two regions at least until the sixth century.[3] Sixth-century copperplate inscriptions found in the Godavari region indicate that Harivarman, of the Pṛthivimūla family, vassals (*sāmanta*) of the Viṣṇukuṇḍin kings, had constructed a new monastery at Gunapashapura for Sri Lankan monks and allocated the revenue of a village for their support: "the village Kattacheruvulu was donated, along with exemptions from all taxation, for the provision of the four requisites for the noble community of monks from the four directions, present and future, living in the great monastery which he himself had built on the hilltop[4] at Gunapashapura."[5] When the Chinese pilgrim, Hsüan-tsang (596–664 CE), visited the region a century later, support for Buddhist monasteries had declined. Hsuan-tsang reports only twenty monasteries remained active while there were hundreds of flourishing Śaivite temples.[6]

Nāgārjuna and Āryadeva advised Sātavāhana dynasty kings and in the Deccan region the Madhyamaka School prospered.[7] Joseph Walser's research suggests Yajñaśri, who ruled from Amaravati (ca. 175–204 CE), as the most likely Sātavāhana patron and recipient of Nāgārjuna's *Ratnāvalī,* which was composed "somewhere in the Lower Krishna Valley."[8] With the decline of royal patronage, Buddhist institutions in the Krishna and Godavari river valleys succumbed to the prevailing tide of medieval Śaivite devotion. One of the few Buddhist sites still active in the seventh century was Jaggayyapeta.[9] A seventh-century inscription on the base of a Buddha image found near the Jaggayyapeta *Stūpa* credits Candraprabhā, "the disciple of a disciple of Nāgārjuna," with installing the image.[10] While it is tempting to identify Candrakīrti with this unknown Mādhyamika, this identification remains uncertain. What is certain is Candrakīrti's vigorous opposition to the military culture that dominated his native South India. Against the lust for power, the pride in position, and the defense of violence, values characteristic of the Śaivite rulers who conquered the Deccan, Candrakīrti argued for generosity, restraint, and nonviolence.

The Viṣṇukuṇḍin Kings and the Tummalagudem Copperplates

Not all the kings who ruled over the Deccan during the sixth and seventh centuries were Śaivite. The Śaivite affiliation of the Viṣṇukuṇḍin dynasty, ruling central and eastern parts of Andhra from the fifth to the seventh century, has been challenged by two medieval copperplate donative inscriptions found in the village of Tummalagudem.[11] These copperplates, were the "hard copies" of less enduring materials that recorded medieval land grants made by a king or his royal administrators to Brahmins or religious institutions. Along with the donation of the land (or the village), the grant provided its recipients with certain privileges or benefits, most often exemption from taxation. While the record of the donation was the ostensible reason behind the copperplates' creation, much of the inscription is dedicated to lengthy and often elaborate praises of the king and his royal ancestors.[12] Both Tummalagudem land grants record the donation of villages to a Buddhist monastery for its maintenance. The anonymous composers of these two copperplate inscriptions depict several Viṣṇukuṇḍin kings as Buddhist patrons. M. Rama Rao identifies three of the Viṣṇukuṇḍin kings, Govindavarma I, Vikramendra II, and Govindavarma II, as "Buddhist devotees." S. Sankaranaryan concedes that Govindavarma I was a Buddhist (as both Tummalagudem plates state) but contends that Govindavarma and Vikramendra II should both be considered Śaivites since other land grants describe them as worshiping at the feet of Śiva.[13] With the exception of the Tummalagudem grant issued in the name of Govindavarma, which salutes the Buddha, Viṣṇukuṇḍin land grants "invariably start with salutations to Śiva—the Lord of Śrīparvata."[14]

The chronology of the Viṣṇukuṇḍin dynasty kings and of the two Tummalagudem copperplates is also disputed. S. Sankaranarayanan and A. M Shastri believe the Govindavarma grant is earlier and that the king identified by Rama Rao and V. V. Mirashi as Govindavarma II is the same person as the fifth-century founder of the dynasty, Govindavarma I. Sankaranarayanan recognizes that the paleographic evidence does not support a fifth-century date for the copperplate he attributes to Govindavarman and suggests original land grant that fallen into disuse was revised during the time of Vikramendravarman II by the Buddhist monks of the Paramamahādevī-vihāra. Sankaranarayan reaches this conclusion because of "the stress on the king's leaning toward the Buddhist religion, the glorification of the Buddha and the Buddhist clergy, and the excessive use of Buddhist technical terms."[15] Mirashi comes to the opposite conclusion: Govindavarma II was different from his namesake and flourished later than Vikramendrabhaṭṭāraka, who issued the other set of Tummalgudem plates. He also rejects Sankaranarayanan's "gratuitous assumption" that the original charter had fallen into disuse: "The real cause of the developed characters is that the grant was made and incised at a later date."[16] I have followed Rao and Mirashi in the belief that the copperplates refer to two different kings—Govindavarma I and

Govindavarma II—and that the copperplate issued by Vikramendra II precedes that of Govindavarma II.[17]

Vikramendra II fought a Pallava king, Siṁhavarma, for control over eastern Andhra Pradesh. Sankaranaryanan's study of the land grants of both kings, indicates "beyond a doubt it was Siṃhavarma, the Pallava, who was the aggressor by invading the Vengi country" and threatening the fortune of Viṣṇukuṇḍin family.[18] One of the Tummalagudem copperplates records that in 566/67 CE the righteous conqueror (*dharmavijayin*), King Vikramendra II, on his return from battle with Pallava forces, which he broke like a twig (*pallavabhaṅga*) gave "for the use of the of noble monks from four directions a village called Irundoro, along with all its custom duties, and with an exemption from the burden of all taxation." The monastic institution that received this generous gift, Paramabhāṭṭarikā Mahāvihāra, takes its name from Queen Paramabhāṭṭarikā, Vikramendra II's great-great grandmother, whose generous support enabled it to be built.[19] The inscription also praises her husband, Govindarāja, the Viṣṇukuṇḍin dynasty's founder, for his "confidence in the Buddha's teachings" and for "the collection of unlimited excellent merit he has acquired by building many great monasteries." Its anonymous composer credits Govindarāja with ornamenting the entire Deccan "with the crest jewels of marvelous *stūpas* and monasteries." One of these monasteries, named after him, is referred to in a fifth-century rock inscription found near Hyderabad.[20] The Tummalagudem copperplate also characterizes this generous couple's grandson Vikramendra I (518–28) as a "preeminent devotee of the Buddha (*paramasaugata*)."

The copperplate inscriptions of Vikramendra II and Govindavarma II both indicate that the kings' transference of property is made to the monastic community.[21] The Paramabhāṭṭarikā monastery's fortunes seem to have declined by the end of the sixth century. The second copperplate inscription records that a later Viṣṇukuṇḍin king, Govindavarma II, restored the monastery's dilapidated and damaged sections. The inscription memorializes the king's donation of two villages to the community, described as "the unsurpassed field of merit, the noble community of monks from the four directions, traveling in three vehicles." It indicates that the king's support extended to the Mahāyāna vehicle of the *bodhisattva* and the lesser vehicle of the disciple and the solitary Buddha. This generous king and his queen supplied the monastic community with a long list of material goods—lamps, incense, sandalwood paste, flowers, banners, food, drink, beds, seats, and medicine. The first items in the list provided for the worship of Buddha; the latter items provided for the monks' support.

Govindavarma's meritorious grant of two villages provides much more than basic necessities for the monks of the Paramabhāṭṭarikā monastery. The copperplate inscription contains considerable detail about the benefits conferred along with the transference of the property.

> Two villages named Ermadala and Penkaparu, preceded by the ritual pouring of water, were given. The treasure hidden underground, deposits underground, fines, tenants' fees, unpaid labor, taxes on the land, a share of the produce, and other supplies provided by the tenants were presented. Soldiers, police, envoys, herdsmen, and royal agents were not allowed entry.[22]

In regard to "treasure hidden underground," Krishna Prasad Babu notes that these villages were located in a district of Andhra Pradesh that once was an iron mining area. Early Indian sources refer to mines as an important item of royal income. The ownership of iron mines also involves control over the supply of iron agricultural implements to the villagers.[23] The legal language transferring the property implies that the monastery had the right to the income provided by a variety of taxes—tolls collected on its roads, taxes paid by tenant farmers who used the land to cultivate crops or graze livestock, and the traditional one sixth share of the grain that the farmers were required to give the king.[24] Govindavarma's grant also specifies immunity from the entry of royal troops and officials. Unless specifically exempted, Nilakantha Sastri writes, villages were liable to visits from royal officers for digging salt, the manufacture of sugar, and arrest of culprits. They also had to accommodate touring officers with beds, boiled rice, milk, curds, grass, fuel, vegetables, as well as providing free labor on specified public works.[25] The grant enabled the monks to employ this unpaid labor for the cultivation of their own agricultural fields.

The king sows the seeds of his generosity in the most fertile of fields, the *Saṇgha*, "the unsurpassed field of merit." In providing generously for the monastic community, the king intends also that merit, the "auspicious roots" planted by his gifts will not be severed. The merit generated by these donations is intended for king's own well-being and also for relieving his mother, father, and all beings of the suffering of complete ignorance.[26] Similar statements about the donor's intention of benefiting parents and others occur in Buddhist donative inscriptions found throughout India. Schopen indicates that when parents are mentioned in Mahāyāna inscriptions as the intended beneficiaries of this implicit transference of merit it is in conjunction with the category of "all beings" and "the merit from that act is always explicitly stated to be for the attainment of supreme knowledge."[27] The transference of Govindavarman's merit to all beings implies that he is a *bodhisattva*-king intent on liberating all beings from suffering.

The Buddhist character of the second Tummalagudem copperplate is transparent. The inscription begins with a invocation to "the fully enlightened and compassionate Lord Buddha, who has shown the wise the path to *nirvāṇa*."[28] The inscription goes on to describe Govindavarma II as a *bodhisattva* whose "great altruistic intention of enlightenment is produced for the sake of protecting the realm of all sentient beings." This royal *bodhisattva* seems intent on perfecting the virtue of generosity. The poet portrays him as beloved by his people because of his generosity in repeatedly giving up all that he owns: villages, fields, gold, elephants, horses, cattle, vehicles, houses, furniture, food, drink, and servants of both sexes. He donates this wealth, which the poet is careful to say that he has acquired properly, to monks, Brahmins, and the poor. In addition to giving away his property, Govindavarma II constructs new temples, monasteries, halls, ponds, and wells, and repairs old ones, an ambitious building project that rivaled that of his namesake, Govindavarma I. The inscription concludes with wish that the Viṣṇukuṇḍin dynasty may rule the earth as long as the sun and the moon remain in the sky. Despite the wishes of this anonymous composer, the Viṣṇukuṇḍin reign soon ended, replaced by Cālukya dynasty kings with a quite different agenda.

The Cālukya Dynasty and Ravikīrti's Panegyric Inscription at Aihole

Mutual conflict among the Cālukya dynasty kings and their South Indian rivals, the Pallavas and the Pāṇḍyas, began in the middle of the sixth century.[29] Pulakeśin I (543–566 CE) established Cālukya sovereignty by erected a hill fortress at Vatapi and performed a horse sacrifice and a golden egg ceremony to proclaim himself as an independent lord. Ali writes:

> Since Vedic times the horse sacrifice had been the liturgical act for articulating an imperial order through combat. A king's performance of the horse sacrifice was a political challenge to other ruling kings. The golden embryo, however, was not a Vedic sacrifice but instead One of the "great gifts" elaborated in the Purāṇas. Future Cālukya kings saw Pulakeśin as not only the performer of Vedic sacrifices but also as having "emerged from the golden egg."[30]

By releasing a horse to roam free for a year and threatening to fight any king who would impede it, Pulakeśin I established himself as lord over all land it crossed. The performance of the golden egg ceremony, in which the royal donor chants "formerly I was born from my mother but only as a mortal, now being born of you, I shall assume a divine body"[31] associates the king with divinity.

Pulakeśin I left his hill fortress of Vatapi in the western Deccan, eight miles from Aihole, where Ravikīrti would celebrate his exploits, to conquer territories bordering the Krishna River. D. C. Sircar regards the Aihole inscription as "fairly clear and trustworthy" in its account of the rise and early history of the Cālukyas, though it suffers from defects common to inscriptions: limits of space, attention to the conventions of poetry, and the willingness of the court poet to exaggerate the accomplishments of his royal patron and his ancestors.[32] Most eulogistic inscriptions are "stiff and pedantic" in style and suggest, as Salomon says, that "becoming a favored poet may have often have had more to do with political than literary skills.[33] Ravikīrti's composition, which takes Kālidāsa's epic poem on the accomplishments of Rāma, the *Raghuvaṁśa* as its inspiration, raises above the pedestrian work of most court poets.[34]

Ravikīrti composed in 634–635 CE a eulogy of the Cālukya dynasty that celebrates their achievements as warriors, not as donors. The changing religious landscape of South India is seen in this stone inscription, which celebrates the construction of a Jain temple, by its royal patron, Pulakeśin II.[35] Ravikīrti portrays (v. 5) the first Cālukya king, Pulakeśin I, also known as Jayasiṁhavallabha, in the thick of combat where "horses, soldiers, elephants, reeled, and fell under the blows of many hundreds of weapons and thousands of blazing swords sparked a macabre dance of headless corpses." His son, Kīrtivarma (567–597 CE), continued the dynasty's eastward expansion. Ravikīrti (v. 9) depicts him as "a deadly night" for his enemies whose fortunes had enticed him. At his death, his younger brother Maṅgaleśa (597–609 CE) took control and through his own violent conquests won his enemies' fortunes (v. 12) "after repelling with the sheen of hundreds of blazing swords the dark mass of [enemy] elephants." Kīrtivarma's son, Pulakeśin II, successfully fought his uncle for control of the kingdom (vv. 14–15).

The remainder of Ravikīrti's poem in praise of the Cālukya dynasty (vv. 15–32) concentrates on the glorious victories of his patron, Pulakeśin II (609–654/5 CE). The court poet depicts (vv. 16–17) this warlord's brilliance overpowering the hostile darkness as he makes his enemies know "the taste of fear." Radiant like Śiva, the destroyer (v. 21), he extends his dynasty's domain further east into the Krishna and Godavari river valleys. In a deceptively beautiful simile (v. 28), Ravikīrti compares the water of the Kunala Lake "red with the blood of men slain with a multitude of weapons" to "the sky red at twilight." At Kunala Lake, Pulakeśin II defeated the Viṣṇukuṇḍin forces and brought eastern Andhra country under

Cālukya control.[36] The Cālukya understood their domain as the hub of the sphere of command of a world ruler. These poets' use of royal titles such as "great king among kings," "paramount overlord," "beloved of earth and fortune" and "worthy of highest honor" emphasizes the overwhelming power of these South Indian kings who considered themselves "rulers not simply of the Deccan but of the entire earth."[37]

Ravikīrti was not the first South Indian poet to employ these striking images to depict the royal occupation of war. Several centuries earlier, the Tamil poet Kāppiyāṟṟukappiyaṉār, wrote of his king's victories on the battlefield:

> Headless bodies dance about
> before they fall to the ground.
> Blood glows, like the sky before nightfall,
> in the red center of the battlefield.
> Demons dance there.
> And your kingdom is an unfailing harvest
> of victorious wars.[38]

This poem and others collected in early anthologies of Tamil poetry (ca. 100–250 CE) speak of an unstable society of small kingdoms at war with one another. The poems glorify the battlefield ("the field of carnage resplendent while arrow-drops rained down and shining swords were lightning in your camp as you gained victory!")[39] Several centuries later, South Indian kingdoms are still at war and anonymous poets attached to royal courts praise their patron's conquests on land grants.

The Timmapuram land grant praises Kubja Viṣṇuvardhana, the younger brother of Pulakeśin II, who, with "the blade of his own sword subdued an entire circle of vassals in his conquest over eastern Andhra Pradesh.[40] Other inscriptions similarly describe the brute force used by Jayasiṁhavallabha, the nephew of Pulakeśin II, in his numerous victories over rival kings in the Krishna and Godavari river valleys.[41] It is not only the skillful use of the sword that makes these Cālukya kings successful in the Deccan. Ronald Davidson draws attention also to the poets' deliberate invocation of an erotic undercurrent to this tide that swept over South India. The divine virility of the Cālukya dynasty's founder is so irresistible that Pulakeśin I easily wins fortune's favor. Pulakeśin II's conquest of Vanavāsī is "rendered in a language that portrays the city as coy as a woman and the warlord as her ardent lover; their embrace depicted as the dalliance of idle courtiers, not the bloody pillaging of a terrified population." While Ravikīrti's use of heroic and erotic sentiments (*rasa*) to describe a royal patron, is not unique, Davidson concludes that Śaivite kings and the court poets who celebrate their victories, seem particularly susceptible to such seductive rhetoric.[42]

Candrakīrti on the Proper Role of Kings

Candrakīrti's rhetoric is far different. He criticizes the king's willingness to allow passion to dominate his behavior, but he directs most of his criticism toward the necessary submission of the king to his Brahmin power brokers. Instead of helping him to make decisions, all their advice makes him appear indecisive and foolish. In a particularly savage analogy, Candrakīrti compares the king to trained monkeys and dogs that must look to their masters for instruction before they act.[43] He is equally forthright in undermining the heroic claims of a king who leads his men into battle. His harsh condemnation of the royal occupation of war may well reflect the persistent military adventures of the Deccan's Chālukya dynasty kings, fueled by belief in their divine right to conquer.

Candrakīrti repudiates the conception of the king's divinity. In the *Mahābhārata*, the sage Bhīṣma informs Yudhiṣṭhira's (12.68.40–47) that the king is a god in a man's form. He can assume any of five different divine forms: Agni's form when he scorches with his anger those who deceive him, the form of the ever-present sun when he sends out spies, Yama when he punishes the wicked, Death when he destroys the wicked, and Vaiśravaṇa, god of wealth, when he grants prosperity to the righteous. Candrakīrti satirizes the divine king's polymorphous nature with the example of a royal dancer. The dancer, through the artifice of cosmetics and costumes, can assume any one of five roles: a king, a minister, a priest, a householder, and a servant. Each of the roles the dancer plays is temporary. Candrakīrti warns the king that his role of king is temporary and the stage he dances on is the cosmos, with its five potential places of rebirth (gods, humans, animals, ghosts, and hell-beings).[44] Not only is the king at present not a god in the form of a man but also he is unlikely to become a god in future because of the perilous nature of his royal role. The king, who abuses his position because of his passion for wealth and women, will reap the consequences of his ignorant and immoral behavior when he is reborn in a far less exalted state.

In Candrakīrti's view, kingship, rather than a divine right, is a human institution. Candrakīrti relies on an account of the king's origins similar to those found in the *Aggaññasuttana* (D III.84–96) and in the *Mahāvastu* (I.338–348). The people of the first eon chose the most capable man to protect the fields and paid him one-sixth of the harvested grain.[45] The king's pride in his royal position is unwarranted because he is economically dependent the taxes his people pay. Though his arguments primarily attack the king's pride, Candrakīrti implies that the people have the moral right to overthrow an immoral king. Only kings who govern with generosity and compassion have legitimate moral authority and are worthy of praise and emulation.

The inscriptions that eulogize Viṣṇukuṇḍin and Cālukya kings describe some of them as world rulers. One Tummalagudem copperplate describes a Śaivite Viṣṇukuṇḍin king, Indrabhaṭṭarakavarma (528–555 CE), as achieving sovereign power over the land of other world rulers through the blows struck by his blazing sword. In his eulogy of Cālukya dynasty's kings, Ravikīrti similarly glorifies Pulakeśin II's use of force to triumph over rival kingdoms in all four directions. Candrakīrti, in contrast, characterizes the world rulers as moral exemplars, who rely on treatises that advocate righteous behavior. These righteous kings protect the people just as they would protect their own beloved sons. In contrast, present day "kings, born in the age of discord (*kali yuga*) who rely on the evil nature of their own opinions, and are devoted to their desire for wealth alone take as authority texts that condone unrighteous behavior." These merciless kings become predators and devastate the entire world. The exercise of war exposes the predatory nature of kings and the devastation their violent propensities inflict on the world. War in medieval India was not a benign affair, as Davidson indicates. The devastation brought about through warfare results from "military foraging, the violence inflicted on crops and citizens outside the battlefield, and such practices as burning of cities, poisoning wells, and enslavement of populations."[46] The violent and ruthless behavior warfare calls for has no place in the Buddhist system of values.

War involves the king in competition with his rivals for land, livestock and the labor of the conquered people. Candrakīrti denounces the king's pursuit of the spoils of war as immoral and dishonorable. Against the opinion that it is right to attack the weak points of an enemy's defense, he argues that if it is not wrong for a king to attack his enemies and reap the spoils of war, then thieves who steal do no wrong. He takes this argument to an absurd conclusion. He implies the thieves who take advantage of ineffective watchmen and steal the property of the rich are not doing anything wrong because they have followed the royal thief's example (and are even better at stealing than he is)![47]

Even more than plundered goods, kings seek fame and honor from the battlefield. Candrakīrti denies that violent actions committed in battle have any redeeming value. As scriptural support for his belief in the king's right to wage war, Candrakīrti has his royal adversary quote *Bhagavad Gītā* (II.37): "If you are killed, you will gain heaven. Or if you conquer, you will enjoy the earth." In the preceding verses (II.31–36), Kṛṣṇa urges the reluctant Arjuna not to fear his own duty, for nothing suits a warrior better than to wage a righteous war. If he fails to wage such a war, instead of fame, he reaps infamy and the contempt of friends and foes alike for his cowardice. In response to this line of argument, Candrakīrti questions why warriors who sacrifice their lives in battle are respected and people who sacrifice their wealth through obsessive gambling, drinking, and sexual activity are not. He regards the warrior's pursuit of honor on the battlefield as a dangerous obsession, which places him in harm's way. The harm a warrior faces comes not only from the blows of his enemies' swords but also from his own deliberate use of weapons. "Surely, how can it be right for someone who has no compassion, who has cruel intentions towards his enemy, who enthusiastically attacks in order to kill, and raises up his sword with a view towards bringing it down on his enemy's head," Candrakīrti asks, "to go to heaven when his enemy kills him?" He emphatically rejects the king's claim that going to heaven is certain for the warrior who dies in battle.

Candrakīrti mocks the royal warrior's belief that "of all kinds of gifts, that of giving the body in battle is the highest"[48] by telling an amusing story of a cowherd's foolish wife who attempts to give her father-in-law the highest of a woman's gifts, her body in bed:

> A certain cowherd's wife treated her father-in-law very disrespectfully while her husband was away from home. When his son returned, the old cowherd told him what had happened. He said: "If your wife ever again treats me disrespectfully, I will not stay in your house!" The cowherd was unafraid of his wife and devoted to his father. Consequently, he reprimanded his wife and told her: "If you ever again treat my father with contempt, you will not live in my house. You should do for him even what is very difficult to do, and you should give to him even what is very difficult to give." "Yes, yes," she promised him. The next time her husband was away from home, she very timidly and with great respect attended her father-in-law. During the day, she washed and oiled his body, presented him with flower garlands, and offered him food and drink. At night, after she had washed his feet with warm water and rubbed them with oil, she took off her clothes, and naked

> she proceeded to enter into an illicit union. She began to climb into his bed. The old cowherd exclaimed: "You evil woman! What have you begun to do?" She replied, "My husband told me that I should do for you what is very difficult to do and give you what is very difficult to give. There is nothing more difficult to do and nothing is more difficult to give." The old cowherd angrily retorted: "This is a good strategy to make me leave! You should be pleased! I will never again stay in this house!" After he said that, he left. His son returned and when he did not see his father, he questioned his wife: "What did you do?" She replied: "Husband, I deprived your father of nothing. With great respect and with pleasure, I bathed him, rubbed him with oil, and gave him food. I offered him everything!" Her husband sharply rebuked her and drove her from his house. After he had appeased his father, he brought the old man back into the house.[49]

This story illustrates the contempt in which Candrakīrti holds the notion of sacrificial death on the battlefield. This wife's misguided effort to serve her lord ends in dishonor and exile. Candrakīrti's comparison of warriors to women may have its roots in fact. Nilakanta Sastri, draws attention to Hsüan-tsang's observation on Cālukya kings' treatment of defeated soldiers: "whenever a general is dispatched on a warlike expedition, although he is defeated and his army destroyed, he is not himself subjected to bodily punishment, only he has to exchange his soldier's dress for that of a woman, much to his shame and disgrace. So many times, those men put themselves to death to avoid such disgrace." Nilakanta Sastri finds corroboration for this curious practice of disgracing soldiers by compelling them to wear women's clothes in Cola inscriptions relating to the Cālukya wars of the eleventh century.[50]

Candrakīrti directs his parting blows to the king's pride in his royal lineage. He undermines the confidence the king has in the purity of his own lineage. He aims a particularly low blow at the king's pride when he implies that the king cannot be certain about his royal birth. Since women often deceive their husbands, the king might in fact be a bastard. If the queen had an adulterous liaison with a lower-class lover, her son would not be a member of the royal class. He concludes that the present-day kings have their origins in the lower class.[51] His comment may reflect the rhetoric of the Pūraṇas rather than the actual class status of the Andhra kings of his time. Sircar notes that inscriptions often fabricate a respectable genealogy for rulers whose ancestors were not from royal lineages.[52] The Tummalagudem inscriptions describe the ancestry of the Viṣṇukuṇḍin dynasty as mixture of the brilliance of both priestly and royal lineages. Sankaranarayanan finds no conflict with this upper-caste designation and the Puranic traditions that designate Andhra kings as *vṛiṣala;* the word may signify "a wicked man" and not "a person of the fourth caste."[53] A later twelfth-century inscription on a pillar at the entrance to the Buddhist temple at Amaravati, however, does depict the ruling monarchs' lower-caste origins: these kings were born from Brahmā's feet.[54]

Righteous Kings and the *Bodhisattva* Ideal

The fourth chapter of the *Catuḥśataka* concludes with Āryadeva's observation (IV.25) that the king's pride in his sovereignty will vanish once he has seen others with equal or superior power. This verse and Candrakīrti's commentary on it suggest that the superior power they have in mind encompasses both the power of the righteous king and that of the compassionate *bodhisattva* whose career chapter 5 of the *Catuḥśataka* examines. King Aśoka (third century BCE) is the model of the righteous king. Aśoka's own edicts indicate his remorse for the violence and suffering caused in the victorious war against the Kaliṅga people and his hope that his successors will renounce the use of force and conquer with by righteousness, since righteousness is of value in both this world and the next. Aśoka's inscriptions, however, never use the title *bodhisattva* to refer to him.[55] Candrakīrti may never read Aśoka's inscriptions, but he is familiar with the legendary stories and refers to the infamous prison that exemplified Aśoka's merciless cruelty before his conversion to Buddhism.[56] After his conversion, Aśoka becomes a righteous king who uses his wealth and power to benefit his people and support Buddhist religious institutions. The *Aśokāvadāna* describes him not only as a righteous king but also as a world ruler who governs the entire Indian subcontinent.[57] These legends, John Strong suggests, the portrait of King Aśoka resembles "the bodhisattva ideal" found in Mahāyāna texts: "like the bodhisattva, he has a curious combination of personal striving for his own enlightenment and compassion for others."[58]

In the *Ratnāvalī,* Nāgārjuna advises the king that he can benefit himself and his people by following Buddhist precepts and ruling in a just, compassionate, and nonviolent manner. He encourages him also to perfect the virtues of a *bodhisattva,* beginning with generosity. The king's wealth should be donated to construct *stūpas,* temples, and Buddha images seated on lotuses (III.31–33). Walser finds evidence of such Buddha images around Amaravati during Yajñaśri's reign.[59] In the *Ratnāvalī*'s fifth and final chapter (V.41–60), Nāgārjuna depicts the royal *bodhisattva* progressing through the stages of the *bodhisattva* path, as he becomes an increasingly more powerful and influential king. On earth the *bodhisattva* becomes a world ruler ruling over the four continents and, in series of ascending heavenly realms, he becomes the lord of the gods. The connection between *bodhisattvas* and world rulers is reinforced by Āryadeva's rhetorical question (V.23): "Why shouldn't a certain [*bodhisattva*], who always is born precisely because of his control over mind, become a ruler over the entire world?" Candrakīrti comments on this verse that *bodhisattvas* chose to be reborn voluntarily as world rulers out of their compassion for people in need.

Close connections between the Buddhist communities of South India and Sri Lanka were maintained as Buddhist monastics, including Āryadeva, traveled from one region to another.[60] Along with these itinerant monks and nuns, there may have come Mahāyāna ideas about righteous kings and compassionate *bodhisattvas*. John Holt points out that evidence for the "fusion of the two ideals of Buddhist kingship and bodhisattva model of piety" can be found in Sri Lankan chronicles and inscriptions. The *Mahāvaṃsa* praises Sirisanghabodhi (251–253 CE) for his compassion and describes him as a "great being," a title that usually refers to Mahāyāna *bodhisattvas*.[61] Holt reports that Mahāyāna supporters brought the worship of the *bodhisattva* Avalokiteśvara to Sri Lanka during a time of Pallava cultural influence in the seventh through tenth centuries. The royal sponsorship of images of Avalokiteśvara connected royal power and the divine compassion of *bodhisattvas*.[62] A tenth-century inscription attributed to Mahinda IV (956–972 CE) concludes with this statement:

> The regulations thus enacted should always be maintained with due regard to the descendants of our dynasty, the Kśatriya lords devoted to the Buddha, who have received the assurance [made by] the omniscient Lord of the Sages, the pinnacle of the Śākya race, that none but the Bodhisattvas would become kings in prosperous Laṅkā . . .[63]

A fifteenth-century inscription refers to Parākramabāhu VI as Bosat Parākramabāhu, and an earlier king, Vijayabāhu IV (1270–72 CE) was popularly known as "Bosat Vijayabāhu."[64] The *Cūlavaṁsa* records the meriorious activities of these royal *bodhisattvas* and other Sri Lankan kings who used their wealth to support Buddhist institutions. Mahinda IV restored temples and monasteries and provided the monks with food, clothing, medicine, and relief from taxation, as well as donations of lamps, incense, flowers, and perfumes for the Buddha. Vijayabāhu built new monasteries, restored ancient ones, supported monks, commissioned images of the Buddha and enshrined his relics. Parākramabāhu VI provided robes for monks, repaired their dilapidated monasteries, had a new monastery built, and donated villages and land for its support.[65]

The last of the kings the *Cūlavaṁsa* praises as an exemplary patron of Buddhism is Kīrti Śri Rājasinha (1747–82 CE).[66] He used his wealth and influence revitalize Buddhism by introducing new ordination lineages from Thailand, sponsoring translations of Buddhist texts and religious festivals, and restoring dilapidated monasteries and temples. The *Cūlavaṁsa* and the numerous land grants issued in Kīrti Śrī's name represent him as tireless patron of Buddhism and all its institutions:

> Having thus revived Buddhism, (the king) repaired all the dagobas [reliquary monuments] and viharas [temples with monastic residences], which had been in ruins . . . [commanding] the produce of the land within [nearby] boundaries to be utilized for the maintenance of the priests.[67]

Land that had become royal property Kīrti Śrī rededicated as "the Buddha's property" so that its income could be used to provide adjacent monasteries with donations of money, flowers, and oil offerings. His meritorious actions place him securely on the *bodhisattva* path. The copperplate inscription indicates that the king's righteous action in returning this property was undertaken "with a view of securing to himself the benefits resulting from such donations, temporally and spiritually, and to attain nirvāṇa."[68] Temporal and spiritual power converge in Kīrti Śrī, described in eulogistic land grants inscriptions as a great monarch descended from "the illustrious race of Mahā Sammata, the first king on earth" and as a *bodhisattva*, "a candidate for Buddhahood."[69]

The references to the first king on earth in inscriptions praising Kīrti Śrī's rule Sri Lanka and in Candrakīrti's advice to an unknown South Indian king are used with similar intent. Both texts allude to Buddhist scriptures' explanation of the first king's origins: he is chosen for his fitness to serve the people and protect them from harm. In contrast, Hindu scriptures emphasize the divine origins of the royal class. The *Rig Veda* (10.90.12) explains that the gods sacrifice a cosmic man and from his the arms create the royal class. The *Mahābhārata* (12.67–20–32) claims that the gods created the first king so that "the law of the fishes" in which the strong consume the weak would not prevail. Buddhist kingship is based on merit not on the will of the gods. Nāgārjuna states in the *Ratnāvalī* that that merit determines who has access to sovereign power (IV.43). Candrakīrti explains that people become kings, not through an accident of birth, but through the deliberate cultivation of meritorious actions. He compares acquiring a kingdom to learning a trade. The proper training provides those who pursue it with a trade; in the same way, the proper moral training makes certain individuals fit to rule a kingdom. [70]

Candrakīrti's royal opponent supports the position expressed in the *Mahābhārata* (12.68.10): If the king does not wield the rod, the strong would steal from the weak, murderers would go unpunished, elders would receive no respect, and all of civilized society would be in ruins. These sums up the advice given to Yudhiṣṭhira, who is reluctant to assume the throne after the bloody battle that guaranteed his right to rule. Candrakīrti argues that if the king cannot rule in righteous manner, in accord with the Buddhist principles of nonviolence, and compassion, it would be better for him to renounce his kingdom. To illustrate his view that compassionate kings benefit both themselves and those to whom they show compassion, Candrakīrti tells the story of a poor washerman who offers an eloquent excuse for ruining the king's clothes:

> The water of the dark daughter of the southern ocean,
> dear to Viṣṇu, known as the Godavari river,
> companion of the Ganges river,
> which covers the shores for washing,
> is not clear, even though the rainy season has ended,
> because the pestle of your maddened elephant's tusk
> has stirred up grains of sand.[71]

In this tale, the king shows mercy but Candrakīrti reminds this king no plea will ever appease the King of Death. The merciless King of Death wields more power than any king on earth and never shows compassion. The king himself is responsible for stains of his unrighteous reign and will suffer the consequences in the life to come.

Conclusion

We have no evidence to suggest that Candrakīrti's arguments persuaded any South Indian king to follow the model of past righteous kings and generously support Buddhist institutions and values. The medieval history of the Deccan suggests otherwise. Large Buddhist institutions required grants of villages to enable to remain economically viable. Without royal patronage, these grand Buddhist monasteries declined and eventually disappeared, and were replaced by Śaivaite temples. A comparison of the two earlier Tummalagudem donative inscriptions with Ravakīrti's panegyric indicates a considerable shift in the conception of the exemplary king. The anonymous poets who praise the Buddhist Viṣṇukuṇḍin kings describe them as generous donors who gave away their fortunes and took pleasure in providing comfort to their people. Ravikīrti, on the other hand, describes the Cālukya king as seducers of the goddess Śrī, who took pleasure in the sport of war.

When Candrakīrti urges the king to renounce the military culture of violence and follow past righteous kings' examples, he has in mind King Aśoka who repudiated warfare and became a celebrated patron of Buddhism. He is familiar with Nāgārjuna's advice in the *Ratnāvalī*[72] to Sātavāhana kings on the characteristic virtues—generosity, compassion, nonviolence—of *bodhisattva*-kings. During Candrakīrti's lifetime, Buddhist monuments and institutions in the Krishna and Godavari river valleys, once generously supported by the Sātavāhanas, suffered from neglect. He may have known of the Viṣṇukuṇḍin kings' patronage of Buddhism, though it was less extensive. Even these kings were not immune from armed conflict: Vikramendra II's gift to the Paramabhāṭṭarikā Mahāvihāra is made on his return home after his success in defeating a Pallava invasion. The Tummalgudem copperplate land grant issued in his name portrays him as a supremely righteous king and conquering through *Dharma* (*dharmavijayin*) the same epithet applied to Aśoka centuries earlier. Tummalgudem land grant of Govindavarma describes him in ways reminiscent of an even earlier Buddhist royal. Like the *bodhisattva* Vessantara, he gives away everything he owns: villages, land, elephants, horses, chariots, gold and jewelry, and servants of both sexes. These inscriptions, which speak of the merit that results in the king's generosity, reinforce the Buddhist belief that merit makes and sustains a king's rule.

The medieval inscriptions at Aihole and Tummalagudem copperplates' imperial histories fail to meet "the contemporary standards of objectivity, precision, and comprehensiveness that guide modern historical thought."[73] Candrakīrti's views on kingship are likewise not guided by objectivity; his references to the righteous kings of the past are intended to transform the behavior of contemporary monarchs. His text reflects the type of historical thought that Jonathan Walters finds characteristic of the medieval Sinhala chronicles. Walters describes the concerns of these chronicles as "kamma-based": The Sinhala chronicles ask these questions: What kind of merit and demerit did the king acquire during his reign? How will this affect his future destiny? Did he promote the Buddha's teachings and exemplify charitable behavior or not?[74] These are the questions that Candrakīrti poses to this unnamed South Indian King. These critical questions that address the king's own welfare and the welfare of his people seem to go unheard and unanswered as a culture of warfare and violence pervaded the Deccan in the sixth and seventh centuries. Buddhists were not successful in retaining patronage of South Indian kings, Davidson writes, because they were not as "open to negotiations about issues of violence, power, and self-aggrandizement as were the medieval Śaiva representatives."[75] Candrakīrti has no intention in his literary dialogue of settling for anything less than the king's full compliance with the Buddhist values of nonviolence, compassion, and self-effacement.

Notes

1. Candrakīrti attacks Dharmapāla (530–561 CE) and Vasubandhu (320–380 CE) for misinterpreting Āryadeva's views. He criticizes in the *Prasannapadā* Bhāvaviveka (500–570 CE) and Dignāga (480–540 CE). His failure to mention Dharmakīrti (600–660 CE) suggests that the latter's works were unknown to him. David Seyfort Ruegg, *The Literature of the Madhyamaka School of Philosophy in India* (Wiesbaden: Harrassowitz, 1981), p. 71, and Tom J. F. Tillemans, *Materials for the Study of Āryadeva, Dharmapāla and Candrakīrti* (Wien: Arbeitskreis für Tibetische und Buddhistische Studien Universitat, 1990), p. 13, suggest 600–660 CE as the likely dates; Christian Lindtner, "Candrakīrti's *Pañcaskandhaprakaraṇa*, I. Tibetan Text," *Acta Orientalia* 40 (1979): 91 proposes 530–600 CE.

2. Lama Chimpa and Alaka Chattopadhyaya, *Tārānātha's History of Buddhism in India* (Simla: Institute for Advanced Study, 1970), pp. 198–199, 203–206.

3. I. K. Sarma, *Studies in Early Buddhist Monuments and Brahmi Inscriptions of Andhradesa* (Nagpur: Dattsons, 1988), 13–23. Cf. Ajay Mitra Shastri, *Early History of the Deccan: Problems and Perspectives* (Delhi: Sundeep Prakashan, 1987), pp. 104–105 and D. Jithendra Das, *The Buddhist Architecture in Andhra* (New Delhi: Books & Books, 1993), pp. 36, 83. For references on the continuance of these relations between South India and Sri Lanka into the fourteenth century, see R. A. L. H. Gunawardhana, *Robe and Plough: Monasticism and Economic Interest in Early Medieval Sri Lanka* (Tucson: University of Arizona Press), 1979, pp. 262–266.

4. D. Jinthendra Das, *The Buddhist Architecture in Andhra* (New Delhi: Books & Books, 1993), p. 82 notes that Buddhists in Andhra preferred hilltops for the establishment of *vihāras*: the hilltops afforded seclusion for the monks and were generally flat, which facilitated the construction.

5. S. Sankaranarayanan, "Two Viṣṇukuṇḍi Charters from Tummalagudem," *Epigrahica Andrica* II (1977): 186.

6. Samuel Beal, *Si-Yu-Ki: Buddhist Records of the Western World* (Delhi: Motilal Banarsidass, 1884 [1969]), vol. 2, p. 221.

7. The chronology of the Sātavāhanas is still uncertain. See G. Yazdani, *The Early History of the Deccan* (New York: Oxford University Press, 1960), vol. 1, pp. 72–147. Etienne Lamotte, *Le Traité de la grand vertu de sagesse de Nāgārjuna*

(Louvain: Institut Orientaliste, 1949, [1966]), vol. 1, pp. xi–xiv, and 1970 vol. III, li–lv discusses the connections between members of this dynasty and Nāgārjuna and Āryadeva. Joseph Walser, "Nagarjuna and the *Ratnāvalī*: New Ways to Date an Old Philosopher," *Journal of the International Association of Buddhist Studies* 25 (2002): 249–262 using a variety or sources—literary, archeological, and art historical—makes a compelling case for the association of Nāgārjuna with the Sātavāhana dynasty.

8. Joseph Walser, Nāgārjuna and the *Ratnāvalī*: New Ways to Date an Old Philosopher," *Journal of the International Association of Buddhist Studies* 25 (2002): pp. 261–262. Two later Sātavāhana kings, Candraśri (210–213 or 210–220 CE) and Puḷumāvi II (213–220 or 220–227 CE), are the other possible patrons.

9. Ronald M. Davidson, *Indian Esoteric Buddhism: A Social History of the Movement* (New York: Columbia University Press, 2002), pp. 90–91.

10. James Burgess, *The Buddhist Stupas of Amaravati and Jaggayyapeta* (Varanasi: Indological Book House, 1887 [1970]), pp. 111–112 and I. K. Sarma, *Studies in Early Buddhist Monuments and Brahmi Inscriptions of Andhradesa* (Nagpur: Dattsons. 1988), p. 16, who writes: "This Candraprabhācarya is identified with Candrakīrti, the author of the *Madhyamakāvatāra*." Given the time gap between the third century date of Nāgārjuna and that of Candrakīrti three centuries later, Sarma's attribution depends on taking the expression "disciple of a disciple" loosely.

11. There are several editions of these copperplates: Vasudeva Visnu Mirashi, *Indological Research Papers* (Nagpur: Vidarbha Samshodhan Mandal, 1982), pp. 135–141; S. Sankaranarayanan, *The Viṣṇukuṇḍis and Their Times: An Epigraphical Study* (Delhi: Agam Prakashan, 1977), pp. 153–156, 172–175 and 1972, 4–20; and M. Rama Rao, "New Light on the Viṣṇukuṇḍins," *Journal of Indian History* 43 (1965): 737–746. The plates were first edited by B. N. Sastri and published in the Telegu journal *Bharati* (June 1965).

12. On the form and content of copperplate inscriptions see Richard Salomon, *Indian Epigraphy: A Guide to the Study of Inscriptions in Sanskrit, Prakrti, and the Other Indo-Aryan Languages* (New York: Oxford University Press, 1998), pp. 114–117 and Daud Ali, "Royal Eulogy as World History: Rethinking Copperplate Inscriptions in Cola India." In *Querying the Medieval: Texts and the History of Practice in South Asia*, ed. Ronald Inden. (New York: Oxford University Press, 2000), pp. 169–171.

13. M. Rama Rao, "New Light on the Viṣṇukuṇḍins," *Journal of Indian History* 43 (1965):746; S. Sankaranaryanan, *The Viṣṇukuṇḍis and Their Times: An Epigraphical Study* (Delhi: Agam Prakashan, 1977), pp. 40, 84.

14. R. Subhramanyan, *The Tuṇḍi Copper Plate Grant of Viṣṇukuṇḍin King Vikramendravarma* (Hyderabad: Government of Andhra Pradesh, 1962), p. 25, who comments: "This need not necessarily be construed that they were sectarian in their outlook. They seem to have allowed absolute freedom for the followers of other creeds particularly, Buddhism."

15. S. Sankaranarayanan, *The Viṣṇukuṇḍis and Their Times: An Epigraphical Study* (Delhi: Agam Prakashan, 1977), p. 38.

16. Vasudeva Visnu Mirashi, *Indological Research Papers* (Nagpur: Vidarbha Samshodhan Mandal, 1982), pp. 127–128.

17. M. Rama Rao, "New Light on the Viṣṇukuṇḍins," *Journal of Indian History* 43 (1965): 743 proposes the following chronology:

Vikramendravarma 450–455
Govindavarma 458–468
Mādhavavarma II 468–518
Vikramendra I 518–528
Indrabhaṭṭārakavarma 528–555
Vikramendra II 555–566
Indravarma 566–570
Mādhavavarma II 570–575
Govindavarma II 575–615

S. Sankaranarayanan, *The Viṣṇukuṇḍis and Their Times: An Epigraphical Study* (Delhi: Agam Prakashan, 1977), 13 suggests a different chronology:

Indravarman 375–400
Mādhavavarman I 400–422
Govindavarman I 422–462
Mādhavarvarman II 462–502
Vikramendravarmana I 502–527
I Indrabhaṭṭārakavarma 527–555
Vikramendravarman II c. 555–572

See also R. Subhramanyam, *The Tuṇḍi Copper Plate Grant of Viṣṇukuṇḍin King Vikramendravarma* (Hyderabad: Government of Andhra Pradesh, 1962), pp. 8–13.

18. S. Sankaranarayanan, *The Viṣṇukuṇḍis and Their Times: An Epigraphical Study* (Delhi: Agam Prakashan, 1977), p. 83.

19. S. Sankaranarayanan, *The Viṣṇukuṇḍis and Their Times: An Epigraphical Study* (Delhi: Agam Prakashan, 1977), p. 36 locates this monastery in western Andhra Pradesh. He identifies Indrapura, the city in which it was built, with "the modern Indrapālaguṭṭa near Tummalagudem in the Ramannapeta Taluk in the Nalgonda District." The Sanskrit text of Vikramendravarman's inscription is given on pp. 172–174.

20. I. K. Sarma, *Studies in Early Buddhist Monuments and Brahmi Inscriptions of Andhradesa* (Nagpur: Dattsons, 1988), p. 22 writes that the rock inscription refers to Govindarāja vihāra as an establishment for followers of the Piṇḍapātika sect, a Theravādin group. See also Gregory Schopen, *Bones, Stones and Buddhist Monks: Collected Papers on the Archeology, Epigraphy, and Texts of Monastic Buddhism in India* (Honolulu: University of Hawaii Press, 1997), pp. 268, 283, n. 47.

21. The fifth/sixth copperplate grants studied by Gregory Schopen, *Bones, Stones and Buddhist Monks: Collected Papers on the Archeology, Epigraphy, and Texts of Monastic Buddhism in India* (Honolulu: University of Hawaii Press, 1997), p. 261, record "the gift of a village which was 'to be used' to provide perfumes, incense and flowers, etc., 'for the Blessed One, the Buddha,' and to provide the requisites for the monks . . .)" Schopen, pp. 265–267, observes that these inscriptions, as well as others which describe the community of monks as headed by the Buddha, indicate that ownership of the villages was transferred to the monastic community as a corporate group, with the Buddha was considered to be the legal head of the group and "owner" of the property. The two Tummalagudem copperplates

similarly note the transference of land to the monastic community but without any explicit reference to the Buddha. The grant of Vikramendrabhaṭṭa simply indicates that the village is given "for the use of the of noble monks from four directions." Govindavarama II's grant of two villages specifies that the donation is dedicated to the use of the noble community from the four directions.

22. See the Sanskrit text in S. Sankaranarayanan, *The Viṣṇukuṇḍis and Their Times: An Epigraphical Study* (Delhi: Agam Prakashan, 1977), pp. 154–155.

23. J. Krishna Prasad Babu, "Social and Economic Transition in 4th–7th Century A.D." In *Social and Economic History of Early Deccan*, ed. Aloka Parasher-Sen (New Delhi: Manohar Publishers, 1993), pp. 131–133.

24. See Dinesh Chandra Sircar, *Indian Epigraphy* (Delhi: Motilal Banarsidass, 1965), pp. 388–400 for a list of the various privileges that could be attached to these land grants.

25. K. A. Nilakantha Sastri, ed. *A History of South India* (New York: Oxford University Press, 1966), p. 166.

26. The translation "complete ignorance" for *nikhiladāridrya* follows from the suggestion of Sree Padma Holt.

27. Gregory Schopen, *Bones, Stones and Buddhist Monks: Collected Papers on the Archeology, Epigraphy, and Texts of Monastic Buddhism in India* (Honolulu: University of Hawaii Press, 1997), pp. 58–61.

28. The copperplate's anonymous author describes the Buddha using the distinctive vocabulary of a learned Buddhist monk. The Buddha is endowed with the ten powers his body is adorned by the four grounds of self-confidence, the eighteen special Buddha *dharmas*, and the thirty-two marks of a great man. On these characteristics see Har Dayal, *The Bodhisattva Doctrine in Buddhist Sanskrit Literature* (Delhi: Motilal Banarsidass, 1931 [1970]), pp. 20–23. The Buddha is further described as having accumulated the collections of merit and knowledge over many immeasurable aeons for the sake of rescuing all sentient beings submerged in the miseries of the cycle of birth and death.

29. See Nilankta Sastri, ed. *A History of South India* (New York: Oxford University Press, 1966) pp. 146–169. On the Cālukya's battles with their rivals for control of Deccan, see also G. Yazdani, *The Early History of the Deccan* (New York: Oxford University Press, 1960), vol. 1, 203–220 and Ronald M. Davidson, *Indian Esoteric Buddhism: A Social History of the Movement* (New York: Columbia University Press, 2002), pp. 34–42.

30. Daud Ali, "Royal Eulogy as World History: Rethinking Copper-plate Inscriptions in Cola India." In *Querying the Medieval: Texts and the History of Practice in South Asia*, ed. Ronald Inden. (New York: Oxford University Press, 2000), p. 186.

31. R. Subramanyam, *The Tuṇḍi Copper Plate Grant of Viṣṇukuṇḍin King Vikramendravarma* (Hyderabad: Government of Andhra Pradesh, 1962), pp. 28. See also 29–33 for his description of the horse sacrifice.

32. Dinesh Chandra Sircar, *Indian Epigraphy* (Delhi: Motilal Banarsidass, 1965), pp. 18–25. See also S. Sankaranarayanan, *The Viṣṇukuṇḍis and Their Times: An Epigraphical Study* (Delhi: Agam Prakashan, 1977), pp. 110–129 who compares other land grants' descriptions of the events Ravikīrti celebrates.

33. Richard Salomon, *Indian Epigraphy: A Guide to the Study of Inscriptions in Sanskrit, Prakrit, and the Other Indo-Aryan Languages* (New York: Oxford University Press, 1998), pp. 235–236.

34. F. See Kielhorn, F., "Aihole Inscription of Pulakeśin II, " *Epigraphica Indica*, vol. 6 (New Delhi: Archeological Survey of India 1900–01 [1981]) *passim* for allusions to Kālidāsa's work. See also Ronald M. Davidson, *Indian Esoteric Buddhism: A Social History of the Movement* (New York: Columbia University Press 2002), p. 69.

35. F. Kielhorn, "Aihole Inscription of Pulakeśin II," *Epigraphica Indica*. vol. 6 (New Delhi: Archeological Survey of India 1900–01 [1981]: 1–12 and Dinesh Chandra Sircar, *Select Inscriptions Bearing on Indian History and Civilization: From the Sixth to Eighteenth Century A.D.* (Delhi: Motilal Banarsidass, 1983), vol. 2. pp. 443–450 have edited the text; the translations are my own.

36. G. Yazdani, *The Early History of the Deccan* (New York: Oxford University Press, vol. 1 1960), p. 215. Cf. S. Sankaranarayanan, *The Viṣṇukuṇḍis and Their Times: An Epigraphical Study* (Delhi: Agam Prakashan, 1977), pp. 111–116.

37. Daud Ali, "Royal Eulogy as World History: Rethinking Copper-plate Inscriptions in Cola India." In *Querying the Medieval: Texts and the History of Practice in South Asia*. ed. Ronald Inden (New York: Oxford University Press, 2000), p. 187.

38. A. K. Ramanujan, *Poems of Love and War* (New York: Columbia University Press, 1985), p. 115.

39. George L. Hart III, *The Poems of Ancient Tamil* (Berkeley: University of California Press 1975), p. 33.

40. Bhavaraju, VenkataKrsna Rao, *History of the Eastern Chālukyas of Veṅgī, 610–1210 A.D.* (Hyderabad: Andhra Pradesh Sahitya Akademi, 1973), p. 86.

41. See the citations given by BhavarajuVenkataKrsna Rao, *History of the Eastern Chālukyas of Veṅgī, 610–1210 A.D.* (Hyderabad: Andhra Pradesh Sahitya Akademi, 1973), pp. 98–106.

42. Ronald M. Davidson, *Indian Esoteric Buddhism: A Social History of the Movement* (New York: Columbia University Press, 2002), p. 79.

43. Karen C. Lang, *Four Illusions: Candrakīrti's Advice to Travelers on the Bodhisttava Path* (New York: Oxford University Press, 2003), p. 191.

44. Karen C. Lang, *Four Illusions: Candrakīrti's Advice to Travelers on the Bodhisttava Path*. New York Oxford University Press, 2003), pp. 89–90, 187.

45. On this myth see John Strong, *The Legend of King Aśoka: A Study and Translation of the Aśokāvadāna* (Princeton: Princeton University Press, 1983), pp. 47–48, Steven Collins, "The Discourse on What Is Primary (*Aggañña-Sutta*)," *Journal of Indian Philosophy* 21 (1986): 317–331, and Ronald M. Davidson 2002, *Indian Esoteric Buddhism: A Social History of the Movement* (New York: Columbia University Press, 2002), pp. 132–133.

46. Ronald M. Davidson, *Indian Esoteric Buddhism: A Social History of the Movement* (New York: Columbia University Press 2002), p. 64.

47. Karen C. Lang, *Four Illusions: Candrakīrti's Advice to Travelers on the Bodhisttava Path* (New York: Oxford University Press, 2003), p. 199.

48. Jan Gonda, *Ancient Indian Kingship from the Religious Point of View* (Leiden: E. J. Brill, 1966), p. l4.

49. For the Sanskrit text see Koshin Suzuki, *Sanskrit Fragments and Tibetan Translation of Candrakīrti's Bodhisattvayogācāracatuḥśatakaṭikā* (Tokyo: Sankibo Press, 1994), pp. 60–62.

50. G. Yazdani, *The Early History of the Deccan* (New York: Oxford University Press 1960), vol. 1, pp. 239–240.

51. Karen C. Lang, *Four Illusions: Candrakīrti's Advice to Travelers on the Bodhisttava Path* (New York: Oxford University Press, 2003), p. 205.

52. Dinesh Chandra Sircar, *Indian Epigraphy* (Delhi: Motilal Banarsidass 1965), p. 24; see also Ronald M. Davidson, *Indian Esoteric Buddhism: A Social History of the Movement* (New York: Columbia University Press, 2002), p. 71.

53. S. Sankaranarayanan, *The Viṣṇukuṇḍis and Their Times: An Epigraphical Study* (Delhi: Agam Prakashan 1977), p. 26. See also Daud Ali, "Royal Eulogy as World History: Rethinking Copper-plate Inscriptions in Cola India," in *Querying the Medieval: Texts and the History of Practice in South Asia*, ed. Ronald Inden (New York: Oxford University Press, 2000), pp. 182–183, on Puranic views of the *kali yuga* kings.

54. E. Hultzch, "Two Pillar Inscriptions at Amarāvatī," *Epigraphica Indica*, vol. 6. New Delhi: Archeological Survey of India (1900–01[1981]): 146–157.

55. On Aśoka's reign and inscriptions see Romila Thapar, *Aśoka and the Decline of the Mauryas* (New York: Oxford University Press, 1963) and S. J. Tambiah, *World Conqueror, World Renouncer* (Cambridge: Cambridge University Press, 1976), pp. 54–72.

56. Karen C. Lang, *Four Illusions: Candrakīrti's Advice to Travelers on the Bodhisattva Path* (New York: Oxford University Press, 2003), p. 143.

57. John Strong, *The Legend of King Aśoka: A Study and Translation of the Aśokāvadāna* (Princeton: Princeton University Press, 1983), pp. 49–56.

58. John Strong, *The Legend of King Aśoka: A Study and Translation of the Aśokāvadāna* (Princeton: Princeton University Press, 1983), p. 164.

59. Joseph Walser, Nāgārjuna and the *Ratnāvalī*: New Ways to Date an Old Philosopher," *Journal of the International Association of Buddhist Studies* 25 (2002): 250–262.

60. Karen C. Lang, *Four Illusions: Candrakīrti's Advice to Travelers on the Bodhisattva Path* (New York: Oxford University Press, 2003), p. 112: "Āryadeva was born on the island of Simhala as the son of the Simhala king. In the end he renounced his status as crown prince and entered the religious life. He then traveled to southern India and became Nāgārjuna's disciple." R. A. H. L. Gundawardhana, *Robe and Plough: Monasticism and Economic Interest in Early Medieval Sri Lanka* (Tucson: University of Arizona Press), 242–267 discusses contacts between Sri Lanka and India in medieval period.

61. John Clifford Holt, *Buddha in the Crown: Avalokiteśvara in the Buddhist Tradition of Sri Lanka* (New York: Oxford University Press, 1991), pp. 57–58. See also Walters 2000, 13, n. 71.

62. John Clifford Holt, *Buddha in the Crown: Avalokiteśvara in the Buddhist Tradition of Sri Lanka* (New York: Oxford University Press, 1991), pp. 74–90; Jonathan S. Walters "Buddhist History: The Sri Lankan Pāli Vaṁsas and Their Commentary." In *Querying the Medieval: Texts and the History of Practice in South Asia*, ed. Ronald Inden (New York: Oxford University Press, 2000), pp. 130–131.

63. Quoted in Jonathan S. Walters "Buddhist History: The Sri Lankan Pāli Vaṁsas and Their Commentary. In *Querying the Medieval: Texts and the History of Practice in South Asia*, ed. Ronald Inden (New York: Oxford University Press, 2000), p. 140.

64. John Clifford Holt, *Buddha in the Crown: Avalokiteśvara in the Buddhist Tradition of Sri Lanka* (New York: Oxford University Press, 1991), pp. 57–60.

65. Wilhelm Geiger, *Cūlavaṁsa: Being the More Recent Part of the Mahāvaṁsa* (New Delhi: Asian Educational Services, 1929 [1992]), vol. 1, pp. 180–200, 215–218. On the types of property donated to monasteries and the monasteries' management of this wealth see R. A. L. H. Gunawardhana, *Robe and Plough: Monasticism and Economic Interest in Early Medieval Sri Lanka* (Tucson: University of Arizona Press, 1979), pp. 34–136.

66. Wilhelm Geiger, *Cūlavaṁsa: Being the More Recent Part of the Mahāvaṁsa* (New Delhi: Asian Educational Services, 1929 [1992]), vol. 1, pp. 274–302.

67. Anne M. Blackburn, *Buddhist Learning and Textual Practice in Eighteenth Century Lankan Monastic Culture* (Princeton: Princeton University Press, 2001), p. 100.

68. John Clifford Holt, *The Religious World of Kirti Śrī: Buddhism, Art, and Politics in Late Medieval Sri Lanka* (New York: Oxford University Press, 1996), p. 35.

69. John Clifford Holt, *The Religious World of Kirti Śrī: Buddhism, Art, and Politics in Late Medieval Sri Lanka* (New York: Oxford University Press, 1996), p. 39.

70. Karen C. Lang, *Four Illusions: Candrakīrti's Advice to Travelers on the Bodhisttava Path* (New York: Oxford University Press, 2003), p. 203.

71. Karen C. Lang, *Four Illusions: Candrakīrti's Advice to Travelers on the Bodhisttava Path* (New York: Oxford University Press, 2003), p. 118.

72. Joseph Walser, Nāgārjuna and the *Ratnāvalī*: New Ways to Date an Old Philosopher," *Journal of the International Association of Buddhist Studies* 25 (2002):215 notes that Candrakīrti quotes from the *Ratnāvalī* sixteen times in his *Prasannapadā* and five times in the *Madhyamakāvatāra*.

73. Richard Salomon, *Indian Epigraphy: A Guide to the Study of Inscriptions in Sanskrit, Prakrti, and the Other Indo-Aryan Languages* (New York: Oxford University Press, 1998), p. 226.

74. Johnathan S. Walters, "Buddhist History: The Sri Lankan Pāli Vaṁsas and Their Commentary," in *Querying the Medieval: Texts and the History of Practice in South Asia*, ed. Ronald Inden (New York: Oxford University Press), pp. 106–108.

75. Ronald M. Davidson, *Indian Esoteric Buddhism: A Social History of the Movement* (New York: Columbia University Press, 2002), p. 86.

CHAPTER 6

Two Mahāyāna Developments along the Krishna River

A. W. Barber

This paper explores two different but related Mahāyāna developments that have originated in whole or part, in the Krishna River Valley of Andhra: the *tathāgatagarbha* (hereafter tathagatagarbha) movement and the *darśana*-based practices that were codified in the *tantras*.[1] In part, this paper is a further development of two earlier publications of mine: "The Two Other Homes of Atiyoga in India,"[2] and "The Practice Lineage of Tathāgatagarbha."[3] In this paper, I will briefly explain the significance of the two movements under consideration, explain my methodology, review research by other scholars (as well as my own), and then indicate the names and teachings of important Mahāyāna Buddhists who are connected to the lines of development under consideration.

At the outset, let me explain why these two Mahāyāna developments of doctrine and practice are treated in the same article. Although they have very disparate origins and lines of development (as far as they can be traced through primary texts and secondary sources), it is clear that by the seventh century CE these lines had merged. Thus, it can be seen that many of the same important historic figures played significant roles in the transmission of both tathagatagarbha ideas and transmutation ideas[4] and practices found in the *tantras*. For the purpose of clarity, however, this chapter will begin by presenting these two lines of development as separate systems.

I have attempted to discover the individuals who were responsible for the development and/or transmission of the tathagatagarbha tradition and the *tantras* in Andhra. That is, first I made a preliminary survey of hagiographical and biographical information[5] and developed a list of qualified individuals. Next, I located texts that are associated with these individuals and within the tathagatagarbha or tantric genres from various collections of Buddhist canonical texts and other secondary sources. With this methodology, I hope to put names to the texts and place them within Andhra history.

Tathagatagarbha

The notion of tathagatagarbha and related terms and ideas[6] was a minor development in the greater context of Indian Mahāyāna Buddhism. There are a small number of *sūtras* that focus on this concept, for example, *Ārya-Tathāgatagarbha-nāma-mahāyāna-sūtra*[7] (hereafter the *Tathagatagarbha sutra*), the *Ārya-Śrīmālādevī-siṁhanāda-nāma-mahaāyāna-sūtra*[8] (hereafter the *Srimala*), and a few others that already assume the concept and relate its significance to other concepts, for example, the *Ārya-Laṅkāvatāra-mahāyāna-sūtra*,[9] and the *Buddha-avataṁsaka-nāma-mahāvaipūlya-sūtra*.[10] There is only one major Indian commentary that focuses on tathagatagrabha, the *Ratnagotravibhāga-mahāyānottaratantra-śāstra*[11] (hereafter the *Ratnagotra*). In addition, there is a large collection of primary *tantric* texts that discuss or utilize this concept, for example, the Tibetan *Kun byed rgyal po'i mdo*,[12] and an extensive collection of secondary *tantric* materials, for example, the *Dohakoṣa*.[13]

In the preponderance of Western scholarly accounts, tathagatagarbha is usually understood to mean the "potential" for awakening.[14] However, as Alex Wayman,[15] Michael Zimmermann,[16] and I[17] have noted, the original meaning of the term was that one is *"already"* or primordially awakened. For example, the *Tathagatagarbha sutra* illuminates the matter metaphorically this way: "inside a casting mold there is a perfectly formed Buddha; the ignorant see the filth of the mold but the wise know that the Buddha is within."[18] Moreover, when one considers the fact that most of the major schools of Buddhism that take tathagatagarbha as their doctrinal foundation for practice understand it to mean "already awakened," it is difficult to understand the persistence of the "potential-for-enlightenment" interpretation in scholarly circles. While it is true that textual accounts vary in presenting one position, the relevant schools clearly took tathagatagarbha to be "already awakened." One only needs to consider the Zen and Mahāmudrā (herafter Mahamudra) schools for important examples. One of the legacies of the "already awakened" interpretation is that the emphasis in praxis shifts from how to gain awakening to how to stop the process of engendering *saṁsāra*. This shift in the focus or purpose of practice is further supported by four logical considerations. First, since originally there is no *ātman* or self, there is nothing to become unaware *in principio*.[19] Second, since cause and effect are part of *saṁsāra*, by following a path that allegedly causes awakening, such a caused experience would still be a matter of *saṁsāra*. Third, the construction of any intellectual schemes to achieve awakening would be matters of conditioned consciousness not the unconditioned. Fourth, pursuit of conditioned schemes only produces conditioned results. Wayman has convincingly outlined the logical development of tathagatagarbha thought within various sects, in particular among Mahāsāṃghikas who were located in Andhra.[20]

While a detailed analysis of the evolutional history of tathagatagarbha is not the intent of this chapter, it should be further noted that this implied "antipath" to awakening was contrary to the norms of most Indian Buddhist assumptions. Moreover, though the Yogācāra school absorbed much of reflective discourse on tathagatagarbha and modified it to fit their aims, tathagatagarbha "thought" never became a philosophical school in India in its own right.

The Early Tathagatagarbha Connection with Andhra

We know from the works of Nalinaksha Dutt's *Buddhist Sects in India*,[21] Dipak Kumar Barua's *Vihāras in Ancient India*,[22] and K. S. Subramanian's *Buddhist Remains in South India*,[23] that the Andhra region was a stronghold of various Mahāsāṃghika subsects. In fact, at least one subsect if not the whole group, was called the "Andhaka." Other subsects that evolved from the Mahāsāṃghikas in the Andhra region were known as the Śailas, Caityas, Uttaras, and Aparas, as reported by Vasumitra and Bhavya.[24] We also know that their parent school, the Mahāsāṃghikas, had a very early and strong presence in the Andhra region. Understanding this is extremely important for ascertaining the development of the tathagatagarbha movement.

In a seminal article entitled, "The Mahāsāṃghika and the Tathāgatagarbha (Buddhist Doctrinal History, Study 1),"[25] Wayman delineated eleven points wherein the philosophical tenets of the Mahāsāṃghikas and the doctrines of the *Srimala* text are in complete agreement. In addition, he developed four major arguments that further support the connection between this school and this text. His arguments are specifically devoted to demonstrating that the most likely locale for the development of the tathagatagarbha articulated in the *Srimala* was Andhra. Wayman also traced a general history of doctrinal development found in the Hīnayāna materials, in particular within the Mahāsāṃghika, as a prelude to what is found in the *Srimala.* The *Srimala* is probably the second *sūtra* in the genre of literature that can be termed tathagatagarbha. The first is the *Tathagatagarbha sutra* itself.[26] A brief review of Wayman's findings is provided below.

Tenets shared by the Mahāsāṃghika and the *Srimala:*

A. The Buddhas are supermundane (*lokottara*),
B. The Tathagatas are devoid of flux (*anāsrava*/outflows) and mundane natures (*laukikadharma*),
C. The Buddha expresses the entire Dharmadhātu with a single sound,
D. All *sūtras* have a final meaning,
E. The material body is unlimited,
F. The Tathāgata's power is unlimited,
G. The longevity of the Buddha is unlimited,
H. After well establishing sentient beings the Buddha has no satisfaction,
I. The self-presence of mind is bright,
J. There is no intermediate state,
K. There is a root consciousness (*mūlavijñāna*).[27]

Arguments Supporting Connections Between the Mahāsāṃghika and the *Srimala:*

1. The *Srimala* is named in the Mahāsāṃghika canon,
2. There is a passage in the *Mahāvastu* (a major Mahāsāṃghika work) that connects the two,
3. The four career-phases in the *Mahāvastu* are embedded in the structure of the *Srimala,*
4. There is a connection between the *Mahāvastu*'s position on the *bodhisattva* stages and the *Srimala*'s position.[28]

Assuming Wayman's findings and based on a careful study of the *sūtras, śāstras,* and various historic works summarized below, we can place the *Tathagatagarbha sutra* along with the *Srimala* in the Andhra region around the third century CE. For the purposes of this study, I have used Buddhabhadra's translation of the *Tathagatagarbha sutra,* as this is the earliest extant version.[29]

Buddhabhadra (fourth through fifth century) was an *anāgāmin* famous for the claim that he had visited the *bodhisattva* Maitreya in his

Tuṣita abode. He was involved in various textual translation projects while living in China, most of which dealt with meditation, *vinaya* (in particular the Mahāsāṃghika *vinaya*), as well as texts teaching the verity of tathagatagarbha.[30] In Buddhabhadra's life and work, we can see a close connection between the Mahāsāṃgika and tathagatagarbha thought.

Given that our dating of Buddhabhadra's version of the *sūtra* is accurate, we also find another interesting connection between the *Tathagatagarbha sutra* and the Mahāsāṃghikas. Buddhabadra's version of the *sūtra* mentions *dhāraṇīs* (ritual incantations that figure dominantly in later *tantric* practice). As is well known, the Mahāsāṃghika had a *Dhāraṇīpiṭaka* as part of their canon.[31]

I will now turn to an argument that further links tathagatagarbha thought to Andhra. The *Tathagatagarbha sutra* declares that four *bodhisattvas* did not realize their already awakened status when this *sūtra* was initially taught by an ancient buddha. Among the listed is Avalokiteśvara. As I have demonstrated elsewhere, there is a strong connection between the *Tathagatagarbha sutra* and the whole of Sukhāvatīvyūha teachings.[32] I attribute the statement that Avalokiteśvara was not one of the *bodhisattvas* who realized his awakening through the tathagatagarbha teachings to the familiarity that the target audience already had with the cultic myths about Avalokiteśvara's connections to other Buddhist liberative teachings (precisely the more śraddhic or confidence-oriented teaching related to the *bodhisattva's* compassion in rescuing suffering sentient beings). If the target audience for the *Tathagatagarbha sutra* was indeed well informed with this orientation of Avalokiteśvara, it would have been difficult for them to accept a new teaching that states a contrary position. Certainly, one place that would well know the mythic corpus of this most popular *bodhisattva* would be the region where his mountain home was located. Mt. Potalaka, according to *The Life and Liberation of Padmasambhava*,[33] is located near a cremation ground called "cooling."[34] In the hagiography of Śrī Siṁha (one of the main tathagatagarbha practice teachers in the Vajrayāna period), it is stated that the cremation ground named "cool blessing" was located near Sri Dhanyakataka.[35] If this is so, then this would place Mt. Potalaka somewhere in Andhra (the commonly accepted location by most scholars[36]).

In summary, Andhra being the place of the inception of the tathagatagarbha teaching is based on the following: Andhra was a stronghold of the Mahāsaṃghika, there are eleven points of doctrinal connections between the Mahāsāṃghika and the *Srimala* (a primary text in this tradition), there are four arguments supporting the connection between these two, there are demonstrated connections between the tathagatagarbha teachings and the Mahāsāṃghika in the life and works of Buddhabhadra who translated tathagatagarbha texts into Chinese, and the *Tathagatagarbha sutra* reflects a close familiarity with the cult of Avalokiteśvara whose cultic center was Mt. Potalaka near Dhanyakataka, known definitively as a major center of Buddhism in Andhra.

The *Tantras*

There are various classifications schemes for the texts that functioned in support of the Vajrayāna movement in India.[37] For our purposes, I have selected a common and popular system to facilitate our understanding of important historic issues. However, I recognize that by viewing Vajrayāna through the lens of later classification schemes, I am partially blinding myself to some of the dynamics and creativity of the time period I wish to investigate. Further, I will not attempt to present a complete disciple-master lineage. Since my goal is only to locate significant individuals who worked or lived in Andhra, such an undertaking is not essential.

For scholarly purposes, Buddhist tantric teachings can be roughly divided into two basic categories: those primarily based on tathagatagarbha and those primarily based on practices of transmutation. As indicated above, the first is connected with the Mahamudra and Atiyoga lines. The *tantras* also contain a written record of the spiritual culture that developed in Indian Buddhism post–400 CE. It should be kept in mind that this distinction in teachings is more functional in nature than anything else, as texts that articulate tathagatagarbha often have ideas based on transmutation and texts emphasizing transmutation often have ideas based on tathagatagarbha. The texts that focus on the "Buddha within," sudden awakening, and related ideas are often placed in a separate class of literature. The second class of texts I have referred to, which focus on changing base elements such as hatred and envy into various types of *prajñā* (wisdom), are generally connected with the tantric *kriyā* through *anuyoga tantras* (see below).[38]

A common way to divide up the entire corpus of Buddhist tantric literature is a fourfold scheme that has several subdivisions. At the lowest level there are the *kriyātantra*s (action *tantras*). The next two levels are the *caryātantra*s (behavior *tantras*) and the *yogatantra*s (union *tantras*). The *yogatantra*s can be further divided between those which are like the *caryā* and *kriyā* and those which are more like the final class: *anuyogatantra*s (superior union *tantras*), which in turn are further subdivided into a lower group called "father" *anuyogatantra*s and the higher group called "mother" *anuyogatantra*s. To date, we have only limited information on the popularity of the *kriyā* and *caryātantra*s in the Krishna River

Valley area, but we know more about the presence of the *anuyoga*-level *tantras*.[39] Most of the information we have comes almost entirely from Tibetan sources.

Whatever the nature of our sources, it is clear that Andhra appears as one of the major locals of legendary or mythic origins for the Vajrayāna. For example, two different traditions within Vajrayāna note that their origins were in Andhra. The first is the Japanese Shingon tradition, which developed from the Chinese Vajrayāna tradition introduced by Śubhākarasiṁha, Vajrabodhi, and Amoghavajra from India. It claims to have originated when Nāgārjuna discovered *tantric* texts in an iron pagoda located in Andhra.[40] Second, the last great tantra to emerge, the *Kālacakra tantra*,[41] was allegedly taught at the great *stūpa* of Amaravati.[42] These are but two examples testifying to the status that Andhra achieved in the minds of the practitioners of Vajrayāna.

Teachers of Tathagatagarbha

The various *sūtras* containing the doctrine of tathagatagarbha usually do not indicate the names of their authors or teachers who might have been associated with them. The first name that we can glean to be connected with tathagatagarbha teachings is Sāramati. According to Chinese information, Sāramati is the author of the *Ratnagotra.* commentary.[43] Although, as Takasaka has pointed out, there are problems with assigning the whole of the *Ratnagotra* to Sāramati. Yet his name in relation to this text has support from several sources.[44] Accordingly, it can be hypothesized that Sāramati was born seven centuries after Śākyamuni's *parinirvāṇa* and was from central India. If we take the fifth century BCE to be the date of the Buddha's *parinirvāṇa*,[45] this would place Sāramati in about the third century CE, reasonably close to the early period of the *Tathagatagarbha sutra* and the *Srimala sutra.* Nakamura[46] roughly assigns Sāramati to 350–450 CE and states that he also wrote the *Mahāyānadharmadhātu-nirviśeṣa-śāstra*[47] and *Mahāyānavatāra.*[48] There may be a confusion in authorship between Sāramati and Stiramati in some cases.

Based on the *Lo yang ch'ieh lan chi,*[49] T'an lin's preface to Bodhidharma's *Erh ju ssu hsing lun*[50] and the *Hsu kao seng chuan,*[51] the next major figure identified in the "lineage" of tathagatagarbha is Bodhidharma, the famous founder of the Ch'an or Zen school in China, who lived in the later part of the fifth century and the beginning of the sixth. He most likely came from Andhra and it is probably from there that he sailed to China.[52] We know that there were well-established trade routes from Andhra to China by these dates. Bodhidharma introduced a "*yogi*"-type tradition in China, which eventually became the Ch'an school. However, because the beginnings of this school in China are in yogic communities, tracing further the Indian history of this line with any accuracy in Chinese sources is a near impossible task. After Bodhidharma's time, connections between the *tantras* and taghagatagarbha in India are very intimate and so we must address the two in relation to one another.

Tathagatagarbha and Tantric Teachers in Andhra

It is quite possible that Padmasambhava (eighth century CE), a master who hailed from Uddiyana and who was massively influential in Tibet, also spent time in Andhra.[53] But Padmasambhava was associated with so many traditions that disentangling history from myth may no longer be possible. Yet he is especially connected to the *anuyoga tantras* of the first division, with texts like the *Sarvabuddhatiśākaṁakraratnakulināma*,[54] and the second division with texts like the *Vajrakīlāyāgnekalpajvala tantranāma*,[55] as well as many more.

We are on a bit firmer ground when considering the lineage of Atiyoga. Based on a study of Padmakarpo's *Tibetan Chronicals*,[56] the *Vairo a'Dra a'Bag*,[57] Dudjom's *Nyingma School of Tibetan Buddhism*,[58] and the *Blue Annals*,[59] we know that in the sixth century, in the Swat River Valley (in what is now modern northeast Pakistan), the tantric master Ānandavajra founded another line of teaching incorporating tathagatagarbha. This is the important line mentioned above called the Atiyoga or Mahāsaṅdhi that is doctrinally linked to the idea of "already awakened" rather than the "potential for awakening," the latter by this time clearly associated with the Yogācāra school. The difference between the teachings of Bodhidharma who established Ch'an, and Ānandavajra is not to be found in the foundational praxis-oriented ideas of the two, but rather simply in the language employed by each to explain tathagatagarbha. While Bodhidharma uses the language and metaphors of the *sūtras*, Ānandavajra uses the language and metaphors of the *tantras*. This is not surprising, given that by the sixth century CE, the Swat Valley was known for being a Vajrayāna center. For Ānandavajra, Atiyoga is considered the pinnacle of all practices and doctrine. In his scheme, he hierarchically considers Hīnayāna, Mahāyāna, and Vajrayāna with Atiyoga as the quintessential learning and practice of the last. Unfortunately, we know nothing about Ānandavajra's predecessors. I have been able to reconstruct the lineage of major figures in the Atiyoga tradition beginning with Ānandavajra and then a descending line that includes Mañjuśrīmitra I,

Vimalamitra I, Mañjuśrīmitra II, Śrī Siṁha, and finally Vimalamitra II. Indubitably, many other individuals were associated and considerably more research is needed in this area. Be that as it may, I have been able to ascertain that Śrī Siṁha (circa 725 CE) was of central Asian origins and that he lived in India. The *Vairo a'Dra a'Bag* states that he lived in a temple near a hall named "Dhahena" located near a lake named Kuta or Kosha. On analysis we can reconstruct this place name as "Dhanyakataka."[60] This is reconfirmed by carefully mapping out all place names in that text indicating the Andhra locale. Thus, it would appear that Śrī Siṁha took the Atiyoga line to Andhra and made his residence at the famous Dhanyakataka along the Krishna River. From here it was transmitted to teachers who then took the line to Tibet and China. But after this date, we find no further reference for this teaching in India. This is conceivably because the next line of development surpassed it.[61] Śrī Siṁha was also connected in a number of the father *anuyoga* tantras such as the *Kamadhatuśvari-tantra*[62] as well as others.[63]

In the seventh century, Saraha,[64] from either Orissa or Vidarbha, founded a new development called Mahamudra. Although this term has several meanings, I will only use it here with regard to a line of teaching that is based on tathagatagarbha doctrine and that, like the Atiyoga, uses the language and metaphors of the *tantras*. The most consequential teachings in the Mahamudra are Saraha's cycle of songs entitled the *Dohakoṣagīti.*[65] Other works of his include the *Dohakoṣa-nāma-caryāgīti,*[66] *Dohakoṣopadeśagīti-nāma,*[67] *Dohakoṣa-nāma-mahāmudropadeśa,*[68] *Kakhadoha-nāma,*[69] *Svādhiṣṭhānakrama,*[70] and many more.[71] He also wrote works in the *Buddhakapāla tantra* cycle.[72] Saraha's disciple was Nāgabodhi.

Unfortunately Nāgabodhi and Nāgārjuna seem to have been confused in our sources. It is nearly impossible to distinguish which facts may be attributed to which individual. It could be that the Andhra associations of Nāgārjuna were unwittingly attributed to Nāgabodhi, but it is also possible that both are connected with the Krishna River Valley area. It is further possible that there was a tantric master named Nāgārjuna, as Nāgārjuna is connected with the *Guhyasamāja-tantra,*[73] the main *tantra* of the father *anuyoga* class as well as other works.[74] However, we do know that Nāgabodhi, Saraha's disciple, was connected with the *Yamāri* cycle[75] of texts and that his disciple was one Savari.[76] Savari was also known as "Saraha the younger." According to Tāranātha's account, he lived during the time of the Pāla dynasty (ca. ninth through tenth centuries).[77] If the current research on the dates of Saraha is accurate, and Savari lived in the ninth century, then we are left with a considerable gap in our historic record.

Accordingly, Savari lived and taught the Mahamudra in the Andhra region as he had learned it from Nāgabodhi who, as I have noted, received the teaching from Saraha. The texts that he is associated with are the *Śrī-sahajopadeśa-svādhiṣṭhāna-nāma*[78] and most important, the *Cittaguhyagaṁbhīrārthagīti-nāma.*[79] His name is also associated with a number of other Vajrayāna teachings such as the *Vajravidāraṇā, Vajrakrodha,* and others.[80] His line of teachings was then transmitted to Virūpa, whose *anuyoga tantric* texts consist of seven works with a focus on the *Yamāri* cycle.[81] Virūpa spent some years in Andhra and transmitted the Mahamudra teachings to many disciples.[82]

From the eighth century, the Krishna River Valley area became a major center of the Mahamudra teachings. The line developing from Savari eventually was transmitted to Naropa and to Maitripa (1007?–1085?), the latter lived in Andhra.[83] He had many students who spread his teaching across India. Our sources are not in agreement as to whether these two were in a lineal succession or whether these masters were contemporaries. Some accounts claim that Maitripa learned the Mahamudra from Naropa, while others make him a direct disciple of Savari. If our dating of Savari is correct it would have been impossible for Maitripa to have trained directly under him. Teachings associated with Maitripa are *Sahajaṣatka*[84] and *Mahāmudrākanakamālanāma.*[85] He is also associated with a number of *tantric* works, particularly the *Cakrasaṁvara* cycle.[86] Of considerable significance is the fact that he is credited with the rediscovery of the *Ratnagotra,* which had been lost around the fourth century in India. As I noted, Maitripa had many disciples who contributed to the development of the Mahamudra teachings. However, how many of these stayed for any length of time in the Andhra region remains unclear at the present stage of my research.

Lower *Tantric* Teachers

According to the scheme presented above, the lower *tantras* consists of the *kriyātantra, caryātantra,* and the *yogatantra* classes. It is important to note that these classes of *tantras* can be practiced by both monastics and nonmonastics. Some of the higher tantric practices were theoretically limited to nonmonastics.

I will first address two known historic figures who were definitely connected to Andhra, but whose accounts lack sufficient information to determine if they should be conclusively listed as masters of the lower *tantras* or the higher *tantras.*[87] Śāntivarman (fifth century), a visitor to Andhra, has been connected with Avalokiteśvara, Hayagrīva, and Ekajatī cycles.[88] Kamalagomin (ca. seventh century) is identified by Tāranātha as visiting Andhra and being connected with the Avalokiteśvara cycle of practices.[89]

We have a limited number of names of individuals in Andhra that are associated with lower *tantras*. All except one of these individuals were *bhikṣus*. These are: Subhākarasiṁha,[90] Buddhaguhya and Buddhaśānti.[91] The one non-monastic is the eminent Candragomin.[92]

Subhākarasiṁha (637–735) was from central India and probably set sail from Andhra on his long trip to China. Having been invited by Emperor Jui tsung, he arrived in China in 716. Emperor Jui tsung (reign 710–712) died before the master arrived, so he was welcomed by the succeeding emperor Hsüan tsung (reign 712–755) and bestowed with the title "National Preceptor." He lived in the capital and was repeatedly called on by the emperor to perform tantric rituals.[93] He translated twenty-one tantric texts into Chinese.[94] The most important of these was the *Mahāvairocana sūtra*,[95] the main *tantra* for the *caryā* class.[96] Candragomin (seventh century), according to Tāranātha, not only visited Andhra but was also connected with the Avalokiteśvara and Tārā cycles.[97] His name appears prominently in the *Tripiṭaka* catalogs with forty-six works accredited. Of particular note is his work on the *Mañjuśrīnāmasaṁgīti*.[98] Buddhaguhya (eighth through ninth centuries) was a disciple of Buddhajñānapāda (eighth century) as well as other masters. He specialized in the *kriyātantra*, *caryātantra*, and *yogatantras* and achieved noted success (*siddhi*) by employing the *yogatantra* techniques. He is said to have had special exchanges with the *bodhisattva* Mañjuśrī and a repeated vision of the *Vajradhatu-mahāmaṇḍala*, a *caryā* level practice listed in the *Mahāvairocana sūtra*. He is reported to have spent time at Avalokiteśvara's Potalaka mountain in Andhra.[99] The *Karmopāya-nāma*,[100] *Dhyānottarapaṭalaṭīkā*,[101] *Vairocanābhisambodhi-tantrapiṇḍārtha*,[102] and *Vairocanabhi-sambodhitantraṭīkā*[103] are some of the more important texts listed under his name in the *Tripiṭaka*, in addition to seventeen other texts.[104] Buddhaśānti (eighth through ninth centuries) was a friend and fellow disciple of Buddhajñānapāda, along with Buddhaguhya. He too specialized in the lower *tantras* and it is reported that he was able to achieve even higher success than his friend, with the aid of Tārā, while at the Potalaka mountain.[105] No works are listed under his name in the Tibetan *Tripiṭaka*. He is said to have finished his days in Uddiyana along the Swat River.

Conclusion

After establishing that the Andhra region was one of the strongholds of the Mahāsāṃghika school, various facts and arguments demonstrating the association of tathagatagarbha thought with this school were noted, in large part due to the work of Wayman. These connections were based on a comparison between the Mahāsāṃghika and the *Srimala*. In this and previous publications, I have also argued that the *Tathagatagarbha sutra* most likely originated in the Krishna River Valley. The *Tathagatagarbha sutra* and *Srimala* are the first two sūtras to emerge that focus on tathagatagarbha thought. In addition to the discussion regarding the emergence of tathagatagarbha thought in Andhra, I provided information that demonstrates an intimate connection between Andhra and the emerging *tantric* form of Buddhism in classic times. That Andhra appears as one of the legendary and mythic centers of Vajrayāna is discerned from a list of famous masters who lived or worked there.

I have also mentioned individuals who can be safely associated with some of the earliest tathagatragarbha texts. In particular, from a careful analysis of the material associated with the *Ratnagotra*, I have been able to identify Sāramati as the first historic figure. Following in the Andhra area was Bodhidharma, the famous founder of the Ch'an school in China who set sail from this area. Leaving behind the material developed along with the Mahāyāna *sūtras*, tathagatagarbha became one of the major concepts in the Vajrayāna movement, in particular in the Atiyoga and Mahamudra teachings. By the sixth century, the tantric and the tathagatagarbha lines of development had merged. I then presented information on a number of historic individuals, providing dates where possible, who were connected with these two teaching systems and were active in the Andhra region. I also provided the names of a number of important texts associated with the Atiyoga, Mahamudra, and the tantric teachings. However, it seems safe to assume that I have only presented the names of the most prominent teachers through the ages and this list should not be understood as either comprehensive or exhaustive.

In conclusion, I have demonstrated that Andhra was clearly a center of tathagatagarbha and tantric teachings. That is, I have shown that Andhra was the locale where there were active developments in both of these teachings from at the least the third century CE up to and including the twelfth century CE, and therefore a region of religious dynamism which is perhaps unsurpassed in the greater history of Indian Buddhism.

Notes

1. By *tantra* here I mean what some classifications have labeled the *anuyoga* and lower *tantras*.

2. A. W. Barber, "The Two Other Homes of Ati-Yoga in India," *Buddhist Himalaya* 1 and 2 (1989), pp. 49–62.

3. A. W. Barber, "The Practice Lineage of Tathāgatagarbha," *Studies in Zen Buddhism*, vol. 77 (1999), pp. 29–45.

4. I take it that the idea of entering into the sphere of *nirvāṇic* power (*darśana*) of a *buddha* or *bodhisattva* is one of the foundational elements in the development of the *tantras*. Further, the idea of transforming base elements such as hatred, and so forth into higher order wisdoms is key to the operations of the tantric process and thus transmutation is an extremely important idea in this material.

5. The "biographical" materials were never composed for the Western historic project and thus from that perspective, leave much to be desired. They tend to be a mixture of history, psychological depictions, doctrinal expressions and yogic maps encapsulating the Buddhist goals in the *modus operandi* of the individuals depicted. Often called "hagiography," but this term is a misnomer as the Buddhist masters are not "saints." Portraying themselves as histories, these accounts are really *modus docendi*. As such they are difficult to work with for historical purposes. For an interesting discussion of much of these consideration see Ronald Davidson, *Indian Esoteric Buddhism: A Social History of the Tantric Movement* (New York: Columbia University Press, 2002), pp. 7–24.

6. See Brian E. Brown, *The Buddha Nature* (Delhi: Motilal Banarsidass Publishing, 1991), David S. Ruegg, *La Théorie du Tathāgatagarbha et du Gotra* (Paris: Ecole Francise d'Extreme Orient, 1969), Paul Williams, *Mahāyāna Buddhism* (London: Routledge, 1991), pp. 96–115.

7. Junjirō Takakusu, ed., *Taishō shinshū daizōkyō* (Tokyo: Daizō shuppan kai, 1922–33), hereafter T; A. W. Barber, ed., *The Tibetan Tripitaka: Taipei Edition* (Taipei: SMC Publishing, 1991); hereafter TP. See T #666, 667; TP #258.

8. See T #310 (48), 353; TP #92.

9. See T #670, 671, 672; TP #107.

10. See T #278; TP #44.

11. See T #1611; TP #5525.

12. See TP #4474.

13. See TP #3068.

14. Williams, pp. 97 ff. indicates both sides of the argument.

15. Alex Wayman, and Hideko Wayman, trans. and eds., *The Lion's Roar of Queen Śrīmālā* (New York: Columbia University Press, 1974), pp. 47–48, states that the idea that we are already awakened and thus Buddhas is found in the *Ārya-Aṅgulimālīya-nāma-mahāyāna sūtra* (T #99 [1077], 100 [16], 118, 119, 120, 125; TP #213). Hajime Nakamura, *Indian Buddhism: A Survey with Bibliographical Notes* (Delhi: Motilal Banarsidass Publishing, 1987), p. 230, claims that the above *sūtra* was "published" in the earliest period of tathagatagarbha textual development.

16. Michael Zimmermann, *A Buddha Within: The Tathāgatagarbhasūtra the Earliest Expositions of the Buddha-Nature Teachings in India* (Tokyo: International Research Institute for Advanced Buddhology, Soka University, 2002) pp. 39 ff. and 50 ff.

17. Barber, "The Anti-Sukhāvatīvyūha Stance of the Tathāgatagarbha Sūtra," *The Pure Land,* 16 (1999), pg. 192.

18. William H. Grosnick, "The Tathāgatagarbha Sūtra," in Donald S. Lopez, ed. *Buddhism in Practic* (Princeton: Princeton University Press, 1995), pp. 92–93, claims that this *sūtra* presents the "potential" for awakening. However, with careful analysis, this is clearly not the case. Instead, the *sūtra* offers multiple examples of the "already awakened" understanding.

19. *Avidyā.*

20. Wayman and Wayman, pp. 42 ff.

21. Nalinaksha, Dutt, *Buddhist Sects in India* (Delhi: Motilal Banarsidass Publishing, 1978) pp. 57–58.

22. Dipak Kumar, Barua, *Vihāras in Ancient India* (Calcutta: Indian Publications, 1969), pp. 199–208.

23. K. S. Subramanian, *Buddhist Remains in South Indian* (New Delhi: Cosmo Publications, 1981), pp. 9–10.

24. Dutt, pp. 57 ff.

25. Alex Wayman, "The Mahāsaṃghika and the Tathāgatagarbha" (Buddhist Doctrinal History, Study 1), *Journal of the International Association of Buddhist Studies* 1 (1978) pp. 35–52.

26. Nakamura, ibid. pp. 229–230, places the two just mentioned plus the *Anuttaraśraya sūtra, Mahāparinirvāṇa sūtra*, and *Mahābherī-hāraka-parivarta sūtra* in the first period of tathagatagarbha development around 350–400 CE.

27. Wayman, Study I. pp. 37–38. My summation wording is slightly different than Prof. Wayman's original wording.

28. Ibid. pp. 39–40.

29. T #666.

30. He translated the *Tathāgatagarbha sūtra* (T. 667), the *Mahāparinirvāṇa sūtra* (T. 5), and the *Avataṁsaka sūtra* (T. 278).

31. Lamotte, Etienne, *History of Indian Buddhism* (English translation), Sara Webb-Boin (Louvain-Paris: Peters Press, 1988, p. 139.

32. A. W. Barber, "The Anti-Sukhāvatīvyūha Stance of the Tathāgatagarbha Sūtra," pp. 190–202.

33. Although this is a much later Tibetan work (fifteenth century), I have found no reason to question this geographic information in general. This Tibetan composition was based on earlier tales and information about India at a time when Indian masters were still coming to Tibet.

34. Toussaint, Gustave-Charles. *Le Dict de Padma* (English translation) Douglas, Kenneth & Bays, Gwendolyn. *The Life and Liberation of Padmasambhava* (Berkeley: Dharma Publishing, 1978), pg. 434.

35. See A. W. Barber, *The Life and Teachings of Vairocana* (Madison: University of Wisconsin PhD dissertation, 1984), pp. 40–41.

36. See Warder, p. 487; Joshi, Lal Mani. *Studies in the Buddhist Culture of India* (Delhi: Motilal Banarsidass Publishing, 1977), p. 257.

37. See Guenther, Herbert. *Buddhist Philosophy in Theory and Practice* (Boulder: Shambhala, 1976), pp. 174 ff. and Alex Wayman, *The Buddhist Tantras* (New York: Samuel Weiser, 1973), pp. 225 ff.

38. There are, of course, different ways of trying to understand the tantric teachings vis-à-vis the Mahāyāna. In general, it seems to me that the *tantras* do not depart seriously from Mahāyāna in terms of doctrine, goal, or cosmological view. In many ways tantric literature expands on existing models without setting off in completely different directions. Thus, I view Vajrayāna as another way of "practicing" Mahāyāna. This position is consistent with some traditional interpretations. However, the issue is far from settled. Although important, this chapter is not the venue for that discussion and I mention it here only to provide the reader with adequate information on the stance that informs this chapter.

39. See F. D. Lessing, and A. Wayman, *Introduction to the Buddhist Tantric System* (New York: Samuel Weiser, 1980), pp. 25 ff.

40. See A. K. Warder, *Indian Buddhism* (Delhi: Motilal Banarsidass, 1980) pp. 488–489; and Yamasaki, Taiko. *Shingon: Japanese Esoteric Buddhism.* Richard and Cynthia Peterson, trans. (Boston: Shambhala, 1988), pg. 8.

41. TP #363. Also see: Gyatso, Tenzin (English translation) Jeffrey Hopkins. *The Kalachakra Tantra* (London: Wisdom Publications), 1985.

42. Warder, p. 350.

43. Takasaki, Jikido. *A Study on the Ratnagotravibhāga* (Roma: Instituto Italiano Per Il Medio ed Estremo Oriente, 1966), pg. 9.

44. Ibid.

45. The dating for the death of Śākyamuni being used by the sources reporting Sāramati's authorship of the *Ratnagotra* is not recorded.

46. Nakamura, ibid., pp. 261–262.

47. T #1626, 1627, however, the Taisho attributes this to Sthiramati.

48. TP #3228; this is attributed to Dhokhindha in Tibetan. T #1634; however, the Taisho attributes this to Sthiramati.

49. T #2092.

50. Yanagida Seizan. "Daruma no goroku—Ninyū shigyō ron," *Zen no goroku,* No. 1 (Tokyo: Chikuma Shobō 1969), T #2837.

51. T #2060. Further, the lineage of Indian "Ch'an" patriarchs can not be historically proven to be authentic. It seems composed of Sarvāstoivāda vinaya lineage, Mahāyāna luminaries, and a few others. See Yampolsky, Philip B. The Platform Sutra of the Sixth Patriarch. New York: Columbia University Press, 1967, pp. 2–111.

52. This is based on: (1) early texts do not mention any Indian kingdom but say "from the south," (2) Andhra being the main center of tathagatagarbha teachings and Ch'an/Zen take this as its fundamental position, (3) Andhra had regular shipping routes to China, and (4) The Pallava dynasty ruling in Andra at the time, traced its origins back to a combined Brāhmaṇ–Kṣatriya heritage noted in the Chinese sources. Other locals have been hypothesized.

53. Douglas Toussaint, and G. Bays, ibid. pp. 167–168, 434.

54. TP #4784.

55. TP #4899.

56. Padma Kar po, *Tibetan Chronicals* (New Delhi: International Academy of Indian Culture, 1968).

57. Manuscript in my personal collection, no publication information.

58. Rinpoche, Dudjom (Jikdrel Yeshe Dorje). *The Nyingma School of Tibetan Buddhism: Its Fundamentals and History* (Boston: Wisdom Publications, 1991), p. 490 ff.

59. George N. Roerich, *The Blue Annals* (Delhi: Motilal Banarsidass Publishing, 1979), pp. 104, 106–108, 168, 170–172, 191–192, 197, 491, 497, 552, 729, 849.

60. See Barber (1989).

61. See Herbert V. Guenther, *Buddhist Philosophy in Theory and Practice* (Boulder: Shambhala, 1976) pp. 208 ff.; Herbert V. Guenther, *Kindly Bent to Ease Us* (Emeryville: Dharma Publishing, 1975), Tulku Thondup Rinpoche, *Buddha Mind* (Ithaca: Snow Lion Publications, 1989).

62. TP #5228.

63. TP #5163, 5748. These are classed *mahāyoga*, which roughly equals father *anuyoga* class in the scheme employed in this article.

64. Roerich, ibid. p. 842 ff. and David Templeman, *The Seven Instruction Lineages by Jo Nang Tāranātha* (Dharamsala: Library of Tibetan Works and Archives, 1983) p. 2 ff.

65. TP #3068.

66. TP #3110.

67. TP #3111.

68. TP #3119.

69. TP #3113.

70. TP #3122.

71. TP #2524, 2527, 2528, 2529, 3179, 3985, 3986, 4129, 4248.

72. TP #424, and TP #2524.

73. TP #442, also see Alex Wayman, *Yoga of the Guhyasamājatantra* (New York: Samuel Weiser, 1980) and Francesca Fremantle, *A Critical Study of the Guhyasamāja Tantra* (London: University of London PhD dissertation, 1971).

74. TP #2662–2667, Vajrapāṇi cycle TP #3049–3051, Hayagrīva cycle TP #3877, and others.

75. TP #2827.

76. Roerich, ibid. p. 869; James Robinson, *The Buddha's Lion* (Emeryville: Dharma Publishing, 1979) p. 37 ff., Templeman, p. 8.

77. Templeman, ibid., pg. 8.

78. D. T. Suzuki, ed., *The Tibetan Tripiṭaka: Peking Edition* (Tokyo: Tibetan Tripiṭaka Research Institute, 1961), #2174.

79. TP #3276.

80. TP #3759, 3760, 3763.

81. TP #2874, 2875, 2876, 2878, 2900, 3129, 3133.

82. TP #3129.

83. Roerich, ibid. pp. 841–843; Templeman, ibid., pp. 11 ff.

84. TP #3076.

85. TP #3282.

86. TP #2201, 3213, 3874, 3875.

87. I have included them here because the information I have suggests that they were mostly connected with the lower *tantric* practices. I present the

information in this section hoping that further research will allow us to make a clear determination regarding this matter in the future.

88. Chimpa, Lama and Chattopadhyaya, Alaka, *Tāranātha's History of Buddhism in Indian* (Simla: Asian Institute of Advanced Study, 1970), pp. 191–195.

89. Ibid., pp. 246–247.

90. Jan, Yun-Hua, *A Chronicle of Buddhism in China* (Calcutta: Visva-Bharati Santisiniketan, 1966), p. 55, and Ch'en, Kenneth. *Buddhism in China* (Princeton: Princeton University Press, 1973), p. 334. He is said to have come from central India and arrived via the sea route. I have tentatively placed him in Andhra because of these two points. Further, Vajrabodhi, the second great Vajrayāna master in China (ca. 720) may have also spent time there.

91. Chimpa and Chattopadhyaya, ibid., pp. 280–281.

92. Chimpa and Chattopadhyaya, ibid., pp. 199–209, and Tatz, Mark, *Difficult Beginnings* (Boston: Shambhala Publications, 1985).

93. See Jan, ibid., p. 55, Ch'en, ibid., p. 334, and Weinstein, Stanley, *Buddhism Under the T'ang* (Cambridge: Cambridge University Press, 1987). pg. 55.

94. T #850, 851, 877, 893, 894, 895, 905, 906, 907, 917, 973, 1068, 1075, 1079, 1141, 1145, 1158, 1239, 1270, 1286.

95. T #848. This text is also known as a *tantra* in the Tibetan system. See TP #494.

96. Lessing and Wayman, ibid., pp. 205.

97. Chimpa & Chattopadhyaya, ibid., pp. 199–209.

98. Works listed: TP #2048, 2609, 3363, 3534, 3541, 3542, 3551, 3679, 3737, 3879, 3903, 3904, 3905, 3906, 3917, 3919, 3920, 3921, 3922, 3923, 3924, 3925, 3936, 4150, 4438, 4443, 4488, 4489, 4491, 4492, 4493, 4494. Also see Alex Wayman, *Chanting the Names of Mañjuśrī* (Boston: Shambhala, 1985).

99. Chimpa and Chattopadhyaya, ibid., pp. 280–281; and Roerich, ibid., pg. 372.

100. TP #3754.

101. TP #3495.

102. TP #3486.

103. TP #3487.

104. Works listed: TP #3184?, 3324, 3451, 3461, 3495, 3496, 3504, 3687, 3751, 3752, 3755, 4528, 4581, 5693. Also see Hakuju Ui, et al., *Tohoku Catalogue of the sDe dGe Edition of the Tibetan Tipitaka* (Sendai: Tohoku Imperial University, 1934), #3914, 4535, 4562.

105. Chimpa and Chattopadhyaya, ibid., pp. 280–283.

CHAPTER 7

Dhanyakataka Revisited

Buddhist Politics in Post-Buddhist Andhra

JONATHAN S. WALTERS

Introduction: The Amaravati Pillar Inscription of Simhavarman

At its core this chapter interprets an inscribed pillar from Amaravati,[1] taken by some scholars as evidence of "later traces" of Andhran Buddhism.[2] After problematizing just what sort of "trace" it represents, I present evidence associating this enigmatic inscription with other quasi-Buddhist activities of a twelfth century royal court in Dhanyakataka, a premodern name of Amaravati (section 1) and I discuss the possible significance of those activities with reference to Indian imperial history, especially in Andhra, both before (section 2) and after its composition (section 3). I conclude with some general reflections on the geopolitical position of Buddhists in post-Buddhist India.

The inscription occupies three faces of an octagonal stone pillar excavated in 1877 at the famous Amaravati *stūpa,* twenty miles northwest of Guntur, Andhra Pradesh.[3] The actual pillar must date from the *stūpa's* Sātavāhana Period heydey (see section 2 below), as it corresponds to other pillars discovered there and one face contains a typical first century, BC Prakrit donative inscription.[4] But florid medieval Sanskrit betrays the much later provenance of the inscription that will concern us here; on paleographic grounds Hultzsch dates it to about 1100 AD.[5]

Like the earlier donative inscription, this one is clearly Buddhist. It opens by invoking, for the reader-listener's "great good fortune," the "particles of dust on the feet of Śrīghana [the Buddha][6] which are poison to rebirth and ever-glistening in the multitude of rays [arising] from the crest gems of the lords of gods and demons" (verse 1).[7] After a mythic genealogy of the Pallava dynasty (verses 2–9) the epigraph introduces Siṃhavarman Pallava, a universal emperor who "for a long time held up the earth whose garments are the oceans, whose pearl necklace is the Ganges and whose earrings are Mounts Meru and Mandara" (verses 10–11).[8] It then breaks into prose (line 28 ff.) to narrate the occasion when Siṃhavarman had ascended Mount Meru to establish the fame of his complete conquest of the directions (*akhila-digvijaya*). "Wishing to remove the weariness produced by roaming throughout the entire surface of the earth," Siṃhavarman "passed several days there overjoyed in his heart due to the tender shade of the yellow sandalwood trees growing on its golden slopes" then returned toward the Pallava country, crossing the Ganges, Godavari, and Krishna Rivers. Just then "he saw the city named Sri Dhanyaghata [= Dhanyakataka] whose chief[9] is the Passionless (*Vītarāga*) [Buddha]" and

> having looked at it with curiosity, he humbly approached the resident deities in charge of protecting the entire place. After greeting them, off in a secluded place . . . he heard Dharma-preaching, and having heard and greeted the . . . liberated [Buddha] he said this: "I too, O Blessed One, shall create a . . . of the Blessed One right here, ornamented with gems, gold and silver." When that was said the Blessed One said: "Excellent, excellent *upā[saka]* Siṃhavarman! Henceforth [in this?] [resplendent] superb Buddha-field[10] . . . among the . . . indeed." Then having saluted [the Buddha] in [Dhanya]ghataka [Siṃhavarman] . . .

Hultzsch guessed that the remainder of the epigraph, which breaks off here, contained some grant to a Buddhist establishment at Amaravati.[11]

This inscription presents numerous epigraphical and historical problems. Despite this guess of Hultzsch's, it likely never did contain an operative portion.[12] In its failure to *do* anything this inscription is quite unlike typical (Pallava, Cālukya, Cōḷa, Gaṅga, Koṭa, etc.) imperial inscriptions of the general period and region; instead, it narrates a past event in a quasihistorical style that is itself very unusual for South Asian lithic discourse. Similarly, whereas typical imperial inscriptions reserve Sanskrit (verse) for the *praśasti* (opening eulogy, corresponding to the versified portion of the Amaravati pillar) and use vernacular prose for the operative portion of the record, here the prose too is in Sanskrit.[13]

This inscription is also unusual for not referring to the specific victories scored in Siṃhavarman's *digvijaya*. It lacks the expected date for Siṃhavarman or the period when it was inscribed, mention of the king who authorized it, information about the patron/s who had it carved, an enforcement clause,[14] and the name and/or aspiration of the scribe himself. Though producing the record must have required effort and expense, instead of a new and appropriately hewn stone this is inscribed on the back of a millennium-old antique; and even so, those responsible chose an ordinary pillar rather than some special piece of the fabulous Amaravati *stūpa* to bear their work.[15] Oddest of all, this inscription reads from bottom to top rather than from top to bottom, which prevented its Orientalist discoverers from making any sense of it at all![16]

The inscription's content is even more troublesome than these strictly formal peculiarities. Thus, it is uncertain who this Siṃhavarman might have been. The inscription's record of his mythic Pallava forebears parallels similar accounts in other Pallava inscriptions, and some of the names of Pallava kings it narrates are likewise known, but on the whole it disagrees with accepted Pallava genealogies[17] and this Siṃhavarman "cannot be identified with any other Pallava king of the same or similar name."[18] Siṃhavarman's identity is further complicated by the fact that this inscription was carved long after the Pallava Period. The script is "the transitional type of the Telugu-Kanarese" rather than the Pallava Grantha characteristic of genuine Pallava imperial epigraphs, and its paleographic date falls in the Cōḷa Period, about two centuries after the last great Pallava emperor, Aparājita, was defeated by Parāntaka Cōḷa (925, AD).[19] Sewell's, and following him Sircar's attempt to negate this anachronism by portraying Siṃhavarman as a vassal of Kūlottuṅga Cōḷa I is hard to accept because Siṃhavarman is a world-conquering monarch, not a "Pallava chieftain," and because Siṃhavarman would then be the sole Pallava known to have reappeared during the Cōḷa Period.[20] Likewise, even if Siṃhavarman were a historical king he would be the sole Pallava known to be particularly Buddhist (let alone an *upāsaka* or pious "eight-precept-holder"), and this otherwise unknown donation of a Buddhist (something) at Amaravati would appear from his absence elsewhere in the epigraphic record to have been his only significant public work. Moreover, as I detail below (section 2) this would appear to be the only donation to the Amaravati *stūpa* made by *any* king of any dynasty in the eight centuries between the rise of the early Pallavas and the production of this very inscription.

Multiplying the inscription's quirkiness is its Hīnayāna ("Lesser Vehicle") tone, despite the predominantly Mahāyāna ("Great Vehicle") orientation of Pallava Period Indian Buddhists (especially, as this volume demonstrates, in Andhra). Thus the Buddha is "Śrīghana" or "Bhagavān" or "Vītarāga" (characteristically Hīnayāna epithets) rather than "Śākyamuni" or "Anuttarasamyaksambuddha" (typical Mahāyāna epithets); Siṃhavarman is a Hīnayāna *upāsaka* rather than a Mahāyāna *bodhisattva*; the very language of the inscription evokes the Hīnayāna context.[21] But the Hīnayāna context makes it difficult to imagine how anyone could have been chatting with the living Buddha during the Pallava Period, at least 1,000 years after his final extinction (*parinibbāna*)! Further complicating the matter is the decidedly theist (Śaiva) tone of the opening *praśasti*. Though as indicated the first verse invokes the Buddha's blessings, it is modeled after the second introductory verse of Bāṇa's classic theist romance, *Kādambarī*.[22] The Pallava genealogy begins with the theist creator (Dhātṛ) and traces the dynasty's lineage through celebrated theist characters like Bharadvāja, Angiras, Sudhāman, Droṇa, and finally Aśvatthāman, Pallava's father. Aśvatthāman was born to found a great dynasty "through the grace (*prasād*) of Śambhu ['Benevolent One' = Śiva]" after his father, Droṇa, "pleased eight-bodied [Śiva] with austerities" (verses 3–4); Pallava's mother Madanī, "maiden daughter of [Indra] the king of gods, surrounded by Apsaras" fell in love with Aśvatthāman the moment she saw him, "like Umā when she was in front of Śarva ['Dart-bearer' = Śiva]" (verses 5–7). When Siṃhavarman sees Dhanyakataka his emotion is one of "curiosity" (*sakatūhalam*)—hardly indicative of a strongly Buddhist king—and he enters the site only after "humbly approaching the resident deities" there.

As a result of these difficulties Siṃhavarman's inscription remains largely unexplained. After editing and translating it, Hultzsch could only caution that "great care should be taken in using the above list [of Pallava kings in the inscription] for historical purposes."[23] Sivaramamurti, who reprinted Hultzsch's edition with a list of his emendations *in extenso* and a new (inferior) translation, has nothing to say about what it means; it is simply categorized among the "miscellaneous pillars" now in the Madras Museum (#II-E-29) and silently left there, framed by two first century BC pillar inscriptions.[24] As noted Sircar and others treat the inscription as evidence of a "later trace" of Andhra Buddhism, but it will now be clear why I question just what sort of trace this is. Beyond this, as far as I have been able to discern, no serious interpretation has been offered.

But we can move beyond this impasse by acknowledging the implication of all these different problems that this is *not* a straightforward Pallava Buddhist imperial inscription; it is best understood as a post-Pallava fabrication. This would explain the sloppy Pallava genealogy; the post-Pallava paleographic date; the use of Andhran-Telugu rather than Pallava-Grantha script; the choice of an antique stone pillar over a new production; the historical-descriptive rather than operative tone;

the omission of a then-modern vernacular, a date, and reference to contemporary kings.

Put differently, I think the text is intentionally mythic; it locates Siṃhavarman in a then-already-ancient Pallava dynasty springing from the Creator during the classical Indian theist *illud tempus*. Siṃhavarman's (universal and unchallenged) conquest of the directions and subsequent tarry on Mount Meru (where he "fixed in the sky a golden canopy made up of the dust that was raised by the edges of the hooves of his horses as they walked on the nuggets of gold that were dug up by the claws on the feet of his elephants wandering about like celestial mountain peaks [themselves]") are also of clearly mythic proportion. If it occurred in mythic time, perhaps the encounter with the Buddha was meant to imply that Siṃhavarman was his contemporary, rather than that the Buddha somehow reappeared in early medieval Andhra (which would anyway have to be explained on the basis of mythic thinking). If that is the case, then perhaps the inscription credited Siṃhavarman with constructing the Amaravati *stūpa* itself, rather than, as Hultzsch supposed, some medieval structural addition to the site (of which there is no archaeological evidence). This inscription would then appear to be a sort of Buddhist *sthala purāṇa* ("local history") for the site of the *stūpa*, which presumably would have served whatever medieval activity invoked that history.[25]

In similar fashion, all the problems I have raised can be read as clues to the identity and project of those who actually carved the inscription. Thus on paleographic grounds alone it can be assumed that they were Telugu-speaking Andhrans. If the inscription was an intentional forgery they likely would have employed a somewhat archaic (but still intelligible) script, which means they might have lived a few generations after the paleographic date of *circa* 1100 AD. The Śaivism of the *praśasti* suggests that they would have been Śaivas themselves, but that like Siṃhavarman they would have taken some special interest in the Amaravati *stūpa* and the Buddha as conceived by Hīnayāna Buddhists. We can likewise suppose that they would have had some stake in the (by then defunct) Pallava Empire, such that claims about how things were then would matter. And we can expect that they would have had some imperial aspirations of their own related to all this, given the inscription's explicitly imperial imagery.[26]

Koṭa King Keta and God Buddha of Sri Dhanyakataka

Searching for the historical location of "Siṃhavarman's" inscription in twelfth century Andhra Pradesh rather than in the Pallava Period bears fruit in directing attention to a second Amaravati pillar inscription, actually two pillars containing a total of six inscriptions, also edited and translated by Hultzsch.[27] These belong to the reign of King Keta II of the Koṭa dynasty, a royal clan of considerable regional power based in Dhanyakataka (modern Amaravati) itself. Though Hultzsch seems not to have noticed the striking parallels between these inscriptions and that of "Siṃhavarman," they lead me to believe that all three Amaravati pillars were probably inscribed in the same historical moment.

The first five inscriptions on the two Koṭa pillars are all dated on the same day in Śaka-saṃvat 1104 (= 1182–1184, AD, depending on how the date is read, which was probably the date of Keta's coronation).[28] They narrate a series of benefactions made by the king and his harem on that all-significant day: (1) Keta donated three villages to the Buddha (called here "Well-Gone-One," *Sugata*, another characteristically Hīnayāna epithet); (2) Keta provided 110 sheep for the maintenance of two perpetual lamps for "Buddha" (in the Sanskrit portion) or "glorious god Buddha" (*Srimadbuddhadeva*) in the Telugu translation; (3) one of Keta's concubines provided 55 sheep for a perpetual lamp for "glorious god Buddha"; (4) another of Keta's concubines provided 55 sheep for a perpetual lamp for "glorious god Buddha" and (5) Keta granted 12 villages to Brahmins for the benefit (*śreyase*) of his father, mother, elder brother, and himself, and changed their names accordingly. Keta's own inscriptions are in Sanskrit and Telugu, those of his concubines in Telugu alone. The second pillar also contains a later inscription dated Śaka-saṃvat 1156 (= 1234 AD) recording a similar benefaction by another of Keta's wives, who had assumed his royal position after his death and gave 55 sheep for the maintenance of a perpetual lamp for "glorious god Buddha." This latter inscription also mixes Sanskrit with Telugu.

Unlike "Siṃhavarman's" pillar, these inscriptions are quite typical of the day. They include an elaborate *praśasti* of the Koṭa dynasty in Sanskrit verse followed by a series of operative commands, in Telugu. They are all carefully dated, and leave no doubt whatsoever about the identity of the king whose pious activities they enact; he, and some of his descendants, are known from numerous other inscriptions that have been discovered in the area.[29] The inscriptions are carved on pillars newly fashioned for the purpose rather than antiques pillaged from the old *stūpa*. And they read in the normal fashion, from top to bottom!

But they contain their peculiarities, too, which associate them with the inscription of "Siṃhavarman." Thus despite these offerings to "god Buddha" the Koṭa kings were Śaiva theists, not Buddhists. The opening *praśasti* (verse 3) describes the clan (*kulaṃ*) as *Amareśvaradevena rakṣitaṃ* ("protected by god Amareśvara" = Śiva as embodied in the Amareśvara Temple at Dhanyakataka, see below) just as they are "the protection of the people" (*rakṣakaṃ nṛīṇaṃ*); Keta is dubbed *Śrīmadamareśvaradeva-divyaśrīpādapadmārādhaka* ("Devoted to the lotus on the glorious divine feet of glorious god Amareśvara [Śiva]") and these Koṭa pillars, which were discovered at the Amaresvara Temple rather than at the site of the great *stūpa*, grant Brahmins four times the number of villages given to "god Buddha." In another telling parallel to the "Siṃhavarman" inscription, Keta is styled *Śrīmattriṇayanapallavaprasādāsāditakṛṣṇave[r]ṇṇā-nadīdakṣiṇaṣaṭsahasrāvanīvallabha* or "(Called) 'The Beloved of the Earth'[30] [i.e., emperor] in six thousand [villages] on the southern bank of the Krishna River by the grace of the glorious [Emperor] Triṇayana ('Three Eyes') Pallava," a throne name that reappears in other inscriptions of this dynasty[31] and which, however obscurely today, indicates a claim to the authority of the Pallavas. Explicitly mirroring the depiction of "Siṃhavarman," "Three Eyes" Pallava is further described as *Catussa-mudramudritanikhila-vasuṃdarāparipālaka* ("Protector of the entire earth adorned in the four oceans"). Though not on the epic scale attributed to "Siṃhavarman," Keta is moreover a king with imperial ambitions, "the lord of a large assembly [of kings]" (*mahāmaṇḍaleśvara*) who is "the [lion] king of various beasts to the rutting elephants Cōḷa and Cālukya" (*Coḍacālukya-madānekamṛgendra*); the forty-three Sanskrit verses that eulogize his ancestors strengthen his claim to imperial power.[32]

As a twelfth century Telugu-speaking Śaiva king with an odd attraction to the Buddha, a claim to the authority of the Pallava Empire, imperial aspirations and a penchant for erecting inscribed pillars at Dhanyakataka, Keta II neatly fits the profile of those responsible for "Siṃhavarman's" inscription (as discussed above). The association of these Koṭa pillars with that of "Siṃhavarman" is also apparent in certain formal similarities among them. Thus the *praśasti* of Keta's inscriptions begins, oddly, not with reference to the Koṭa dynasty but rather with a depiction of the site reminiscent of "Siṃhavarman's" antiquarianism:

> Oṃ! There is a city, Śrī Dhānyakaṭaka,
> the door to the city of gods;
> Where Amareśvara Śambhu [Śiva] is worshipped
> by [Indra] the Lord of the Gods.[33]
> Where nearby is god Buddha,
> worshipped by the Creator (Dhātṛ),
> [and] where there is a lofty stūpa,
> well ornamented with various ornaments.[34]

In addition to the historical-descriptive tone and this sole epigraphic reference to the Amaravati *stūpa* (other than "Siṃhavarman's") made between the third century Ikṣvākus and modern times, Keta's name for the city parallels "Siṃhavarman's" inscription. "Dhānyakaṭaka" (softened to "Dhānyaghaṭa" or "Dhānyaghaṭaka" in the latter) is a Sanskritization of the old Prakrit name for this site,[35] which though standard in modern scholarly usage seems to have originated in these very inscriptions. As in the "Siṃhavarman" inscription here too that city is given the honorific prefix *Śrī*, another invention of these very inscriptions reflecting Keta II's focus on the site as his royal capital (another throne name was "Lord of the excellent city of Sri Dhanyakataka" [*Śrīdhānyakaṭakapuravarādhīśvara*]). Even the Telugu softening of "*ka*" to "*gha*" in "Siṃhavarman's" inscription is witnessed in the Koṭa epigraphs; that dated Śaka-saṃvat 1156 donates the lamp to "god Buddha who is pleased to reside at Sri-Dhanyaghati."[36] Similarly, the Koṭas, like "Siṃhavarman," are reckoned descendants of the theist Creator Dhātṛ, whom Keta also portrays as a worshiper of the Buddha;[37] "Siṃhavarman" and Keta II both style Śiva "Śambhu," describe the Amaravati *stūpa* as "well ornamented" (*maṇi-kanaka-rajata-vicitraṃ* and *nānā-citra-sucitritaṃ* respectively) and spell the name of the Krishna River "*Kṛṇṣave[r]ṇṇā*." Siṃhavarman is made out to be Siṃhavarman II, bearing his grandfather's name; in one place Keta II, likewise named for his grandfather, is even styled "Keta the Grandson" (*Manma-Geta*).[38]

If these similarities convincingly associate Keta II with "Siṃhavarman's" inscription, that still-anomalous historical location remains to be explained. Why did Keta, a devotee of Śiva, thus honor "god Buddha" with villages and lamps, and install him in the temple of his favored deity on the very day of his coronation?[39] This is what Hultzsch has to say:

> It appears . . . that the majority of the villages were granted to Brāhmaṇas, but that, in spite of that, and though Kēta II. and his predecessors were worshippers of Śiva-Amareśvara, he granted three villages and two lamps to Buddha, and two further lamps were granted to Buddha by two inmates of his harem. This proves what is already suggested by the second verse of the inscription, that at the time of Kēta II. the Buddhist religion continued to have votaries in the Telugu country and was tolerated and supported by the Hindū rulers of Amarāvāti. I hope I am not unjust to Kēta II. if I suggest that his gifts to Buddha were a case of *'Cherchez la femme!'* The two *dēvīs* of his who granted lamps to Buddha may have been Buddhist *upāsikās* and may have induced him to join them in making donations to their own god, though he professed the Śaiva creed. It may have been to atone for his apostasy

> that he subsequently granted a large number of villages to Brāhmaṇas, as recorded in the inscription.[40]

There are several problems here. First, installing the Buddha as a god in a Śaiva temple is not necessarily indicative of tolerance and support for "the Buddhist religion" as such; the Koṭas' "Buddhism" was couched in a Śaiva idiom.[41] Second, it is doubtful that these gifts to "god Buddha" were some regretted "apostasy," given that they and the greater gifts to Brahmins were commissioned on the same day and in a stroke of the same chisel. Third, because these gifts were part of Keta's coronation festival and thus the constitution of his rule, it is difficult to believe that they represented no more than a whim to please a couple of concubines. Fourth, this could hardly explain why Keta II's widow, in the inscription of AD 1234, would also make such a gift on assuming his political position (she makes no claim to being an *upāsikā*).

Underlying these qualms with his interpretation is my sense that Hultzsch underdetermines the significance of ceremonially installing gods and inscribing lithic records. As the imperial imagery in both Keta's and "Siṃhavarman's" inscriptions signals, these were politically consequential acts; both worshiped the Buddha while celebrating the consolidation of real-world power (and carving inscriptions was quintessentially imperial throughout premodern South Asia). A more satisfactory explanation of Keta's pieties, including the "Siṃhavarman" inscription, would locate them in the imperial contexts of the day. I attempt to do this in the next section.

Dhanyakataka as an Imperial "Key Site"

Long before—and long after—Keta II, Dhanyakataka attracted the attention of powerful Indian rulers who established their lordship over vassal kings and chiefs, in part, by engaging them in pieties performed there. Acts of worship, restoration, and enlargement demonstrated the ruler's ability to command and improve the imperial space of predecessors, and marked the site with innovative art, liturgies and sectarian affiliations which the royal court deemed most appropriate for the age. There were numerous "key sites" like Dhanyakataka throughout the Subcontinent; such practices were ubiquitous, and leaving permanent records of them produced the bulk of premodern South Asian inscriptions.[42]

Dhanyakataka's imperial significance was as old as Indian empire itself, as evidenced by the Mauryan Buddhist (third century BC) remains there.[43] Elsewhere I have reconstructed the imperial centrality enjoyed by Amaravati and other prominent *stūpas* in Andhra (Jaggayapeta, Nagarjunakonda) and Madhya Pradesh (Sanci, Bharhut) in the centuries following the Mauryas, when Buddhist thought and practice still dominated South Asian imperial politics.[44] At these sites, Śunga Period (second through first century BC) Buddhists encircled simple Mauryan bricked *stūpas* with distinctive stone railings bearing "medallion" carvings of religious scenes, transforming these landmarks of Aśoka Maurya's paradigmatic first South Asian empire into landmarks of their own. Sātavāhana Period (first century BC to early third century AD) Buddhists added exquisite carved gateways (*toraṇa*) to complete as it were the Śunga railings. In the succeeding Ikṣvāku Period (third through fourth century AD) Buddhists added ornate altar-platforms ornamented with five "*āyaka*" pillars.[45] These successive layers of improvement rendered the *stūpas* easily decipherable symbols of about six centuries of Buddhist imperial history in the southern Subcontinent. The penchant of artists at these sites, especially Amaravati, to carve composite pictures of the *stūpas* carefully delineating each of these distinctive imperial ornaments suggests the centrality of that history in their patrons' understanding of the monuments.[46]

The Amaravati *stūpa* flourished under the Sātavāhanas in particular because Dhanyakataka served them as an imperial capital. Archaeological remains still testify that huge wharves at this and other great *stūpas* along the Krishna River[47] as well as a brick wall connecting them together[48] provided Dhanyakataka strategic control in the Krishna River trade and strong defenses (about one-half mile from the *stūpa*, at Dharanikota, there is also an ancient brick fort [*koṭa*] from which Keta II's dynasty apparently later derived its name). From this position of power the Sātavāhanas improved Amaravati[49] and the other *stūpas* of its ilk (their carved gateways at Sanci are world famous),[50] thereby outdoing Mauryan and Śunga Period predecessors. After conquering the western Indian Buddhist Kṣatrapas they similarly became great patrons of the formerly Kṣatrapa cave temple at Nasik (Govardhana), where Sātavāhana inscriptions specifically humbled the conquered predecessors and apparently recognized the preeminence of monks from Dhanyakataka.[51]

But Buddhists became increasingly insignificant in South Asian imperial history after the decline of the Sātavāhanas (and corresponding rise of Śaiva and Vaiṣṇava theists), especially in the southern Subcontinent. There, the Ikṣvākus who succeeded the Sātavāhanas were the first great Indian emperors to erect inscriptions and monuments in honor of theist deities (here Śiva as Mahāsena) rather than the Buddha;[52] they boldly advertised (in a fashion that would become standard for subsequent

Indian imperial formation) that their religious activities took such theist forms as Vedic sacrifice, gifts of cash and cows to favored Brahmins, and the construction of theist temples at originally Buddhist "key sites."

This is not to say that the Buddhists had simply disappeared into Hinduism (as one long-lived theory would have it); neither had they been suddenly obliterated by anti-Buddhist foes (as follows another well-known theory). Though the ideological construction of imperial power at the top (say as the grace of Śiva, in the Ikṣvāku and later the Pallava formulations, or as the descent of Vṣṇu in Gupta or Rāṣṭrakūṭa thought) took a radical turn that set Indian imperial politics forever on a non-Buddhist course, the implications of this change continued to be worked out in individual kingdoms for many centuries. This was true even in regions (such as Andhra) where the Buddhists were reduced to an oppositional status[53] before dying out altogether, and especially the case in those fringe regions (such as Nepal and Sri Lanka) where Buddhists continue even today to wield power in shifting relations with domestic and pan–South Asian theists. Long after theism had come to dominate Indian imperial formation, as late as the twelfth century AD, occasional Buddhists (especially Sinhalas and Pālas) exercised imperial aspirations and for centuries after the Sātavāhanas a sufficient number of Buddhists remained in at least some of the kingdoms that constituted any particular empire to necessitate that they—and their theist overlords—create some space for Buddhist thought and practice.[54]

Varied and sophisticated discourses and practices created that space. In the earliest, Ikṣvāku constellation, the emperor's theist practices were counterbalanced by Buddhist construction projects directly continuous with those of the Sātavāhanas, sponsored by his female relatives, who embellished the *stūpas* of Andhra Pradesh (including Amaravati but especially at the Ikṣvāku capital Nagarjunakonda) with state-of-the-art art on those distinctive *āyaka* platforms and pillars. Their Buddhist inscriptions open with eulogies of the emperors praising their theist practices but vastly outnumber the strictly theist inscriptions endowing several Śaiva temples that were also built around the Ikṣvāku citadel at Nagarjunakonda; likewise those temples appear to have been much less impressive than the newly ornamented Buddhist monuments. This continuing public support for Buddhist imperial projects would have served the otherwise theist Ikṣvākus well, providing place to the still large number of Buddhists and Buddhist kingdoms in the region and presenting a Buddhist face to the largely Buddhist transregional Krishna River trade (see Sree Padma's chapter).

These new theist empires welcomed Buddhists of a particular sort. Those highlighted in the Ikṣvāku inscriptions were among the most radical of the day: Bahuśrūtīyas, Mahīśāsakas, Aparaśailas, and Abhayagirivihāravāsi Theravādins from Sri Lanka.[55] It has been conjectured that the *Śrīmālā-Siṃhanāda-sūtra* was composed by Buddhists at Nagarjunakonda (see Barber's chapter),[56] and as the site's name implies there are also conflicting indications that locate the great Mahāyāna dialectician Nāgārjuna and his Mādhyamaka Buddhist school in Andhra Pradesh, at Nagarjunakonda itself, or at Dhanyakataka/Amaravati.[57] These Mahāyāna or proto-Mahāyāna groups—in obvious dialogue with the newly hegemonic theists—were effecting important changes in the very structures of the old imperial Buddhist thought and practice.

However much their new prominence certainly (and intentionally) further dislocated the (Hīnayāna) sorts of Buddhists who had enjoyed such status earlier,[58] Mahāyāna Buddhists of the ilk sponsored in the transitional Ikṣvāku imperial projects did thrive within the subsequent, more exclusively theist imperial spheres of the early Pallavas (Śaivas, fourth and fifth century AD), the Guptas (Vaiṣṇavas, fourth through sixth century AD), the Vākāṭakas (Vaiṣṇavas, fifth through sixth century AD), the later Pallavas (Śaivas, seventh through tenth century AD), the Cālukyas of Badami (Vaiṣṇavas, seventh through ninth century AD), the Rāṣṭrakūṭas (Vaiṣṇavas, eighth through tenth century AD), even the Cōḷas (Śaivas, tenth through thirteenth century). Mahāyāna Buddhists similarly dominated South Asia's remaining Buddhist kingdoms (e.g., of the Pālas, the Sinhalas and in the Himālayan world).[59] Their revised Buddhist ideas and liturgies were appropriate to the new theist context,[60] while the theists in turn scripted such Buddhists into their own discourses and practices.[61] This new, post-Sātavāhana constellation of power is manifest throughout Xuanzang's account of seventh century South Asia, where Mahāyāna Buddhists consistently outshined Hīnayāna Buddhists but, as he regularly admits with dejection, the "heretics" (theists) outshined both.[62]

Andhra Pradesh, too, witnessed the post-Ikṣvāku pattern favoring Mahāyānists within an increasingly theist context, which was after all an Andhran innovation. As many of the essays in this volume make clear, Pallava Period Mahāyāna Buddhists thrived in Andhra.[63] Yet perhaps due to its significance in earlier imperial formations—when the relative positions of Buddhists and theists were reversed, and Mahāyāna Buddhists played no role—after the Ikṣvākus the Amaravati *stūpa* apparently received no imperial patronage at all. Though even as late as Keta II it obviously remained an impressive monument, and there were sporadic Buddhist pilgrims to it even if the famous Xuanzang was not, tellingly, among them,[64] beginning with the advent of the early Pallavas in the fourth century AD the Amaravati *stūpa* fell into neglect.[65] Its very stones were carted off to build wells, tanks, temples, and later mosques[66] as the earth gradually devoured it, until more recently British archaeologists carted off more of it (including "Siṃhavarman's" pillar) to Indian and Western museums.

But Dhanyakataka itself did not decline along with its famous *stūpa*. Rather, as was the pattern at originally Buddhist "key sites" throughout the Subcontinent, its imperial significance was recast in theist terms. The construction and enlargement of Amaresvara Temple on the river bank, where Keta II installed his own inscriptions, corresponded directly to the ruination of the *stūpa*. Coping stones from the *stūpa* were pillaged for the temple's foundation, and the fifteen-foot-tall white marble *lingam* in the central shrine there is said to be an old Ikṣvāku *āyaka* pillar![67] That temple may be very ancient: Sewell was told of (but not shown) an inscription there dated Śaka-Saṃvat 478, which would place its origin early in Pallava history.[68] The temple is centrally integrated into Andhran Śaiva tradition and practice,[69] and was certainly well established by the early twelfth century, when the wife of a vassal of Kūlottuṅga Cōḷa I made improvements there.[70]

Thus Keta's additions to Amaresvara Temple improved on the improvements of imperial predecessors in the region, recapitulating in theist terms the ancient pattern of development of Buddhist "key sites" like the Amaravati *stūpa*. This pattern persisted into modern times at Amaresvara Temple, where later members of Keta's own dynasty,[71] their successors in Andhra Pradesh among the thirteenth through fourteenth century Reḍḍis,[72] their successors among the imperial kings of Vijayanagar,[73] and their successors up to the nineteenth century[74] recorded in stone inscriptions the additions made and the rites performed in the process of consolidating power.[75] Ironically, this reconfiguration of Dhanyakataka as a Śaiva "key site" was so complete that today even the Buddhist *stūpa* is known as "Amaravati," a name that derives from the theist temple that displaced its one-time glory.

Yet as the case of Keta II makes clear the Buddhists, though gone, were not entirely forgotten; they remained potential players in the politics even of a post-Buddhist Andhra. As mentioned there were instances when Sinhala and Pāla Buddhists challenged theist overlordship altogether, and I highlight one such Buddhist ruler below; on a smaller scale Buddhist challenges within the theist context had some precedent in the history of Andhran oppositional politics.[76] Though it is sometimes unclear what sort of Buddhists participated in this oppositional politics, in at least one case and probably more they were political allies from Sri Lanka, which remained Buddhist despite the pan–South Asian shift to theism.[77] Alliances of this sort would have made sense in political situations where Sri Lankans and Andhrans faced a common imperial aggressor in the Tamil country.[78]

This sort of situation might account for why Buddhists suddenly reappeared in Keta II's Andhra, too. Keta II challenged the imperial powers of the day, in his case as a lion to those rutting elephants Cōḷa and Cālukya. How, despite his fortified position in Dhanyakataka, was this possible? In thinking about alliances it is significant to note that he was crowned, and endowed "god Buddha," during the final triumphant years of the last great Sri Lankan Buddhist imperial aspirant, Parākramabāhu I of Polonnaruwa (1153–1186 AD). This ruler drove the Cōḷas out of Sri Lanka—where with one exception (Vijayabāhu I, 1055–1110) they had dominated the scene since the early eleventh century—and he harassed them on the mainland, too; like all Sri Lankan rebels against imperial overlordship Parākramabāhu was a virulent Hīnayāna Buddhist, and was the only such king making such imperial inroads in the southern Subcontinent of Keta II's day.[79] Perhaps installing the Buddha in Śiva's temple ceremonially enacted real Buddhist participation in Keta's Śaiva polity: if indeed Keta II and Parākramabāhu I had entered into some sort of alliance, their ability to effect a squeeze-play against the Cōḷas might help explain how both were able to make stands against those powerful rivals. Is this then why Keta II adopted the throne name *Pratāpalaṃkeśvara*, "he whose power is the King of Sri Lanka"?[80] "*Laṃkeśvara*" was the motto on some Sri Lankan coins of the period.[81]

There is a bit of Sri Lankan evidence that further suggests this possibility, discovered at a site in eastern Sri Lanka which Buddhists call Velgam *vehera* (Buddhist temple) and Śaivas call Nātanār *kōvil* (Śaiva temple). This originally Buddhist complex (including an ancient *stūpa*), like a counterpart on the western seaboard too, became a focus for Cōḷa religious activity in Sri Lanka after Rājendra Cōḷa I defeated Anurādhapura and its imperial alliance in the early eleventh century.[82] On both coasts Cōḷa imperial inscriptions boasted in Sanskrit and Tamil that as Rāma defeated Rāvana so they had defeated the Sinhala king, and these triumphant Cōḷas granted both temples immunities and privileges after renaming them *Rājarājaperumpaḷḷi* for Rājendra Cōḷa's father. These pious acts stood in stark contrast to the Cōḷas' otherwise infamous destruction of Sri Lankan Buddhist sites,[83] and signaled a Cōḷa attempt to take command of the Buddhist alliance network, formerly centered on Anuradhapura, which at its strongest embraced anti-Cōḷa kingdoms in the southern Subcontinent as well as Southeast Asia and Indonesia. The shrines built at these privileged sites—resembling the Śiva temples constructed by the Cōḷas at Polonnaruwa when it was still their imperial outpost[84]—greeted Buddhist traders arriving at Sri Lanka's coasts with a "Buddhism" that bore the distinctive mark of the Śaiva Cōḷas, and that realized its greatest expression at Nāgapaṭṭanam, the Cōḷa Buddhist seaport on the Kāveri River where the Buddhist kings of Śrī Vijaya, formerly staunch allies of Anuradhapura, constructed the first of many Buddhist temples there in league with Rājarāja Cōḷa I.[85]

Excavations at Velgam *vehera* revealed numerous Cōḷa Period Tamil inscriptions which, significantly echoing the unusual practices at Amaresvara Temple, endow perpetual lamps to the Buddha through the investment of live animals.[86] More interesting still, post–Cōḷa Sinhala inscriptions discovered there prove that when Sinhala kings like Parākramabāhu I reasserted themselves in the later days of Polonnaruwa, they reclaimed the site of Velgam *vehera* and its original name. These also endow perpetual lamps to the Buddha through the investment of live animals,[87] appropriating what seems to be an originally Cōḷa practice. One of Polonnaruwa's last kings, Kalinga Nissanka Malla (1187–1196), visited the site personally as an explicit symbol of restoration after the Cōḷa invasions.[88] Thus in the politics of later Polonnaruwa it made sense to donate animals as endowments of perpetual lamps to the Buddha in reclaimed Cōḷa temples as part of the latter-day challenge to Cōḷa imperial supremacy, which of course is precisely what Keta II and his wives did too.

If these suggestions help illuminate what was going on when Keta II celebrated his coronation with lamps for "god Buddha" at the Amaresvara Temple, then perhaps we can also make a little more sense of his strangest act, the erection of "Siṃhavarman's" pillar. It is impossible to know whether the narrative of Siṃhavarman's visit to Dhanyakataka was an invention of the day, or reiterated an earlier local tradition, but either way it invoked Dhanyakataka's very real history as a Buddhist imperial site, on which Keta now had an opportunity to capitalize. Though treated like a god in a Śaiva structure, the Buddha also had another presence at Dhanyakataka as at Velgam *vehera*, where his relics were interred in ancient *stūpas* studded with centuries of Buddhist remains. Perhaps Keta II's coronation activities included rituals or other celebrations at the site of the *stūpa* as well as at the Amaresvara Temple; perhaps the old pillar was reerected as part of a restoration project there. The *stūpa* is after all highlighted in Keta's Amaresvara Temple *praśasti* as the Buddha's actual residence in Dhanyakataka ("nearby"—but not in—Śiva's abode), and presumably it was the source of the Buddha statue(s) which Keta installed at the latter. In such a context the "Siṃhavarman" inscription would have had real significance, providing as it does an imperial pedigree for the *stūpa* and a precedent for Śaiva kings in Dhanyakataka—even paradigmatic emperors of the mythic past—to also venerate the Well-Gone-One there. Making Siṃhavarman a *Pallava* king invoked a period when the position of Buddhists in Andhra Pradesh, if not halcyon, was at least considerably different than it had become by the time of the later Cōḷas, and given Keta's own claim to Pallava authority it rendered doubly fitting that he thus imitate his imperial predecessor (and the Creator!) by honoring the Buddha—no doubt after first requesting permission from "the resident [Śaiva] deities [at Amaresvara Temple] in charge of protecting the whole place."

The scenario I have presented may also shed some light on the unusual choice to make the inscription read upward from the bottom. Given the claim of the priests of Amaresvara Temple, reported to Sewell in 1877, that the oldest inscription there was written "upside down, in characters of the Tretā Yuga," it is possible that the "Siṃhavarman" pillar was produced to parallel an existing epigraph at the place (or that both were forged at the same time). Or, it is possible that this pillar was staged to be "discovered" during Keta II's rites; figuring out how to read it would have made for as thrilling a show of discovery as it did in Hultzsch's day, especially if the text then turned out to edify visiting Buddhists (say Sri Lankan imperial representatives at Keta's coronation) or answer some type of objection (say from the priests of the Amaresvara Temple or a pro-Cōḷa faction in the court) or enliven some particular liturgical practice (say something connected with the inscription's characterization of Dhanyakataka as a "Buddha-field" or place sanctified by the Buddha's actual presence there). A third and very different possible reason for that upside-down engraving is that this mythic association of the Pallavas with the Amaravati *stūpa*, and the challenge to Cōḷa hegemony it encoded, might have mattered enough to constitute dangerous knowledge that needed to be disguised in twelfth century Andhra Pradesh. It is likely that on first glance, reading from top to bottom, twelfth century Cōḷa inspectors would have taken it to be a largely unintelligible fragment, as did the first nineteenth century Orientalists who studied it.

A Fourteenth Century Visit to Dhanyakataka

As a short postscript on this admittedly conjectural interpretation of the "Siṃhavarman" pillar, I want to point out that an analogous situation emerged a century and a half after Keta II. Because this event—the visit to Dhanyakataka of (Sīlavaṃsa) Dharmmakīrtti (I), a fourteenth-century Sinhala Buddhist monk—is better documented than the Buddhist activities of Keta II there, it helps substantiate the general picture I have painted, and anyway is interesting in its own right as the *latest* trace of a Buddhist political presence at Dhanyakataka, if not in the whole of the Andhra country.

Dharmmakīrtti visited Dhanyakataka in connection with the mid-fourteenth century emergence of the Gampola (Gangasiripura) kingdom in Sri Lanka's central highlands.[89] Two men working in the name of Gampola's first king (Bhuvanaikabāhu IV, 1341–1351) called the shots in its establishment, the chief minister (*agämäti*) Sēnā-Laṃkādhikāra and this same monk (Śilavaṃsa) Dharmmakīrtti.[90] The minister and the monk both claimed descent, in the *Meheṇivara* and *Gaṇaväsi* (= *Lämäni, Lambakaṇṇa*) lineages respectively, from the Śākyan princes who according to the inscriptions I will mention presently (and very old Sri Lankan traditions) brought a branch of the Sacred Bodhi Tree to Sri Lanka during the paradigmatic establishment of Sinhala Buddhist kingship in its position of friendly and mutually beneficial submission to the Indian empire of Aśoka Maurya; it was in their very genes to be facilitators of Sri Lankan participation in Indian empire.[91] Simultaneously, the chief minister Alakeśvara—who had exercised similar power during the reign of Parākramabāhu IV (1302–1326) of Kurunagala and who (or whose son?) effectively ruled Gampola after Bhuvanaikabāhu's reign—arose as a semi-independent ruler[92] at Rayigama in the southwest, later establishing the fortress of Srijayavardhana-Kotte from which attacks by the Jaffna kings were repelled and to which the Gampola kings eventually shifted at the end of the fourteenth century.[93]

When this new constellation of Sinhala Buddhist political power (with Gampola as the seat of kingship and Rayigama/Kotte the semi-autonomous seat of military and economic power and defense) had first been worked out, in 1344/5, all three of the illustrious men I have mentioned—the monk Dharmmakīrtti and the ministers Sēnā-Laṃkādhikāra and Alakeśvara—issued complementary Sinhala inscriptions recording the completion of their construction projects at three now-famous Buddhist temples: Gadaladeniya and Lamkatilaka near Gampola, and Kalaniya near Kotte, respectively. I will focus here on Gadaladeniya, where Dharmmakīrtti's inscription highlights his visit to Dhanyakataka, but as I have argued in other work all three temples obviously were constructed in concert with each other, installing the unlikely divinity Vibhīṣana as the guardian of western Sri Lanka and, I argue, thereby constituting the Sinhala kings, like their rivals in Jaffna, in a position of submission to the great Vijayanagar Empire.[94]

This historical context is significant to the case at hand because Dharmmakīrtti's inscription at Gadaladeniya, carved prominently on a rock face along the old ascent to the temple, makes clear that building it (and constituting these new political arrangements) was the Sri Lankan counterpart and result of his visit to Dhanyakataka. Indeed, according to the inscription Dharmmakīrtti mobilized all sorts of people from throughout the kingdom to construct his temple—the most important are named at length with details of the endowments they made—precisely in order to build "in Sri Lanka too" a stone temple like that he encountered abroad:

> His Holiness[95] Dharmmakīrtti the Sthavira [senior monk], [who was] born in the *Gaṇaväsi* lineage [which] carrying the Sacred Bodhi [Tree] came [from India] to the island of Śrī Laṃkā, [restored] in Jambudvīpa [India] at Śrī Dhānyakaṭa[ka][96] a two-storied image house [with] plentiful gold and gems . . . [textual lacuna] [Dharmmakīrtti] being desirous to construct in Sri Lanka too an image house made of stone so that it will last a long time, [securing the support of][97] lords of the earth such as kings, heirs apparent, ministers, generals, judges . . . chiefs, . . . [another kind of] chief, . . . scribes, . . . and high and low folks such as *kṣatriyas, brāhmaṇas, vaiśyas, śūdras* and [people of various communities] such as Sinhalas and Tamils . . . army . . . [textual lacuna, then the inscription proceeds here to describe the actual construction of Gaḍalādeṇiya.][98]

The Indian context looms large here. Dharmmakīrtti's descent from Indian imperial emissary-princes and his visit to Dhanyakataka are highlighted; there is a tradition that he was even trained in India.[99] The inscription opens with a Sanskrit *śloka*—which like its heavily Sanskritized Sinhala prose similarly marked the Indian context—and Dharmmakīrtti's account of the temple's construction names the southern Indian sculptor he brought to oversee the work and details the theist deities painted attending on the Buddha images in the two central shrines there. The art and architecture of his all-stone shrines made (and despite a later Kandyan roof on the main image house and some Kandyan era repainting still make) the Indian context even more blatant, representing a unique and startling mixture of early Vijayanagaran theist and classical Sinhala Buddhist styles.[100] This highlighting of the Indian theist context in the construction and endowment of Sinhala Buddhist Gadaladeniya (and its sister temples Lamkatilaka and Kalaniya)[101] was fully consistent with Vijayanagar's newly constructed centrality for Gampola's *real politik*.[102]

We are fortunate that there also survives a literary account of this last Buddhist visit to Dhanyakataka, in the *Saddharmaratnākaraya* of Vimalakīrtti who was a pupil of (Sīlavaṃsa) Dharmmakīrtti (I)'s pupil (Jayabāhu) Dharmmakīrtti (II):

> Dharmakīrtti, the forest-dwelling monk of Palābatgala, was respected by all the people due to the fame and reputation he attained in his own country and abroad. He became an unrivalled master of the *śāstras* and *āgamas*, of various languages and so forth, and of the facts of his own religion (*samaya*) and other religions. Aspiring to supramundane Buddhahood he conducted himself in virtuous ways like generosity, morality, and meditation, gathering up skill to overcome Kāma who gives pleasure in this desert of existence. He did *pūjā* with vast amounts of rice, flowers, lamps and so forth wherever he went [in Sri Lanka]. Then, in another country, he [restored] a stone *vihāra* named Śrī Dhānyakaṭaka which had fallen into ruin, making it, in workmanship, exactly as it originally had been. In that stone image house was an 18-cubit (about 27-foot) tall white marble statue of the Lord [Buddha]. It was always given [just a simple] water bath (*jala-snānaya*). [On the first day, after this daily water bath already had been performed,] Dharmakīrti the Sthavira (Elder) did *pūjā* by smearing [the marble Buddha statue] with scented paste about two inches [thick]. Then he decorated it with *sevu vattiya* flowers [so plentiful that] the stem of one was touched by the stems of [the others around it]. On the second day, in the morning, that stone statue of the Lord [Buddha] looked like it was made of flowers. [Then he performed an appropriate water bath:] first he gave it a water bath with scented water. Second he bathed it with pots of sesame oil. Third he bathed it in milk. Fourth he rubbed it with scented powder then he gave it [another] water bath, making it exceedingly pure with clear water. Then he did *pūjā* with five thousand balls of rice, fifty at a time, offering [additional] plates full of milk-rice and rice and curries, and he also set out sweets. After that, for the entire day, he lit nine thousand lamps with sesame oil, and did *pūjā* with two hundred million *idda* flowers and five million seven hundred thousand jasmine flowers. Having done various *pūjā*s in this connection, returning to his own country which was the Island of the Sinhalas, mobilizing much merit, he built . . . the Saddharmatilaka at Gaḍalādeṇiya.[103]

The water bath already occurring there might have been some (anyway low-level) *pūjā* performed by the Śaiva priests of Amaresvara Temple, but it might also have been no more than an attempt to keep the place washed while the Buddhist was visiting; the building housing the image had to be restored to its former condition before the *pūjā* could proceed. The lack of mention suggests that there survived not even a single Koṭa perpetual lamp for the Buddha where formerly there had been five, but at least for that day thousands of precious sesame oil lamps glowed in his honor amidst mountains of fragrant flowers and delicious food. At least for that day, Dharmmakīrtti showed his theist hosts just how a Buddha image ought to be treated—on a grander scale, just precisely the way Buddha images at Gadaladeniya are treated even today.

It should be noted that neither this literary passage, nor the inscription, makes any mention of the Amaravati *stūpa*, which by the mid-fourteenth century might not even have been recognizable as such. Rather, Dharmmakīrtti's sumptuous *pūjā* must have been performed at the Amaresvara Temple, before the very Buddha image that 150 years earlier had been installed and honored with perpetual lamps by Keta II and his wives. I have found no archaeological or inscriptional evidence to suggest that there were any other Buddhas to worship in fourtheenth-century Dhanyakataka, and the Gadaladeniya inscription contains internal evidence that Dharmmakīrtti read or was read Keta II's inscriptions at Amaresvara Temple. Thus Dharmmakīrtti refers to the site as *Sri Dhanyakataka*, adopting both the Sanskritization and the honorific of the Koṭa inscriptions. The two deities who stand out in Dharmakīrtti's Gadaladeniya inscription as attendants on the Buddha are Śakra (= Indra) and Brahmā (= Dhātṛ), both of whom figure prominently in the Sanskrit portion of Keta's inscription (which Dharmmakīrtti easily would have understood; it is not known whether his "mastery of various languages" included Telugu or not). Most tellingly, the Sanskrit verse which opens the Gadaladeniya inscription points directly to the first verse of Keta II's Sanskrit *praśasti* by invoking the rare epithet "Śrīghana" in declaring that Dharmmakīrtti has built "a glorious temple for the Glorious [Buddha]," *Śrīghanaśrīvihāraṃ*.[104]

Dhanyakataka was a logical choice for the site where, preceding and paralleling the ceremonial establishment of Vijayanagar's significance for Gampola, the Vijayanagar kings ceremonially enacted their part of their bargain by providing space for a continued Sinhala Buddhist presence within their theist world. This required a site with a history of Buddhist associations still remembered in the fourteenth century, yet which still maintained real-world significance in then-contemporary theist religious and political formations, leaving open only two possible venues in the regions Vijayanagar commanded directly or at least could enforce its will on. There were the old Pallava and Cōḷa sites at Kanchipuram and Nagapattanam on the southeast coast, where occasional Buddhists enacted their lingering presence in the Indian world as late as the seventeenth century,[105] and where Sēnā Laṃkādhikāra reportedly also built a Buddha image house of stone![106] And then there was the Amaresvara Temple, where a 150-year-old stone image house already existed, where if my speculations in section two are on the mark ceremonial enactment of relations with Sinhala Buddhist kings had a good precedent, and where there had once been a great Buddhist *stūpa*—then-surviving only in Keta II's *praśasti*—which both in history and in myth had been visited by the great Indian emperors of the past.

Conclusion: Andhra-Lankan Relations and Buddhist Geopolitics in Later Medieval South Asia

In an attempt at making some sense of the Amaravati Pillar Inscription of "Siṃhavarman" I have taken the reader across wide expanses of time and space because I do not think that any piece of historical evidence can be properly understood in isolation from the pasts encapsulated in the minds of the people who produced it and the futures that they helped to create, or in isolation from their dialogue with others (in this case foreign kings and followers of other ways of life), which gave it shape in their own present. The "Siṃhavarman" pillar means virtually nothing in isolation from these diachronic and synchronic dimensions of its own history (in fact Hultzsch dismissed it from the beginning as unreliable evidence for studying even those), and for that reason more than a century after its publication it remains the basis for little insight into the phenomenon of which it is nevertheless taken as important proof: the "survival of Buddhism" in post-Buddhist Andhra Pradesh. By opening up the interpretation of this strange epigraph, I have been able to go further than Hultzsch in suggesting possibilities for its historical location and purpose.

I have argued that "Siṃhavarman's" inscription was probably forged for the late twelfth century Andhran Koṭa King Keta II, in some connection with installing the Buddha in the Amaresvara Temple on the day of his coronation. I have tried to substantiate that argument by analyzing numerous ideological, lexigraphical, and stylistic similarities between Keta's own pillar inscriptions and that of "Siṃhavarman," which once stood just a short distance apart. Taking as my lead the (overlapping) imperial imagery in these inscriptions, moreover, I have tried to make sense of Keta's rather odd decision to do this, in the context of establishing his own kingship, by asking just how such an act could have been meaningful in his political-imperial situation. My answer, that Keta II may have entered into some sort of alliance with or submission to King Parākramabāhu I of Polonnaruwa, in Sri Lanka, has a threefold basis: (1) the absence of any other Hīnayāna Buddhist kings whose imperial claims in the southern Subcontinent could account for the Well-Gone-One's unexpected reappearance in Andhran politics at that time; (2) some shreds of evidence in both Koṭa and Sinhala inscriptions suggestive of such political and religious links between the anti-Cōḷa policies of Dhanyakataka and Polonnaruwa; and (3) epigraphic evidence of the history of Buddhist and Śaiva imperial patronage of Dhanyakataka before and after Keta II, which elucidates the politically significant context of religious pieties there and demonstrates that more than a century after Keta's reign, that ancient site was most certainly a focus for constituting Sinhala Buddhist roles within contemporary theist imperial formations.

The inscriptions of "Siṃhavarman" and Keta II and his wives, like Dharmmakīrtti's fourteenth-century visit to Dhanyakataka,[107] have been taken as evidence that "Buddhism"—by which scholars mean to imply living Andhran Buddhist communities—somehow persisted in Andhra Pradesh late into the medieval period. My interpretation casts doubt on this sole substantive conclusion drawn to date from these documents. While some practicing Buddhists might still have existed somewhere in medieval Andhra—if so, they certainly would have been enamored of Keta II, and edified by Dharmmakīrtti's *pūjā*!—I doubt that these inscriptions are evidence of them. Keta II erected "Siṃhavarman's" pillar at an archaeological ruin which (at least as far as the epigraphic and archaeological evidence goes) had not been improved or even regularly maintained for centuries; Dharmmakīrtti's visit suggests that after Keta's widow-successor relit a lamp for "god Buddha" in 1234 no one attended even to that small acknowledgment of Dhanyakataka's Buddhist past, or kept up the shrine that housed him; Dharmmakīrtti's *pūjā* was likewise a one-time affair. Yet for the 800 years it had fallen into neglect Keta still knew that the "curious" monument on the hill was a Buddhist *stūpa*, and in however revisionist a fashion the "Siṃhavarman" inscription reflects knowledge of its one-time Buddhist imperial significance. Similarly, it remained for the kings of Vijayanagar to know to send Dharmmakīrtti to Amaresvara temple, perhaps because Keta's inscription there still identified the occupant of that stone image house as the Well-Gone-One even if the priests showed him no more regard than providing ordinary water. Rather than a "dying flame of South Indian Buddhism"[108] this evidence shows us that what survived in later medieval Andhra Pradesh was a pattern of transregional (or more properly interregnal) imperial formation whose Buddhist past, when necessary, could still be mobilized in the service of political relations with then-present Buddhists because those Buddhists—in Sri Lanka, anyway—no doubt also remembered their long-established links with Andhra and apparently *wanted* the Buddha to have a continued presence there, perhaps precisely because he no longer did have one.

Understanding just how such seemingly local religious acts—lighting a lamp, offering a *pūjā*, installing a new deity—had geopolitical implications, in this or any other instance, is no easy task. Even when a surviving inscription or copperplate grant alerts us to the fact that unlike the millions of now-forgotten lamps lit or *pūjās* performed daily in medieval South Asia *this one* had special significance, reconstructing the context of that significance—the complex diplomacy, clever mutual-positioning, and search for religious and historical authenticity that were the very stuff of premodern South Asian imperial politics—requires painstaking piecing together of clues, and imagination. The evidentiary record is of course sometimes incomplete, but even where evidence of both sides of any particular such alliance does still exist to study—as is the case with Gampola and Vijayanagar, perhaps Dhanyakataka and Polonnaruwa, and other, earlier alliances still[109]—because these kings did not leave us evidence in forms that would be easily recognizable today (say, written constitutions and treaties, demographic surveys, personal correspondence, or deep scars of war), it remains a challenge to understand just what this is evidence *of*. I hope that even if some of my specific arguments and speculations in this chapter prove less than convincing, it at least points to the arena wherein we need to locate relics like the "Siṃhavarman" pillar, which anyway improves on the silence produced to date.

For all its significance, Dhanyakataka was only one of countless such religio-political "key sites" in late medieval Andhra Pradesh and the rest of South Asia. Some of them (e.g., Bodh Gaya, Velgam *vehera*) were like Amaravati former Buddhist sites whose Buddhist past was still remembered despite a theist overlay; some (e.g., Jagannatha) were former Buddhist sites whose Buddhist past had been obliterated;[110] some (e.g., Kancipuram, Nagapattanam, Thanjavur) were originally theist sites that created space for Buddhists in an already-post-Buddhist South Asia, or not (e.g., Srisailam); still others (e.g., Gadaladeniya, Lamkatilaka, Kalaniya) remained or were constructed to be adamantly Buddhist against all odds, keeping Buddhicized theist deities in their place like "god Buddha" was kept at Amaresvara Temple. Whether theist or Buddhist (or whatever combination thereof), each of these sites has its own complicated history of patronage, multireligious encounter, and change, which when recovered enriches our understanding of the development of Indian theist imperial formation in every period and region, and of the complex history of negotiating Buddhist space within it.

Notes

1. E. Hultzsch, "No. 32. A Pallava Inscription from Amarāvatī," in E. Hultzsch, ed. and tr., *South-Indian Inscriptions, Tamil and Sanskrit* (Madras: Government Press, 1890), pp. 25–58. Throughout this paper I have followed Hultzsch's text including his later emendations, but all translations of Indic language texts and epigraphs in this paper are my own, unless otherwise noted.

2. D. C. Sircar, *The Successors of the Sātavāhanas in Lower Deccan* (Calcutta: University of Calcutta, 1939), p. 40; Ramaprasad Chanda, "No. 13—Some Unpublished Amaravati Inscriptions," in *Epigraphia Indica XV* (1919–20), p. 261.

3. Robert Sewell, *Report on the Amaravati Tope and Excavations on Its Site in 1877* (Varanasi: Bhartiya Publishing House, 1973 reprint), p. 37 [#17].

4. Jas. Burgess, *Notes on the Amaravati Stupa* (Varanasi: Prithivi Prakashan, 1972 reprint), p. 50.

5. E. Hultzsch, "No. 10—Note on the Amaravati Pillar Inscription of Simhavarman," in *Epigraphia Indica X* (1909–10), pp. 43–44.

6. "Śrīghana," meaning something akin to "glorious one," is an epithet for the Buddha which occurs—albeit rarely—in the Pāli (e.g., *Dīpavaṃsa* 1:11 and 2.1) and Sanskrit traditions (e.g., according to the St. Petersburg Dictionary in Amara, Hemachandra, and the *Nāradapañcharātra* [cited in Hultzsch, "Note on the Amaravati Pillar Inscription of Simhavarman," p. 43, n. 2]). The concluding prose passage of the inscription makes certain in its explicit use of the terms "Buddha" and "Bhagavan" that he is the subject of this passage and of the other epithets used for him in the inscription (*Vītarāga, Bhaṭṭāraka, Aparajanmānaṃ*). Cf. section three below (esp. n. 104) on the reappearance of "Śrīghana" in Sri Lanka during the 1340s, following Dharmmakīrtti Sthavira's visit to Dhanyakataka.

7. This is an obvious imperial image, in which the divine rulers of the universe and their demonic doubles submit to the greater power of the Buddha by placing themselves beneath his feet, just as their worldly counterparts, theist and aboriginal leaders (or perhaps friendly kings as well as enemies), submit to his political homologue, the Buddhist world-conquering emperor. Siṃhavarman's conquest of the four directions establishes him as such a homologue to the imperial Buddha; he approaches Mt. Meru protected on all sides "by all his vassals and tributaries, heroes in battle" (l. 31–32). Invoking this very image, "[by Siṃhavarman] in nighttime the darkness was transformed into dawn with the light [arising] from the crest gems of various vassal kings" (verse 10). On imperial imagery in the inscription see also n. 8, below.

8. Here "the earth" means the entire Indian Subcontinent, imagined as a decked-out woman: her sari blowing in the wind is the play of the oceans on the western and eastern coasts of the southern Subcontinent, which would be her body; the course of the Ganges defines her neckline in the Gangetic Plain; the eastern and western cosmic mountains, her earrings, locate her head in the Himālayas. On the imperial logic of the sexualized earth (the king is the lover of this earth/woman/the empire) and its importance in the pan–South Asian imperial ideology of this period, see Daud Ali, "Royal Eulogy as World History: Rethinking Copper-plate Inscriptions in Cōḷa India," in Ronald B. Inden,

Jonathan S. Walters and Daud Ali, *Querying the Medieval: Texts and the History of Practices in South Asia* (Oxford: Oxford University Press, 2000), pp. 197–203, 207–212. For a similar imperial image of the island of Sri Lanka in about this same period, see Jonathan S. Walters, "Lovely Lady Lanka: A Tenth-century Depiction," in *Sri Lanka Journal of the Humanities*, XIX, Nos/ 1 & 2 (1993, publ. 1995), pp. 45–56.

9. *Bhaṭṭāraka* is a term reminiscent of centuries-earlier epigraphs—perhaps part of the author's attempt to make this appear to be an archaic record (see below)—and strikes me as an odd epithet to apply to the Buddha.

10. Here *buddhakṣe[traśrī . . .]* seems to designate Dhanyakataka itself, as the fragmentary word which follows it appears to be in the locative case. To the extent that the inscription understands Dhanyakataka as a place visited by the historical Buddha at least when Siṃhavarman was there (the Buddha's one-time presence there is also marked in the numerous carved Buddha-footprint slabs discovered at Amaravati and the other great *stupas*), and given the presence of his relics in the *stupas* themselves, this would be consistent with Hīnayāna understandings of Buddha-fields as actual places in the ordinary world sanctified by such past presence (see Bhikkhu Ñānamoli, tr., *The Path of Purification (Visuddhimagga) of Bhadantācāriya Buddhaghosa* [Singapore: Singapore Buddhist Publication Centre reprint, n.d.], p. 455 [Vism. 414] for the authoritative commentator's threefold explanation of Buddha-fields as the places the Bodhisatta-Buddha dwelt, the finite but massive scope of the power of the Buddha's protective *suttas* [*parittas*], and the infinite range of his own clairvoyance) rather than, as in various Mahāyāna traditions, parallel universes fashioned for the succor of the faithful.

11. Hultzsch, "A Pallava Inscription from Amarāvatī," p. 25.

12. Hultzsch's own account of the inscription (reproduced in note 10, below) makes clear that the breakage of the top of the pillar only obscured some of the characters in the last lines of the inscription; there was not room for an additional, extended operative portion.

13. Sheldon Pollock, "The Sanskrit Cosmopolis, 300–1300: Transculturation, vernacularization, and the question of ideology," in Jan E. H. Houben, ed., *Ideology and Status of Sanskrit: Contributions to the History of the Sanskrit Language* (Leiden: E. J. Brill, 1996), pp. 87–107.

14. If this were a genuine Pallava grant we would expect an indication that infractions would be punished corporeally; inscriptions of the period and region to which this belongs paleographically tend more often to invoke a curse on those who break the command (e.g., being reborn as a dog).

15. It is possible that at the time the inscription was engraved, the pillar occupied some central position vis-à-vis the entire Amaravati *stupa*, or even that it was reerected as part of some new construction there, but the haphazard excavation of the *stūpa* prevents us from ever knowing what that position might have been. However it is also possible, given the scenarios I present below, that the pillar might have been chosen precisely because it was common, obscure, even already broken off at the top.

16. Hultzsch, "A Pallava Inscription from Amarāvatī," p. 25 writes: "The subjoined Sanskrit inscription is engraved on three sides of an octagonal pillar,

which was excavated at Amāravatī by Mr. R. Sewell and sent by Dr. Burgess to the Madras Museum. The top of the pillar and some letters of the uppermost lines of the inscription have been broken off. The inscription has hitherto remained a puzzle, as each line seems to end incomplete. Finding, that the first words of some lines were connected with the last words of the following ones, I was led to suppose that the inscription must begin from the bottom and not from the top. Curiously enough, this really is the case. If the inscription is read upwards, we find that it consists of eleven complete verses and of a prose passage, the end of which is lost through the mutilation of the pillar at the top." Compare Burgess, *Notes on the Amaravati Stupa*, pp. 49–50: "[The pillar] bears part of a long Sanskrit inscription, each line of which breaks off incomplete, as if it had been continued on an adjoining slab or pillar."

17. Hultzsch, "A Pallava Inscription from Amarāvatī," p. 25.

18. Hultzsch, "Note on the Amaravati Pillar Inscription of Simhavarman," p. 43.

19. Ibid.

20. Sewell, *Report on the Amaravati Tope*, p. 37; Sircar, *The Successors of the Sātavāhanas in Lower Deccan*, p. 40.

21. Thus the prose section, in particular, reads like something right out of the Hīnayāna sūtras: "*. . . dharmmadeśanām aśṛnot śrutvā cāparajanmānaṃ [upagamya abhi] vandy' edam uvāca: 'aham api bhagavan bhagavato. . . .' Evam ukte bhagavān uvāca: 'sādhu sādhu upā[saka] Siṃhavarman. . . .'* "

22. Hultzsch, "Note on the Amaravati Pillar Inscription of Simhavarman," p. 43.

23. Hultzsch, "A Pallava Inscription from Amāravatī," p. 25.

24. S. Sivaramamurti, *Amaravati Sculptures in the Madras Government Museum. Bulletin of the Madras Government Museum, New Series, General Section, vol. IV* (Madras: Tansi Press, 1977), pp. 174, 285–288.

25. There is an extensive, parallel Śaiva *sthala purāṇa* tradition associated with the nearby Amaresvara Temple, which roots itself in the *Skanda-purāṇa*. This maintains that the central *lingaṃ* at the site is the foremost of five pieces of the *lingaṃ* in Tāraka's throat, which Subramānya broke in order to slay that powerful *rākṣasa*. *Devatas* were instructed by Śiva to worship all five pieces lest their destructive power multiply. Bṛhaspati told Indra to locate the piece that is now known as the Amareśvara *lingaṃ* at the site on the Krishna River where the river flows north to south rather than west to east. Here, according to *Skanda-purāṇa*, sage Nārada had instructed the ancient *ṛṣis* to bathe daily, assuring their salvation because Kṛṣṇā himself created this spot (according to the *sthala purāṇa*, for the very purpose of bearing the Amareśvara *lingaṃ*). This is also a place where gods (*amara, devatā*) hid during the war with the demons (*sura, rākṣasa*), and hence it is "full of gods" or "Amarāvatī." It is equated with Benares (Amareśvara is Viśvanāth, the Krishna is the Ganges), and worshiping or dying there is considered to produce the same soteriological effects. For details see Shri N. Ramesan, *Temples and Legends of Andhra* (Bharatiya Vidya Bhavan, n.d.), pp. 2–9. Consulted at URL: http://www.hindubooks.org/temples/andhrapradesh/amaravati. The other four shrines (Bhimarama in Kakinada, Ksirarama

in Palakollu in W. Godavari District, and Draksarama and Kumararama [Kotipalli in East Godavari District] were within Cālukya territory, which may point to another layer of Dhanyakataka's imperial history. For epigraphic confirmation of Cālukya power in this region see Bhavaraj V. Krishnarao, "Tadikonda Grant of Ammaraja II," in *Epigraphia Indica XXIII* (1935–36), pp. 161–170.

26. See notes 7 and 8, above, for detailed analyses of the anyway obvious imperial imagery in the inscription.

27. E. Hultzsch, "No. 15.—Two Pillar Inscriptions at Amaravati," in *Epigraphia Indica VI* (1900–1901), pp. 146–160.

28. That this was the day of Keta's coronation is indicated by the epithet *Saṃprāptarājyonnatiḥ* ("attained of being raised up to the kingdom") in verse 44 of the inscription (again as the simplified *Samprāptarājyaḥ* ["attained kingdom"] in verse 47). See Hultzsch, "Two Pillar Inscriptions at Amaravati," pp. 148, 155, n. 2. and corresponding Sanskrit text. Two additional inscriptions (no's. 257 and 264 of 1897) at the Amaresvara Temple also bear this date, the latter in very much the same language (ibid., pp. 148 and 154, n. 1). On the year in which this occurred, see ibid., p. 147, n. 6.

29. Hultzsch, 1894–95; Hultzsch 1900–01b:159–160; there are many additional inscriptions of Keta and his relatives at the Amaresvara Temple (cf. below, n. 75).

30. On this imperial imagery, which directly echoes that describing Siṃhavarman, see above n. 8.

31. E. Hultzsch, "No. 16.—Yennamadala Inscription of Ganapamba," in *Epigraphia Indica III* (1894–95), p. 95.

32. These epithets stress their close relationship with the gods; thus Bhīma, Keta II's great-grandfather, was "Amareśasaṃkāśo" ("having the appearance [or being in the proximity] of the Lord of Gods [or of Amareśvara]," l. 11).

33. That is, "Amareśvara"—a play on the meaning of Śiva's local name.

34. Hultzsch, "Two Pillar Inscriptions at Amaravati," pp. 148–49.

35. Variously Dhaṃñakaṭaka or Dhaṃñakaḍaka (Chanda, "Some unpublished Amaravati Inscriptions," pp. 259, 262–63), Dhaññakaḍa (E. Hultzsch, "No. 8.—Mayidavolu Plates of Sivaskandavarman," in *Epigraphia Indica VI* [1900–01], pp. 85–86) or Dhanakaṭa (Jas. Burgess, *Report of the Buddhist Cave Temples and Their Inscriptions (Archaeological Survey of Western India, V)* (Varanasi: Indological Book House, 1964 reprint), pp. 110–111). On the identification of Dhanyakataka and Amaravati see also Jas. Burgess, *The Buddhist Stupas of Amaravati and Jaggayapeta in the Krishna District, Madras Presidency* (Varanasi: Indological Book House, 1970 reprint), p. 13.

36. Hultzsch, "Two Pillar Inscriptions at Amaravati," p. 159; his translation of the Telugu.

37. For example, lines 8, 77. This ancient Vedic creator/sustainer is identified in classical sources with Brahmā/Prajāpati, so this reference may well point to Koṭa knowledge of the story of the Buddha's Enlightenment, in which he is approached by Brahmā and begged to preach the Dharma (for a study of the earliest telling of the story see Jonathan S. Walters, "*Sutta*s as History: Four Approaches to the *Sermon on the Noble Quest (Ariyapariyesanasutta)*," in *History of*

Religions Journal 38, 3 [February 1999], pp. 247–284); the Buddha was in fact, as the Koṭas would have it, *Dhātrā prapūjitaḥ*. The Koṭas claimed descent from the feet of the Creator, which Hultzsch takes to mean that they were royal Śūdras.

38. Hultzsch, "Two Pillar Inscriptions at Amaravati," p. 157.

39. As mentioned above, the Koṭa pillars were discovered at the Amaresvara Temple on the bank of the river, not at the site of the *stūpa*; like other Koṭa inscriptions here, they seem to record endowments to the temple itself. Sivaramamurti. *Amaravati Sculptures in the Madras Government Museum*, mentions in passing (p. 8) that three Buddha statues of the "late medieval period," which may have been those installed by Keta, were removed from the Amaresvara Temple and taken to the Madras Government Museum in recent times.

40. Hultzsch, "Two Pillar Inscriptions at Amaravati," p. 148.

41. In addition to the fact that the Buddha was installed as a god in a temple dedicated to Śiva, this is quite apparent in the unusual practice of investing live animals in exchange for ghee to feed perpetual lamps, which seems to have been an originally Śaiva practice of the Cōḷa Period adopted in the Buddhist context. Thus, the father of the wife of Keta II who donated the lamp to "god Buddha" in 1234 earlier had given fifty-five sheep for a lamp for Mahādeva/Śiva; Hultzsch, "Two Pillar Inscriptions at Amaravati," pp. 159–160. On the investment of live animals for perpetual lamps cf. below, section two [esp. n. 86] on Velgam *vehera*).

42. My understanding of the role of religious ideology in the history of Indian imperial formation has been shaped through my work as a student of Ronald B. Inden. On the general parameters of this history—and the important corrective it makes to classical (Orientalist) Indology—see Ronald B. Inden, *Imagining India* (Oxford: Basil Blackwell, 1990); Ronald B. Inden, "Introduction: From Philological to Dialogical Texts" (pp. 3–28) and "Imperial Purāṇas: Kashmir as Vaiṣṇava Center of the World" (pp. 29–98) in Inden, Walters and Ali, *Querying the Medieval*. Much of my own work to date has been concerned to trace Buddhist roles in this imperial history, see especially Jonathan S. Walters, *Finding Buddhists in Global History* (Washington, D.C.: American Historical Association, 1998) and Walters, "Buddhist History." Richard Davis, *Lives of Indian Images* (Princeton: Princeton University Press, 1997) tracks this sort of imperial one-upmanship with specific reference to religious art objects as similar "key sites."

43. Chanda, "Some Unpublished Amaravati Inscriptions," p. 259.

44. Jonathan S. Walters, "Stupa, Story and Empire: Constructions of the Buddha Biography in Early Post-Aśokan India," in Juliane Schober, ed., *Sacred Biography in the Buddhist Traditions of South and Southeast Asia* (Honolulu: University of Hawaii Press, 1997), pp. 160–192. I argue that calendrical festivals and rites as well as festivals celebrating the succession of new construction and/or restoration projects at the *stūpa*—which were funded and organized by a wide variety of Buddhists (royalty, families of wealthy merchants and other leading citizens, craft guilds, towns, special committees, and leading monks and nuns) from throughout the empire, often with the participation of the emperor himself—drew this diverse body of people together in contexts where the soteriological efficacy of their collective and individual pieties was proclaimed, and

where their tangible religio-political association helped to constitute the reality of the empire itself. The names and often brief biographical details of the donors of each component in each new construction project were carefully inscribed on the objects they donated (the Prakrit donative inscription on "Siṃhavarman's" pillar is of this type), making the *stūpas* veritable Constitutions of the successive empires which improved them, and which in the process left their distinctive stylistic and liturgical marks upon them.

45. On this distinctive architecture trait see A. H. Longhurst, *The Buddhist Antiquities of Nāgārjunakoṇḍa, Madras Presidency (Archaelogical Survey of India Number 54)* (Delhi: Manager of Publications, 1938); Elizabeth Rosen Stone, *The Buddhist Art of Nāgārjunakoṇḍa* (Delhi: Motilal Banarsidass, 1994). For post-Buddhist use of one of the Amaravati *āyaka* pillars as a Śiva lingam, and a suggestion that even the Ikṣvākus might have conceived of them this way, see below, n. 67.

46. Stone, *The Buddhist Art of Nāgārjunakoṇḍa,* presents photographs of a wonderful array of these illustrations, usually found carved on drum slabs from the various *stūpas.* For Ikṣvāku Period examples from Amaravati see figs. 67, 72, 97, 102, 150, 153, 154. For parallel examples from Nagarjunakonda see figures 100, 115, 124, 143, 144, 145, 146, 147, 148, 149, 151, 152; for another parallel from Jaggeyapeta, fig. 99. At Nagarjunakonda there are also examples which emphasize the particularly Ikṣvāku addition to the sites (*āyaka* platforms and pillars) by omitting the earlier stages, e.g., figs. 93, 94, 101, 104, 105 (Stone dubs this the "Site 9 Style," see pp. 46–47 where however it will be clear that I would disagree with her account of the reason for omitting the railings etc. in these carvings); for mirror images from Amaravati, which lack the *āyaka* pillars and thus are presumably pre-Ikṣvāku, see figures 71, 95, 96. For a useful, modern 3-D drawing of what the composite Amaravati *stūpa* looked like under the Ikṣvākus, see fig. 16.

47. On the 250 feet long, 50 feet wide, 6 feet high above the water wharf at Nagarjunakonda see Longhurst, *The Buddhist Antiquities of Nāgārjunakoṇḍa,* p. 8; for remains of the wharf at Amaravati see *Indian Archaeology—1963–64—A Review*: 2–3 and *Indian Archaeology—1962–63—A Review:* 1–2.

48. For remains of the wall at Nagarjunakonda, Longhurst, *The Buddhist Antiquities of Nāgārjunakoṇḍa,* p. 3 and *Indian Archaeology—1957–58—A Review:* 5–9. For similar remains at Amaravati, *Indian Archaeology—1963–64—A Review:* 2–3; *Indian Archaeology—1962–63—A Reviewl* 1–2; *Indian Archaeology—1964–65—A Review:* 2–3.

49. Jas. Burgess, *The Buddhist Stupas of Amaravati and Jaggayapeta,* p. 100 (#1); the inscription records the donation, under the Sātavāhana emperor Vāsiṣṭhaputra Śrī Pulamavi, of a "wheel of dharma" (*dharmacakra*) for the Caityaka School, which is said to be in possession of the Great Stūpa. The remains of distinctively Sātavāhana carved gateways at Amaravati makes certain that this record barely scratches the surface of Sātavāhana work at the site.

50. For an inscription directly associating Śrī Sātakarni Sātavāhana with the Sanchi *toraṇa* see Alexander Cunningham, *The Bhilsa Topes* (London: Smith, Elder, and Co., 1854), p. 264 (#190). The inscription broadly proclaims across the upper center of the southern gateway that it was the "gift of Vāsiṣṭhiputra

Ānanda, artisan of King Śrī Sātakarni." Sanchi had been an especially important focus of Buddhist imperial practice during the Śunga Period, which (in addition to their assumption of overlordship in Madhya Pradesh) may be why the Sātavāhanas lavished such attention on it. On the transregional imperial significance of Sanchi during the Śunga and Sātavāhana Periods see Jonathan S. Walters, "Mapping Sāñchi in a Whole Buddhist World," in P. D. Premasiri and C. Witanachchi, eds., *Lily De Silva Felicitation Volume* (Peradeniya, Sri Lanka: University of Peradeniya, 2002).

51. The second Gautamiputra Śrī Sātakarni Sātavāhana funded his improvements at Nāsik by donating a field that formerly had been used by his predecessor, the Kṣatrapa Usabhadatta (Burgess, *Report of the Buddhist Cave Temples and Their Inscriptions,* p. 104 [#13]). For other relevant inscriptions there, of his mother and his son, see ibid., pp. 104–114 (#14–#21). Burgess's #19 (see p. 111, n. 19 and n. 20 for his reconstruction) reads: "to be administered by the Bhadrāyanīya Nikāya [Buddhist school], by the monks in the Queen's cave who are the mendicants from Dhānyakaṭaka" (*Dhanakaṭasamanehi . . . bhikhuhi devileṇavasehi nikāyena Bhadāyaniyena patikkaya).* This reconstruction has been challenged by E. Senart "No. 8.—The Inscriptions in the Caves at Nasik," in *Epigraphia Indica VIII* (1905–06), pp. 67–69 and K. Gopalachari, *Early History of the Andhra Country* (Madras: Madras University Press, 1976), who also question the identification of "Dhanakaṭa" with Dhānyakaṭaka (which I however find credible, given both the lexigraphical and paleographical fluidity of the lithic Prakrits). On Sātavāhana work in the Western cave temples see also Vidya Dehejia, *Early Buddhist Rock Temples: A Chronology* (Ithaca: Cornell University Press, 1972), pp. 19ff. and G. Bühler, "The Nānāghāt Inscription," in Jas. Burgess, *Report on the Elura Cave Temples and Brahminical and Jaina Caves in Western India* (Varanasi: Indological Book House, 1970 reprint), pp. 59–74. Burgess, *Report of the Buddhist Cave Temples and Their Inscriptions,* p. 114 (#22) is another Sātavāhana inscription from this site. Cf. below, n. 65, for a stark reversal of this grant (the order comes from a new imperial capital to Dhanyakataka, which is thereby rendered the outpost) during the time of the early Pallavas.

52. There certainly were earlier theist kings—and from the time of Aśoka himself theists and other non-Buddhists (such as Jains and Ājīvakas) also received some token share of imperial support and patronage—but their power must have been quite local because with one exception (the Heliodorus pillar, itself rather odd) they left no inscriptional record of their imperial claims and practices, and pre-Ikṣvāku "hard" evidence of theist art and architecture, especially in the south, is likewise scanty in comparison with the extensive Buddhist remains there.

53. See below, n. 76–78 on Buddhist politics in the time of the Viṣṇukuṇḍis and Harivarman.

54. Xuanzang (Samuel Beal, tr., *Si Yu Ki: Buddhist Records of the Western World* [Delhi: Motilal Banarsidass, 1981 reprint]) makes clear that in seventh-century India during the rise of the later Pallavas Buddhist space was still being worked out in theist India, in different ways and degrees within the various kingdoms ranging from obliterative attacks to peaceful coexistence and even royal patronage of them. See especially 1:209–227 for Śīlāditya Harṣa's spectacu-

lar failure to ritually (re)enact Buddhist kingship, which vividly exemplifies the complexity and gravity of the sorts of religio-political pieties that are discussed in this chapter.

55. For discussions and citations to relevant epigraphs see Jonathan S. Walters, "Mahāyāna Theravāda and the Origins of the Mahāvihāra," in *Sri Lanka Journal of the Humanities* XXIII, nos. 1 and 2 (1997), pp. 100–119; Walters, "Buddhist History," p. 111n.

56. Alex and Hideko Wayman, trs., *The Lion's Roar of Queen Śrīmālā: A Buddhist Scripture on the Tathāgatagarbha Theory* (New York: Columbia University Press, 1974), pp. xi, 1–2; Elizabeth Rosen Stone, *The Buddhist Art of Nāgārjunakoṇḍa* (Delhi: Motilal Banarsidass, 1994), pp. 13–17.

57. The Tibetan historian Tāranātha states that Nāgārjuna himself constructed the stone wall around the Amaravati *stūpa* and built one hundred and eight temples within it (Lama Chimpa Alaka Chattopadhyaya, tr., *Tāranātha's History of Buddhism in India* [Delhi: Motilal Banarsidass, 1990], p. 107). Not only the Mahāyāna, but also the Vajrayāna is said to originate here (345): "It is well-known among the scholars that Śrī Dhānya-kaṭaka was the place where Mantra-yāna was originally preached. But what is written in the glosses by some older Tibetan scholars in defiance of this is unknown in India. To write that this place—the name of which should be known even to the foolish Tibetans—was called Saddharma-megha-viśālagañja is due only to a bias for what is baseless and to the tendency of placating (the older scholars). This is nothing but the way the fools befool other fools. Sensible persons do not take it as a serious statement at all." For epigraphic confirmation of the presence of Nāgārjuna's school in this region (at the Jaggayapeta *stūpa*) cf. Burgess, *The Buddhist Stupas of Amaravati and Jaggayapeta,* pp. 111–112. For some of the historical problems with this association, see Nalinaksha Dutt, "Notes on the Nāgārjunakoṇḍa Inscriptions," in *Indian Historical Quarterly* 7, 3 (September 1931), pp. 651–653.

58. The evidence from Sri Lanka, anyway (see Walters, "Buddhist History," pp. 121–125) would indicate that such anti-Mahāyānists as the Mahāvihāravāsi Theravādins (who, as the seventh-century Chinese pilgrim Xuanzang put it [Beal, *Si Yu Ki,* I: 247], "opposed to the Great Vehicle and adher[ed] to the teaching of the Little Vehicle") were from the very beginning at best grumbling participants in this new, theist-and-Mahāyānist world order, and often belligerent critics of it; what had been the mainstream imperial ideology of the early post-Aśokan Period, so beautifully embodied in the Amaravati *stūpa,* had become after the Sātavāhanas a displaced, out-group position. Indeed, many Mahāyāna *sūtras* would imply that *stūpas* themselves lost their significance in the process. A Sri Lankan king contemporary with the Ikṣvāku building project, who favored the Mahāyāna Theravādins, actually punished Sri Lanka's Hīnayāna Mahāviharans for their "various transgressions" by forcing them to copy Mahāyāna *sūtras,* and he did so in an inscription carved on a stone pillar that was brought to Sri Lanka from Andhra Pradesh! (Jonathan S. Walters, "Mahāsena at the Mahāvihāra: The Interpretation and Politics of History in Medieval Sri Lanka," in Daud C. Ali, ed., *Invoking the Past: The Uses of History in South Asia* [Oxford: Oxford University Press, 1999], pp. 328–329).

59. But even within still-Buddhist kingdoms this transition did not occur smoothly or overnight; Mahāyāna and Hīnayāna Buddhists—and further subsects of them—corresponded complexly to political factions that favored (and whose fortunes waxed and waned in relationship to) different imperial contestants in the larger Subcontinent. Thus for example, most Sri Lankan Buddhist kings after the Ikṣvāku Period seem to have been content with the new imperial situation, acknowledging vassaldom to theist emperors like the Guptas, Pallavas, Pāṇḍyas, and Rāṣṭakūṭas and giving prominence at home to the Mahāyāna Buddhists, ideas, and practices favored in the imperial centers, but occasional Sri Lanka kings (Dhātusena in the fifth century, Mahinda IV in the tenth century, several eleventh through thirteenth century kings of Polonnaruwa) attempted to rebel against their (theist) overlords on the basis of (Buddhist) imperial aspirations of their own, and whenever they did so the otherwise out-group Mahāvihāra ("Hīnayāna") Theravādins suddenly emerged in the limelight, in the end displacing Sri Lankan Mahāyāna permanently! Similarly, we find Buddhist factionalism and Sri Lankan civil war at their most fevered pitch whenever the imperial situation on the mainland was undergoing a period of transition from one form of theism to another, because the different theisms of the mainland all had their implications for the relative position of the different nontheisms (Buddhisms) on the Island. Even as late as the fourteenth century, in the *Nikāya Saṃgrahaya* of Dharmmakīrtti (I)'s pupil Dharmmakīrtti (II) (see below), Hīnayāna Sri Lankan monks had to rail, at length, against all the Mahāyāna and Tantric texts which were *not* spoken by the Buddha!

60. Pantheons of transcendentalized buddhas and bodhisattvas making "descents" into the world or forming its very substance allowed the Mahāyānists to discuss—and respond to (adopt, adapt, reject, counter, nuance, undermine, ridicule)—the theological discourses which emerged in *Purāṇas* (mytho-historical and ritual compendia) sponsored by various theist imperial courts (on which see Inden, "Imperial Purāṇas"); in this milieu Mahāyāna Buddhist philosophical thinking matured through similar "dialogical" encounter with theist movements like the Vedānta and Mīmāṃsa. So too in practice: Mahāyānists and theists developed their iconographies, *pūjā* practices, chanting traditions, attitudes toward books, pilgrimage circuits and so forth in obvious dialogue with each other, so much so that images of Avalokiteśvara Bodhisattava and Lord Śiva could be interchangeable (for a famous instance see Walters, "Buddhist History," pp. 133–34) and Mahāyāna protective *dhāraṇī* chants were sometimes indistinguishable from Śaiva *mantras*.

61. Thus for examples the Guptas could conceive of the Buddha as an *avatāra* of Viṣṇu, the Pallavas could include a Buddhist temple as one of the "Five Vehicles" constitutive of the empire carved from a mountain at Mahābal-lipuram, the Rāṣṭrakūṭas could conceive the giant copper *aiḍuka stūpa* in their capital at Kanauj an equivalent of the Śiva lingam and both as symbols of Viṣṇu's all-surpassing glory (see Inden, "Imperial Purāṇas," pp. 87–89); the Cōḷas could construct "Rājarāja Cōḷa Buddhist Temples" with oddly Śaiva features on the western and eastern seaboards of a conquered Buddhist Sri Lanka and could allow Mahāyānistic Javanese kings to build a Buddhist temple in their own Buddhist center at Nagapattanam (see below).

62. Samuel Beal, tr., *Si Yu Ki: Buddhist Records of the Western World.*

63. On the contrary, the greatest of the "Lesser Vehicle" Theravādin scholar-commentators, Buddhaghoṣa, though an Andhran native had to go to Sri Lanka's Mahāvihāra to find the "authentic" early scriptures and commentaries because they did not exist in his fifth-century Andhra (nor at Bodh-Gaya, where he first set his search); it is an interesting fact that many of the great Theravādin commentators and early Sinhala authors came to Sri Lanka from Andhra in a similar search for the "authentic" early Buddhist texts and practices (Rev. A. P. Buddhadatta, "Who Was Buddhaghosa?" in his *Corrections of Geiger's Mahavamsa, etc.: A Collection of Monographs* [Ambalangoda, Ceylon: Ananda Book Company, 1957], pp. 142–157).

64. Scattered remains of visits by Chinese and Tibetan Buddhists as late as the ninth century have been discovered at Amaravati and associated *stupas* (Krishna Murthy, *Glimpses of Art, Architecture and Buddhist Literature in Ancient India,* pp. 51–54)

65. This stark transformation of Dhanyakataka's significance was signaled for his own day and posterity by one of these early Pallavas, Śivaskandavarman of the late fourth century, AD, who while still heir-apparent issued a command on copper plates (Hultzsch, "Mayidavolu Plates of Sivaskandavarman") from the new imperial capital at Kanchipuram to an official at Dhannakada, ordering the latter to grant protection and immunities to a village near there which he had gifted to two Brahmins. He does not mention the *stūpa* or the Buddhists who surely still lived in that vicinity then (perhaps even in that village granted to the Brahmins?), and as far as I know no later Pallava inscription—except of course "Siṃhavarman's"—mentions the site at all.

66. Robert Sewell, *Lists of the Antiquarian Remains in the Presidency of Madras, Vol. I., Archaeological Survey of Southern India* (Madras: Government Press, 1882), pp. 63–64.

67. K. Jamanadas, *Tirupati Balaji Was a Buddhist Shrine* (1991), ch. 6 (consulted at URL: http://www.dalitstan.org/books/tirupati). It may very well be that the Ikṣvākus themselves considered the *āyaka* pillars, which remain something of a mystery in the scholarship, to have been representative of their favored deity Śiva, in which case the transferal of one to the central shrine of a Śiva temple would have represented a smooth transition from Ikṣvāku patronage of the *stūpa* to the (early Pallava?) origins of the Amaresvara Temple.

68. Sewell, *Lists of the Antiquarian Remains in the Presidency of Madras,* p. 64: "At the northern door of the *garbhālayam* is an inscription said to be "upside down, in characters of the Tretā Yuga" (!), but said to contain nevertheless the date "Ś.Ś. 478, cyclic year Yuva." All of this sounds thoroughly unreliable. The priests will allow no European even into the outer prākāra." See below on the possibility that this was a counterpart to "Siṃhavarman's" inscriptions. An early Pallava date for the emergence of the Amaresvara Temple would correspond neatly to the tone of Śivaskandavarman's copperplate grant; see n. 65 above.

69. See above, n. 25.

70. Sewell, *Lists of the Antiquarian Remains in the Presidency of Madras,* p. 64, reports the existence of an inscription "[o]n a pillar south-west of the *mukhamaṇḍāpam,* Ś.Ś. 1030 (AD 1108). Grant by the wife of Prōli Nāyuḍu, a

dependent of 'Kulottuṅga Choḍa Goṅka Rāja.' This is Kulottuṅga Chola I, *alias* Koppara Keśarivarmā, *alias* Vīra Chola."

71. Hultzsch, "Yannamadala Inscription of Ganapamba."

72. Sewell, *Lists of the Antiquarian Remains in the Presidency of Madras*, p. 64.

73. H. Lüders, "Amaravati Inscription of Krishnaraya of Vijayanagar; Saka-Samvat 1437," in *Epigraphia Indica VII* (1902–03), pp. 17–22.

74. Sewell, *Lists of the Antiquarian Remains in the Presidency of Madras*, p. 64.

75. These have been collected by K. V. Subrahmanya Aiyer, ed., *South Indian Inscriptions (Texts): Vol. VI: Miscellaneous Inscriptions from the Tamil, Telugu and Kannada Countries* (Madras: Government Press, 1928), pp. 104–134 (nos. 215–249). Not knowing Telugu, I am unable to make adequate use of these inscriptions, which surely would allow for a more nuanced reconstruction of the patronage of the Amaresvara Temple from Cōḷa times to the present than I can offer here.

76. Thus in the fifth and sixth centuries when the hegemony of the Śaiva Pallavas was temporarily destabilized by the Vaiṣṇava Guptas and Vākāṭakas, the powerful Viṣṇukuṇḍi dynasty arose in Andhra Pradesh; Dhanyakataka was one of their three major centers. Though the dynasty before and after him was decidedly theist, and even he boasted the Vedic rituals performed by his ancestors, Viṣṇukuṇḍi Govindavarman I (ca. 422–462, AD) was partial to some Buddhists, issuing an imperial copperplate charter that survives as a remarkable document of his familiarity with Buddhist doctrine and practice. See S. Sankaranarayanan, *The Viṣṇukuṇḍis and Their Times (An Epigraphical Study)* (Delhi: Agam Prakashan, 1977), p. 13 for a reconstructed genealogy of this dynasty. For the text of the copperplate inscription, ibid., pp. 153–155. Sankaranarayanan (155–156) carefully lines up the details of Govindavarman's exposition of the Dharma with passages in Nāgārjuna's *Dharmasaṃgraha*, a believable connection given the evidence that points to Andhra as the home of the great Madhyamaka philosopher (see n. 57 and corresponding text above). However, these details are not characteristically Madhyamaka, in fact they are shared in large measure even by contemporary Pāli works like Buddhaghosa's *Visuddhimagga*, and further work needs to be done comparing (for consistency and style) these interesting details in the copperplate charter with the extant textual sources before Sankaranarayanan's interpretation should be taken for gospel. Though the dynasty thereafter was exclusively theist, a century later when the Viṣṇukuṇḍis's vassals began to raise arms against them, once again Buddhists—suddenly as it were—appeared on the scene. The challenger Prithivīmūla (before 535, AD) made gifts to Brahmins, but authorized his son Harvivarman to build a "great monastery" for the Buddhists; both theist and Buddhist copperplate grants, which together exemplify the complexity of Buddhist-theist dialogical encounters, survive from this royal house.

77. Govindavarman I does not stipulate what sort of Buddhists received his largesse, but Harivarman provides the detail that at least in his case they were Sri Lankans (Sankaranarayanan, *The Viṣṇukuṇḍis and Their Times*, p. 187: "*[U]ddiśya Tāmbraparṇṇīyāt(yān) śāsana[ṃ] Harivarmmanā [/] rājña kṛtaṃ=iha*

stheyyād=idam=ā-chandra-tārakaṃ(m) //." "This order is made by King Harivarman with respect to the [Buddhist monks] of Sri Lanka, and it should remain thus here until the moon and stars [disappear]").

78. Govindavarman's grant was inscribed just when Sri Lankan Buddhist king Dhātusena (455–470, AD) had successfully rebelled against his "*Dāmila*" (Tamil, probably early Pallava) overlords; Harivarman's grant coincided with subsequent civil wars that raged in Sri Lanka among factions supporting and supported by different imperial contenders on the mainland, which ended only when Anuradhapura acknowledged the overlordship of the later Pallavas, 636, AD (Walters, "Buddhist History," pp. 120–124). Working together Govindavarman I and Dhātusena would have been able to produce a powerful squeeze play against their mutual rivals in the Tamil country. Given the virulent Hīnayāna Buddhist ideology that framed Dhātusena's victories it would moreover make sense that for his part Govindavarman I should constitute such an alliance through a ceremonial act of patronage of Buddhist institutions (and corresponding permanent record thereof). In the same way, Harivarman's grant to Sri Lankan Buddhist monks would make sense if they represented an Anuradhapuran faction that supported him against the later Viṣṇukuṇḍis, and/or that he supported in Sri Lanka's civil strife at that time.

79. On Sri Lankan Buddhist empire and the history of its challenges to Cōḷa hegemony see Walters, "Buddhist History," pp. 125–146.

80. Hultzsch, "Two Pillar Inscriptions at Amaravati," p. 152, l. 115–116. Hultzsch translates (156), "resembling the lord of Lankā (Rāvana) in valour" but there is no indication (i.e., the inclusion of *viya* or *iva*) that this is meant as such an analogy. With one possible exception I will mention presently, the remainder of his throne names are directly descriptive of his actual virtues, however metaphorical they may be; my translation treats this one in the same way by parsing the compound as *yasya pratāpaḥ Laṃkeśvaraḥ*. "Whose power is the King of Sri Lanka" bears obvious similarity to another of his throne names (l. 113), *Vibhavāmarendra*, which Hultzsch similarly translates (155), "resembling the lord of gods (Indra) in power," again without any textual warrant for taking this as such an analogy. In the latter case, given that *Amarendra* is a play on *Amareśvara* paralleling that already witnessed in the opening stanza of this inscription (see above, n. 33), and that the epithet "Devoted to the lotus on the glorious divine feet of glorious god Amareśvara [Śiva]" directly follows this one, I think it makes more sense to understand Amareśvara Śiva (or his devotee Indra the king of gods) *as* Keta's power, a divine counterpart to his human protector (Parākramabāhu I, a king of kings).

81. H. W. Codrington, *Ceylon Coins and Currency* (Colombo: Government Printer, 1924), esp. pp. 54, 72, 81 discusses these coins, which he dates to the late tenth century; others associate them directly with the reign of Parākramabāhu I (cf. *Indian Antiquary II*: 249).

82. Jonathan S. Walters, "Buddhist History: The Pāli Vaṃsas and their Commentary," in Ronald B. Inden, Jonathan S. Walters and Daud Ali, *Querying the Medieval: Texts and the History of Practices in South Asia* (Oxford: Oxford University Press, 2000), p. 142.

83. George W. Spencer, "The Politics of Plunder: The Cholas in Eleventh-Century Ceylon," in *Journal of Asian Studies* 35, 3 (1976), pp. 405–419.

84. Senarat Paranavitana, *Glimpses of Ceylon's Past* (Colombo: Lake House, 1972), pp. 165–166.

85. Walters, "Buddhist History," pp. 142–143.

86. One such lamp was actually discovered, a fine bronze object of south Indian craftsmanship, inscribed in eleventh-century Tamil, "the sacred perpetual lamp donated by Eranāḍaṇ Kaṇḍaṇ Yakkaṇ" (Paranavitana, *Glimpses of Ceylon's Past*, p. 168; A. Velupillai ["No. 11.—Two Short Inscriptions of Velgam Vihara," in *Epigraphia Zeylanica VI, I* (1973), p. 90] translates, "A sacred perpetual lamp endowed by Kaṇṭaṉ Yakkaṉ of the Cōḷa country"). For additional Tamil endowments of animals for lamps to the Buddha at this site—one of them dated in the twelfth year of the reign of Rājendra Cōḷa [a fragment of whose imperial *praśasti* was also discovered at the site] and another in the twenty-fifth year of an unnamed Cōḷa king—see Velupillai, "Two Short Inscriptions"; A. Velupillai, "No. 20.—Four More Inscriptions from Natanar Kovil or Velgam Vihara," in *Epigraphia Zeylanica VI, I* (1973), pp. 88–92; ASCAR 1953 p. G-22; Malini Dias, "Section IV: Inscriptions—800–1200 AD," in Nandadeva Wijesekera, ed., *Archaeological Department Centenary (1890–1990), Commemorative Series, Volume Two: Inscriptions* (n.p. [Colombo]: State Printing Corporation, 1990), p. 159.

87. Malini Dias, ed., *Epigraphical Notes Nos. 1–18* (Colombo: Department of Archaeology, 1991), pp. 59–60.

88. Don Martino de Zilva Wickremesinghe, "No. 29. Poḷonnaruva: Prītidānaka-maṇḍapa Rock-Inscription," in *Epigraphia Zeylanica, Volume Two, 1912–1927* (London: Oxford University Press, 1928), pp. 176–177.

89. Gampola was established as the latest in the series of ever-more-remote and short-lived fortress-capitals of the Simhala Buddhist kings that characterized the period after the fall of Polonnaruwa (thirteenth through fourteenth century): Dambadeṇiya, Yāpahuwa, Panduvas-nuwara, Kuruṇägala. These were weak kingdoms on the defensive from south Indian rulers as well as the increasingly powerful Tamil kingdom of Jaffna; their sovereignty was largely limited to central, southwest, and southern Sri Lanka, and even there, petty rulers regularly challenged them.

90. S. Paranavitana, "No. 12. Gaḍalādeniya Rock-inscription of Dharmmakīrtti Sthavira," in *Epigraphia Zeylanica*, Volume IV (1933–41; London: Oxford University Press, 1943), pp. 95–96.

91. These lineages also established (perhaps fictive) kinship relations between them, and both were in fact closely interconnected genealogically with various rulers of Kuruṇagäla and Gampola. The minister belonged to the *meheṇavara* lineage descended from Prince Bodhigupta and the ex-nun (*meheṇi*) Sunandā, which included Vikramabāhu III (1357–74) and Vīrabāhu Äpā (1391/2–1397/8) of Gampola (Mudiyanse, n.d.: 4–5). The *gaṇaväsi* family of the monk claimed descent from Prince Bodhigupta as well as Prince Sumitra (Paranavitana, "Gaḍalādeṇiya Rock-inscription of Dharmmakīrtti Sthavira," p. 96) and tradition holds that the monk was a brother of King Parākramabāhu IV of Kurunagala (1302–1326;

Nandasena Mudiyanse, *Art and Architecture of the Gampola Period (1341–1415 AD)* [Colombo: M. D. Gunasena and Co., n.d.], p. 12).

92. Alekeśvara claimed descent in both the *Meheṇivara* and the *Gaṇaväsi* lineages, and also married his sister to Sēnā-Laṃkādhikāra! The famous Persian traveler Ibn Batuta considered him the actual king of the Island when he visited it in 1344 (Mudiyanse, *Art and Architecture of the Gampola Period,* pp. 7–11).

93. The monk Dharmmakīrtti (who is said to have lived to be 110) remained a very powerful figure in Gampola even after the chief-ministership of Sēnā-Laṃkādhikāra had been assumed by Alakeśvara, with whom Dharmmakīrtti likewise worked in concert; this monk-and-minister alliance persisted for the remainder of the Gampola and early Koṭṭe periods between the former's pupils and the latter's political successors.

94. Jonathan S. Walters, "Vibhīshana and Vijayanagar: An Essay on Religion and Geopolitics in Medieval Sri Lanka," in *Sri Lanka Journal of the Humanities, Golden Jubilee Commemoration Double Volume* (1991–92, publ. 1994), pp. 129–142; Jonathan S. Walters, *The History of Kelaniya* (Colombo: Social Scientists Association, 1996), pp. 48–60. Vijayanagar had arisen in the southern Subcontinent only a few years earlier (1336 AD), and subsequently collected taxes/tribute from all three Sri Lankan polities of the later fourteenth century (Gampola, Kotte, Jaffna) in addition to intervening in internal strife to keep the balance of power among them largely status quo. Vijayanagar's thoroughly theist kings understood themselves as earthly counterparts of Rāma/Viṣṇu, and consciously mapped both the capital itself and their empire at large according to the geography of the great Indian epic *Rāmāyana;* Vibhīṣana, of course, is the brother of the evil king of Laṃkā, Rāvana, who in the *Rāmāyana* betrays him to effect Rama's conquest of Laṃkā. As the kings of Vijayanagar are homologues of Rāma so the Sinhala rulers are homologues of Vibhīṣana, a homology that works out in Sri Lankan submission to Vijayanagar. This is spelled out in fourteenth- and fifteenth-century Sinhala literature (largely composed by the pupillary successors of Dharmmakīrtti [I] and his counterpart the chief monk at Kalaniya for the descendants of these kings and ministers of Gampola and Kotte), according to which after the end of the *Rāmāyana* Vibhīṣana is crowned king of Laṃkā by his friend Rāma, and he is said to have "protected" Sri Lankan kings who have worshiped him ever since. Thus Rāma (Vijayanagar) grants kingship to Vibhīṣana (Gampola and Kotte), upon which worship of Vibhīṣana (ritualized Sri Lankan submission to Vijayanagar's overlordship) becomes the cause of the protection (including military intervention, as in 1378) of Buddhist kingship in western Sri Lanka (where Vijayanagar intervention was most crucial, and where the Alakeśvaras were the real contenders against Jaffna). In this literature Vibhīṣana actually resides in western Sri Lanka (Kalaniya); separate shrines to him were established at the temple restored by Alakeśvara and also on the (western) rampart of the fort (Kotte) he constructed nearby. But for all his popularity among fourteenth- and fifteenth-century Sinhala elites, Vibhīṣana is not worshiped anywhere else in South Asia and appears not to have been worshiped in Sri Lanka either until these very temples were constructed in the early 1340s; even there, other than

as a local deity he has enjoyed no political significance since the fall of Vijayanagar and Kotte in the sixteenth century (Gampola had long since ceased to be anything but a town), which makes very clear the *specifically* imperial-political motivation for his worship.

95. This is Paranavitana's translation of *pādayan vahanse*, an appropriate one.

96. The Sinhala gives *Śrī Dhānyakaṭaye*. Paranavitana reads this as *-kaṭakaye*, and it is certainly possible that the inscriber omitted a letter. *Saddharmaratnākaraya* gives *-kaṭakaya*, which would indeed be the proper Sinhalization of the Sanskritization of this old Prakrit name.

97. This follows Paranavitana's interpretation ("Gaḍalādeṇiya Rock-inscription of Dharmmakīrtti Sthavira," p. 106, n. 4).

98. Paranavitana, "Gaḍalādeṇiya Rock-inscription of Dharmmakīrtti Sthavira," p. 103.

99. Mudiyanse, *Art and Architecture of the Gampola Period*, p. 11.

100. Mudiyanse, *Art and Architecture of the Gampola Period*, pp. 71, 89; Paranavitana, "Gaḍalādeṇiya Rock-inscription of Dharmmakīrtti Sthavira," pp. 90–91.

101. Lamkatilaka and Kalaniya similarly embodied the new situation by incorporating Indian theist architecture, art, and ritual; Sānā-Laṃkādhikāra and Alakeśvara similarly highlighted their own Indian descent in their respective inscriptions.

102. As is evident in an extensive lithic record, all three temples became "key sites" patronized by successions of later kings of Gampola and Kotte, who at Gadaladeniya carved their own inscriptions above and around Dharmmakīrtti's (the same is true at Lamkatilaka; at Kalaniya, where there is no natural rock face for inscriptions, Alakeśvara and his successors erected stone slabs).

103. V. D. S. Gunavardhana, ed., *Saddharmaratnākaraya* (Colombo: Samayavardhana Pothala Samagama, 2001), pp. 499ff.

104. This unusual epithet also opens the *Śāsanāvatāraya* or *Nikāya Saṃgrahaya* of (Jayabāhu) Dharmmakīrtti (II), and likewise Wäliwiṭa Dhammaratana's Kandyan Period *Pariśiṣṭhaya* on that text (Rev. Ambagaspiṭiye Vimala, ed., *Ūṇapurṇa Pariśiṣṭhaya sahita Nikāya Saṇgrahaya hevat Śāsanāvatāraya* [Gampola: Central Printers, 1999], pp. 1, 80).

105. R. A. L. H. Gunawardana, *Robe and Plough: Monasticism and Economic Interest in Early Medieval Sri Lanka* (Tucson: University of Arizona Press for the Association of Asian Studies, 1979), pp. 262–263, 265; K. Krishna Murthy, *Glimpses of Art, Architecture and Buddhist Literature in Ancient India* (New Delhi: Abhinav, 1987), pp. 94–97.

106. *Śāsanāvatāraya* or *Nikāya Saṃgrahaya* (composed by Dharmmakīrtti [I]'s pupil, Dharmmakīrtti [II]) states: "the lord of ministers named Sēnā-Laṃkādhikāra Senavirat [commander of the armed forces] who was born in the *Meheṇavara* lineage, having dispatched various precious things such as pearls and gems, caused to be built at Kanchipuram an image house made of stone" (*Niks.* ch. 12, para. 4: Vimala, *Nikaya Sangrahaya*, p. 62). There is no inscriptional or detailed

textual evidence for reconstructing this act, but it obviously belongs to the same context as Dharmmakīrtti's visit to Dhanyakataka.

107. Paranavitana, "Gaḍalādeṇiya rock-inscription of Dharmmakīrrti Sthavira, p. 98; H. B. M. Ilangasinha, *Buddhism in Medieval Sri Lanka* (Delhi: Sri Satguru Publications, 1992), p. 189.

108. Paranavita, "Gaḍalādeṇiya rock-inscription of Dharmmakīrtti Sthavira," p. 98.

109. For an ancient example see Walters, "Mapping Sāñchi in a Whole Buddhist World."

110. Scholars have adduced a great number of examples of modern theist shrines whose Buddhist origins have been forgotten or erased, see Krishna Murthy, *Glimpses of Art, Architecture and Buddhist Literature of Ancient India*, pp. 55–57, 65–72, 93–99; Jamanadas, *Tirupati Balaji Was a Buddhist Shrine*; K. Jamanadas, *Decline and Fall of Buddhism (A Tragedy in Ancient India)* (Gondwana: Ambedkar Library, 2000; consulted at URL: http://www.dalistan.org/books/decline.) The interest in recovering the Buddhist roots of theist "key sites" is not merely antiquarian; some Buddhists (especially Dalits) like South Asians of all religions participate in battles over the religious affiliation of sacred space that needless to say have real-world consequences even today (in other words, many of these places remain "key sites" even within the modern South Asian political milieu—for a Sri Lankan example, Walters, *The History of Kelaniya*). Though the Buddhist entrees into this ongoing politics of space have not generated the level of violence witnessed in the Hindu-Muslim confrontation at Ayodhya, for example, they have in some instances (on Bodh Gaya see Jacob N. Kinnard, "When the Buddha Sued Visnu," in John Holt, Jacob N. Kinnard, and Jonathan S. Walters, eds., *Constituting Communities: Theravāda Buddhism and the Religious Cultures of South and Southeast Asia* [Albany: SUNY Press, 2003], pp. 85–106) moved from scholarship to the realm of social action. The impact of the 2003 discovery of Buddhist ruins underlying both Hindu and Muslim layers at Ayodhya remains to be seen.

Place Names

Adilabad
Amarāvatī
Amareśvara
Āndhra
Āndhradeśa
Anurādhapura
Assakas
Bāmiyān
Bhārhut
Bhaṭṭiprolu
Bhīmārāma
Bihār
Bodh Gayā
Būdigapalle
Chagaṭūr
Chandraketugarh
Chintaprille
Cinnamanur
Dhaññakaḍa
Dhānyaghaṭa
Dhārāṇikota
Dhenukaṭaka
Dhulikatta
Diamabad
Dīpaldinne
Dongatogu
Drakṣārāma
Ermadāla
Gaḍalāḍeṇiya
Galabhagutta
Gamtur
Ganga-Yamuna Doab
Gaṇgasiripura
Ghanṭasāla
Godāvarī
Gummaḍidurru
Guṇapāśapura
Guṇtupalle
Guttikonda
Himālaya
Inamgoam
Irundoro
Jagannātha
Jaggayapeṭā
Jaggayyapeṭa
Kāñcipuram
Käḷaṇiya
Karimnagar
Karṇāṭaka
Kaṭṭacheṛuvulu
Kesarapalle
Khammam
Kondapur
Kotilingala
Koṭṭe
Kṛṣṇā River
Kṣīṛārāma
Kumārarāma
Kunāḷā Lake
Kuruṇägala

Kuruṇgäala
Kurnool
Laṁkātilaka
Lumbinī
Mādhya
Mādhya Pradesh
Mahāboobnagar
Mahārāṣṭra
Mathurā
Muktyala
Nāgapaṭṭanam
Nāgārjunakoṇḍa
Nāsik
Nasthullapūr
Nizamabad
Nellore
Padra
Panḍukal
Pāṭaliputra
Pedda Vegi
Peddabankūr
Peddaganjām
Peddāpurapuguṭṭa
Peṇkapaṛu
Pōlakonḍa
Pratiṣṭāna
Praksham
Raidur
Rājagṛha
Sāñci
Śaiva Amereśvara
Śālihuṇḍam
Sāmanta
Saṇkaram
Sārnāth
Siṁhavarman
Śravastī
Srī Dhanyaghātī
Srī Dhānyakaṭaka
Śrī Laṇkā
Śrījayavardhana Koṭṭe
Śrīparvata
Śrīśailam
Tungabhadra
Uḍḍiyāna
Vaddamānu
Vātāpi
Veṇgī
Vidarbha
Yelesvaram

Biographies of Contributors

A. W. Barber received his PhD in Buddhist Studies from the University of Wisconsin-Madison and has focused his research on Buddha-Nature and Pure Land forms of Buddhism. He was the editor of the 72 volume *Tibetan Tripitaka: Taipei Edition* and author of many scholarly publications in English and Chinese.

Bart Dessein is Professor at Ghent University, Department of Languages and Cultures of South and East Asia. He obtained his PhD in 1994 from Ghent University on the Tsa A-pi'-t'an Hsin Lun, Samghavarman's Chinese translation of Dharmatrata's *Samyuktabhidharmahrdaya (T. 1552). He has published mainly on Sarvastivada philosophy.

John Clifford Holt is William R. Kenan, Jr., Professor of Humanities in Religion and Asian Studies at Bowdoin College, Brunswick, Maine, USA. His books include *The Buddhist Visnu* (2004), *The Religious World of Kirti Sri* (1996), *Buddha in the Crown* (1991), for which he won an American Academy of Religion Award for Excellence, and *Discipline: The Canonical Buddhism of the Vinayapitaka* (1981). Among the books he has edited is *Constituting Communities: Theravada Buddhism and the Religious Cultures of South and Southeast Asia* by SUNY Press (2003). He has published more than forty articles in journals, collected essays, and encyclopedias.

Jacob Kinnard is Associate Professor of Comparative Religion at the Iliff School of Theology. He is the author of *Imaging Wisdom: Seeing and Knowing in the Art of Indian Buddhism* (RoutledgeCurzon, 1999) and *The Emergence of Buddhism* (Greenwood 2006), and coeditor of *Constituting Communities: Theravada Traditions in South and Southeast Asia* (SUNY, 2003); he has written numerous articles on a variety of topics in South Asian Religions. He is the editor of the Religion, Culture, and History series for Oxford University Press/AAR.

KAREN C. LANG is a Professor of Buddhist Studies in the Department of Religious Studies at the University of Virginia. She teaches undergraduate and graduate courses on Buddhism and reading courses in Sanskrit, Pāli, and Tibetan languages. Her research interests focus on the intellectual history of Indian Buddhism. Her publications include *Āryadeva's Four Hundred Verses: On the Bodhisattva's Cultivation of Merit and Knowledge,* and *Four Illusions: Candrakīrti's Advice on the Bodhisattva's Practice of Yoga* and numerous articles on Indian Buddhist philosophy and literature.

SREE PADMA is currently administering the Inter-Collegiate Sri Lanka Education (ISLE) Program, a study abroad program in Sri Lanka. She has been a research associate in the Department of History and Archaeology at Āndhra University, Visakhapatnam, Āndhra Pradesh, where she completed her PhD. She has taught at Harvard University as a lecturer and research associate in women's studies and history of religions and at Bowdoin College as assistant professor of history. She is the author of *Costume, Coiffure, and Ornament in the Temple Sculpture of Northern Andhra* (Agam Kala Prakasan, 1991). She has published several articles on the cultural links between the Āndhra coast and South and Southeast Asia. She is currently working on a book of folk goddesses in Āndhra Pradesh.

JONATHAN S. WALTERS (BA, Bowdoin; AM, PhD, University of Chicago) is Professor of Religion and Asian Studies at Whitman College, Walla Walla, Washington. He is the author of *The History of Kelaniya* and *Finding Buddhists in Global History*, coauthor (with Ronald Inden and Daud Ali) of *Querying the Medieval: Texts and the History of Practices in South Asia* and coeditor (with John Holt and Jacob Kinnard) of *Constituting Communities: Theravada Buddhism and Religious Cultures of South and Southeast Asia*, in addition to numerous scholarly articles. His research focuses on the history and religion of Sri Lanka, where he has conducted fieldwork since 1982.

Index

Abhidharma 4, 45, 46–62, 109
afterlife, belief in 13, 15, 19, 110
Amaravati (*stūpa*): 14, 110, 113, 115, 117, 118, 119; analysis of sculpture 88–97; aniconic thesis 84–88, 90–92, 96–97; art and architecture 81–82, 83–84; becomes theist temple 181; dating of remains 84, 96, 101n10; decline of 180–81, 201n65; discovery/excavation of 82–83; early history 84; early writings on sculpture 86–88; hegemonic interpretation of Buddhist art 82; imperial importance of 178; influence of 82, 97–100; influence of sculpture 5; multivalent function of sculpture (narrative, venerative, mimetic) 82, 84–86, 87–88, 90–97, 98–100; under Sātavāhanas 178. *See also* Siṃhavarman pillar
arhat: and *bodhisattva* 44, 56, 57, 65; and Buddha 55–56, 58–59; and defilement 49; defining quality of 49; and five points of Mahādeva 61, 65; status of 44, 53, 54–57, 61, 65
art: influence of philosophy 119–20. *See also* art/architecture, Buddhist
art/architecture, Buddhist 3–4, 81–82; as aniconic 4, 84–88, 90, 91, 92, 94–96, 97, 118; distorted western understanding of 83–84, 88; and Buddhist philosophy 119–20; iconic "explosion" in 99
Andhra (Pradesh): belief in afterlife 13, 15, 19, 110; *bodhisattva*-kingship in 131, 132; *bodhisattva* worship in 113; Buddhist schools in Krishna valley region 41–43; *caitya* worship in 41, 62, 110; decline of Buddhism in 11, 12, 29–30; dynasties in 128–35; early Buddhist supporters 25–26; early historic period 20–24; and indigenous religious cults 3, 13–20, 22–24, 25, 28, 37n67; emergence of Buddhism 1, 3, 13, 21–25, 35n48; Sri Lankan Buddhism, influence on 5–6, 107, 114–22, 128, 140–41; Sri Lankan Buddhism, political alliance with 8, 181–89, 203n78; Mahāsāṃghika in 4, 110–13, 153, 161; and Mahāyāna in Andhra 4, 7, 151–52, 153–56, 180, 199n57, 202n76; megalithic period 16–20; merit transfer 26, 110–11, 116, 121; myths of origin 106; neglect of in buddhology 2; neolithic/chalcolithic period 12, 13–15, 16; pre-/protohistory of 3–4, 12–20, 110; royal support for Buddhism 25, 128–32; schism between Mahāsāṃghika and Sthāviravādin 5, 42, 43–45, 61, 65, 68, 70n34, 70n35, 70n38106, 107–10; spread of Buddhism 11, 12, 13, 25–28, 29, 30; *tantras* 7, 151–52, 157, 158–61, 162; *tathāgatagarbha* 7, 151–56, 157–59, 162; trade 16,